INDIVIDUAL AND FAMILY THERAPY: TOWARD AN INTEGRATION

INDIVIDUAL AND FAMILY THERAPY: TOWARD AN INTEGRATION

Fred M. Sander, M.D.

JASON ARONSON
NEW YORK • LONDON

Copyright © 1979 by Jason Aronson, Inc.

ISBN: 0-87668-400-2

Library of Congress Catalog Number: 79-91901

Manufactured in the United States of America

for Joelle, Stephen
and Jason

CONTENTS

PART I
The Emergence of Family Therapy

PART II
The Literature of Individual and Family Interaction

ACKNOWLEDGMENTS

Interest in the interdisciplinary study of psychology was first stimulated in the Department of Social Relations at Harvard twenty years ago. In those years unification of psychology, sociology, and anthropology was still thought a possible dream. The Kluckohns, Henry Murray, John Spiegel, Talcott Parsons, and my faculty advisor, Kenneth Keniston, gave direction.

Psychiatric training at the Albert Einstein College of Medicine helped to sustain that ideal. The chairman of the department, Milton Rosenbaum, allowed the competing biological, psycho-analytic, and social psychiatric approaches a balanced representation that is rare in present-day training programs. Jose Barchilon's teaching of psychoanalytic concepts through the reading of classic novels influenced me in applying this approach to the teaching of family therapy. Israel Zwerling supported the development of a family studies section that became a nationally known family therapy training program. Iconoclastically led by Andrew Ferber, the training program exposed trainees to the varied schools of family therapy; in this context Chris Beels and I developed the first comprehensive course in the literature of the field. As a fellow in social psychiatry I spent one day a week at the

Family Institute (now the Ackerman Family Institute), where Nathan Ackerman conducted family interviews that convinced me that family treatment was a genuine paradigm shift that would shed new light on psychiatric disorders and offer new therapeutic opportunities.

Training at the New York Psychoanalytic Institute was an invaluable and constant reminder that intrapsychic forces are ultimately what make family systems and patterns as resistant to change as they are. A seminar in the Institute's Extension School on psychoanalysis and the social sciences led by Martin Wangh and Daniel Yankelovich supported the attempt to integrate depth psychology with social processes. The contributions made to that seminar by Joel Kovel and Leon Balter (who have applied psychoanalytic concepts to the institution of racism and to group behavior) have encouraged me in my attempt to apply psychoanalytic ideas to family systems concepts. Another Extension School seminar, which I chair, on the topic of psychoanalytic theory and family process, has provided further collegial support.

Those who have read individual chapters and offered valuable criticism and encouragement include Martin Bergmann, Charles Socarides, Kurt Eissler, Eleanor Galenson, Lewis Kirshner, Richard Ellman, Peter Buckley, and Marvin Nierenberg.

Slightly different versions of chapter 2 (The Emergence of Family Therapy) and chapter 4 (Schizophrenia and the Family) first appeared in *Family Process* (vol. 9, no. 3, 1970; vol. 10, no. 2, 1971) and are reprinted with permission. Chapter 5 (Freud on Marriage and the Family) first appeared in the *Journal of the American Academy of Psychoanalysis* (vol. 6, no. 2, 1978) and is reprinted with the permission of John Wiley and Sons. Chapter 7 (The Family Therapy Literature) is republished with minor changes from *The Primer of Family Therapy* edited by Don Bloch, with the permission of Grune and Stratton. Parts of chapter 8 were originally published in *Family Process* (vol. 13, no. 4, 1974; vol. 17, no. 4, 1978) and are reprinted with permission.

Indebtedness to the innumerable psychoanalysts and family therapists whose writings have influenced my thinking will be acknowledged throughout the text.

My students and patients, who were the least biased by theoretical allegiances have helped me keep an open mind regarding the potentialities and the limitations of individual and family therapy.

My wife Joelle, a writer and teacher of writing, has helped make the book more readable. Our sons, Stephen and Jason, daily remind me that individual and family forces are always at work, sometimes clashing, sometimes in harmony.

At a deeper level the interest in interdisciplinary approaches probably stems from having escaped Nazi Germany with my parents when I was two and having to integrate two languages and cultures. My parents' difficulties as well as fortitude in resettling when they were in their middle years are among those forces that contributed to this book and are in the end not measurable.

PREFACE

["Paradigms"] I take to be universally recognized achievements that for a time provide model problems and solutions to a community of practitioners.
— T.S. Kuhn, *The Structure of Scientific Revolutions*

Guildenstern: (quietly) Where we went wrong was getting on a boat. We can move, of course, change direction, rattle about, but our movement is contained within a larger one that carries us along as inexorably as the wind and the current....
— Tom Stoppard, *Rosencrantz and Guildenstern Are Dead*

We see an enormous drill tapping the furnace; slowly moving across the troughs are five men, all of them young. They wear asbestos hoods and coats which extend to the ground. Since they all wear glasses under the hoods, it is hard to distinguish between them.
— From the screenplay, *The Deer Hunter*

When we see *Hamlet* and hear the hero of that play ask "To be or not to be?" we join countless audiences that have been caught up in his struggles and choices. At the end of the sixteenth century Shakespeare was portraying the emergence of an individualism

that the preceding age would not have understood, an individualism that we now, four hundred years later, are beginning to
question. Reflecting this shift, Tom Stoppard in *Rosencrantz and
Guildenstern are Dead* rewrote *Hamlet* by placing these two
minor characters and their individual insignificance at center
stage. Once enmeshed in the Hamlet drama their lives are as
determined as the toss of a two-headed coin. The play, in fact,
opens with, and at intervals is punctuated by, the tossing of a coin
that always comes up heads. There is no longer the illusion of
personal destiny, choice, individuality, or even chance. As their
ignominious death nears they conclude that "our movement is
contained within a larger one that carries us along as inexorably
as the wind and current." They have little autonomy or control
over their lives, and we can identify with that situation as well as
with Hamlet's.

Further reflective of this cultural obsession with how little we
can control the course of our lives is the 1979 Academy award-
winning film, *The Deer Hunter*. From the earliest scenes in the
steel mill and at the wedding, through the repeated Russian
roulette torture sequences in Vietnam, the mass evacuations, and
finally in the singing of "God Bless America," the individual
characters are unable to separate themselves from the pressure of
group processes. They must ultimately pull the trigger pointed at
their own heads. At about the same time, the Three Mile Island
nuclear reactor accident served to reinforce the foreboding sense of
contextual forces over which we have lost control.

This book is about this sociocultural shift of emphasis from the
primacy of the individual to the impact of his context as it is
manifested in the emergence of the theories and techniques of the
family therapy movement. It is the outgrowth of my experience as
a student, teacher, and practitioner of both individual psychoanalytic therapy and family therapy. Having completed my
general psychiatric residency, I came to the position that
psychoanalytic theory and the emerging family systems approaches offered the most compelling explanations of the clinical
problems encountered in my work. (In my essentially outpatient
practice I of course did not see the more severe disorders, in which

biological determinants can play a more significant role.) Psychoanalytic theory and the family theories, however, continue to be taught as if they are mutually exclusive, if not contradictory. Many of my psychoanalytic colleagues wondered how unconscious conflicts could be elicited and worked through in the context of a patient's family. As Freud had remarked early on, it would be like conducting surgery with the patient's relatives looking on in the operating room. My family therapy colleagues, on the other hand, wondered how anyone could be treated in isolation from the family. It would be like treating the symptom rather than the underlying illness. Where dreams were for Freud the royal road to the unconscious, Minuchin would claim, seventy-five years later, that symptoms are the royal road to family structure. In clinical practice the decision to do individual or family therapy was less of a problem, as I have come to view these modalities as appropriate to different clinical problems and situations. Nonetheless, whether individual or family therapy was conducted, the respective theories served to enhance my understanding and management of each case.

In trying to understand the opposition of these modalities I found T. S. Kuhn's *The Structure of Scientific Revolutions* most illuminating. In this study of the history of physics he details the natural evolution of accepted scientific theories, their ultimate insulation and inevitable resistance to methods and data that call into question their underlying principles. These underlying principles constitute the paradigmatic nature of any science. His analysis has great relevance for the relationship of the individual and family therapy paradigms explored in this book, as psychoanalysis and the emerging family systems theories represent scientific revolutions that have challenged the preceding ways of viewing mental disorders.

Just as psychoanalysis was resisted in its early development, the family systems approaches are now similarly challenged. New models (paradigms) for conceptualizing data are inevitably opposed by practitioners of any science because of issues of territory and power as well as the psychological comfort in espousing accepted views. A new paradigm is experienced as heretical. Freud claimed that psychoanalysis was thus revolutionary, comparable to the Copernican and Darwinian heresies that had earlier shaken accepted views of human existence. The family systems theories represent the latest challenge to egocentric conceptions. Where Freud noted how determined by unconscious intrapsychic forces we were, the new family systems theories emphasize how much of our behavior and thought is determined by familial and cultural patterns. This view is not a new one. Various philosophies and religions have for millenia noted that we are shaped by larger forces. More recently the social sciences, most notably anthropology and sociology, have documented the power of cultural and social determinants. Our increasing awareness of how overdetermined our thinking, feeling, and behaving are has led to waves of "consciousness raising" comparable to the "unconsciousness raising" of the psychoanalytic mode.

I have chosen to illustrate some of the questions raised by this new therapeutic paradigm in the discussion of several dramatic plays. Often it is the artist who intuits and reflects these creative revolutionary conceptions of ourselves. For example, the family systems revolution was anticipated by T.S. Eliot in *The Cocktail Party*. In 1969, in the midst of teaching and learning the rudiments of family therapy, I saw a revival of this play and had been expecting an esoteric evening removed from clinical concerns. Though psychiatrists are frequently portrayed on the stage, I was unprepared to see one treating a family group. In persuing the program notes I saw that the play was first produced in 1949, just before the family therapy movement began, and introduced the play into a course on the literature of family therapy. For some time I had used imaginative literature as a way of teaching this new field (see chapter 7), and this book in part grows out of this approach.

More recently I had occasion to reread *Hamlet* and discovered that it better illustrates the conflict of the individual and family therapy paradigms than any other work I have come across. Hamlet, surrounded by manifest family pathology, is repeatedly singled out as an "identified patient." Most identified patients are part of such inexorable family dramas. In order to understand this almost universal (paradigmatic) process of identifying a patient, chapter 1 examines the paradigm shift in the question, What is the matter with "What's the matter with Hamlet?"?

Chapter 2 discusses the emergence of family therapy as reflected in *The Cocktail Party* and introduces some theoretical questions and technical problems raised by this new modality. Areas of overlap between religion and psychotherapy are also reexplored. In treating a family group, the therapist often finds himself called upon to nurture, advise, judge, or guide, thereby assuming quasi-priestly functions. These all imply transference demands that the individual psychoanalytic approach seeks to resolve primarily through interpretation rather than through gratification or enactment.

Having introduced the central notion of the shift to the family as unit of study and treatment we turn in chapter 3 to the interrelationship of individual personality development and the family life cycle. This is explored in a discussion of the role of childlessness in Edward Albee's *Who's Afraid of Virginia Woolf?* In complex ways each person's experience in his family of origin is reworked in his family of procreation. Childlessness aborts this intergenerational sequence, bringing "the family" as a perpetuating institution to an end. George's and Martha's traumatic pasts are transformed in the raising and subsequent annihilation of their fantasied child.

Chapter 4 turns logically to the next stage of the family life cycle, the relationship of the newborn and his family. In the infancy years, individuation from the symbiotic phase of development is set in motion. Disturbances in this "psychological birth" process have been implicated in psychiatry's most elusive disorder, schizophrenia. In Eliot's play *The Family Reunion* a young man recovers from his hallucinatory psychosis through corrective experiences with an old friend and an aunt. Eliot deals throughout with individuation and symbiosis while also underlining the difficulties with separation and change so frequently encountered in families with a "schizophrenic" member.

In the next part (chapters 5-7) relevant psychoanalytic and family therapy writings are introduced. Freud's writings on marriage and the family are reviewed in chapter 5 to show that, despite the insistence on the individual modality, psychoanalytic theory is deeply grounded in the interplay of the individual and his or her family. Chapter 6 expands upon this by noting psychoanalytic writers who have more recently considered in detail the interface between intrapsychic and interpersonal forces. Chapter 7 describes an eclectic course for family therapy trainees that include the writings of those family therapists and theorists who dispense with psychoanalytic concepts. The student is thus exposed to the fermenting, diverse, and as yet uncrystallized field of family therapy.

It is understandable that pioneers in the field had to develop their ideas in opposition to the individual paradigm. To this day, however, the individual psychoanalytic mode of treatment, despite its comprehensive theory of personality development, avoids application to the family unit. It is ironic that this most comprehensive and potentially universal theory remains the basis of treatment of a very small number of patients. The integration of psychoanalytic theory with some of the emerging family systems concepts would greatly expand treatment possibilities while also contributing to further advances in theory.

In the last part we turn to some application and integration of these modalities. In chapter 8 we discuss the clinical theories and approaches of various family therapists. Haley, Minuchin, Bowen, and Whitaker are viewed from the perspective of the individual approach. In chapter 9 we move from the family dramas of the stage to those that present themselves to the clinician. The chapter reviews those factors that influence and bias the choice of individual or family therapy before turning to two brief cases that illustrate the use of family therapy in rather commonly occurring individual/family crises. In one case the treatment is brief and self limited; in the second, family treatment prepares the ground for more extensive individual treatments. These cases suggest possible criteria for the use of these modalities.

Finally in chapter 10 we turn to another play, Oscar Wilde's *Salome*, which is also the libretto of Strauss's opera, to show how individual and interpersonal concepts can complement one another. The play brings us full circle back to the first chapter. Her family's structure and history is identical to Hamlet's. Her oedipal conflict is acutely aggravated by her collusive triangular interaction with her mother and stepfather (and uncle), which moves her closer to an incestuous tie with him. Its resolution is in the direction of a more homosexual tie. She is reconciled with her rival mother as her rage turns against her stepfather and John the Baptist, both substitutes for her dead father. Psychoanalytic examination of the imagery in her sexual advances toward John and her later attitude toward his decapitated head show that she is largely motivated by yearnings for a good preoedipal mother and by rage over the frustration of that yearning.

New York City
May 1979

Part I

THE EMERGENCE OF FAMILY THERAPY

Chapter One

THE PARADIGM SHIFT

This inexhaustibility of meaning which makes Shakespearean criticism a matter for a lifetime, proves, in a sense, that his literary characters are potentialities of practically inexhaustible complexities. This makes it also understandable why critics disagree (and will never find agreement).
— K. R. Eissler, *Discourse on Hamlet and* Hamlet

Something is rotten in the State of Denmark
— *Hamlet* I. iv. 100

The ancient Greeks had for the most part already sketched out the spectra of views regarding the nature of mental illness. Major sociopolitical changes between the Homeric period and the flowering of "the Greek miracle" brought about the emergence of unprecedented individual autonomy together with increasingly differentiated views of madness. Three models of the mind, rudimentary, to be sure, had already become manifest. (Simon and Ducey 1975).

In the Homeric model there was no clear mind-body distinction or clear-cut boundaries between what was inside and what was outside a person. Mental events seemed to reflect external forces, and therapy for mental distress took the form of outside agents, be they drugs or epic songs sung by bards. Thus an early interpersonal model of mental illness was established.

By the time of Plato there was a far more differentiated view of the human "psyche." The beginnings of a mind-body split and a conflictual division between the rational functions and the irrational or appetative functions were described. Madness resulted from inner psychological conflict correctable by greater self-knowledge and philosophy. The psychological (psycho-analytic) model.

Hippocrates soon after introduced the medical model with its emphasis upon the disturbances of the brain and the imbalances of the body's humors. Treatment required the restoration of balance through drugs and various regimens. The interpersonal, intrapsychic, and biological models of the mind were thus already established as logical types that came to form the basic paradigm of psychiatry. The subsequent history of psychiatry largely consists of the detailing of the specific nature of these inner and outer demons and how their complex interaction cause an individual to become ill.

While the confluence of biological, psychological, and socio-logical factors in the "causation" of mental illness is accepted by most, there is nonetheless a natural tendency for practitioners to favor one of these particular points of view. The field of psychiatry itself also tends at one period or another to favor a particular point of view. During the past few decades American psychiatry has shifted from a psychoanalytic (1940s and 1950s) point of view, to a social psychiatric emphasis (1960s) and now again to a biological orientation. These somewhat rapid shifts have led some observers to see psychiatry as going through an "identity crisis." Such an observation does not do justice to the relation of psychiatry to the wider social system. As the boundaries of almost all the other medical specialities have become narrower and narrower (creating a different sort of a crisis in terms of the doctor-patient relationship), the boundaries of psychiatry have become more difficult to define. Prior to the differentiating and specializing trends of the modern era, medicine, including psychiatry, overlapped with religion. More recently, with the rise of science, religions have significantly declined in their influence, and psychiatry, as well as a host of self-help movements, has tried to fill the void (see chapter 2). The social psychiatric movement of the 1960s failed in part because it was too messianic in trying to solve America's spiritual malaise. Now that it is clear that social psychiatry was oversold and that any future national health insurance will not subsidize such wide-scale "healing," psychiatry has begun to tighten its ship and focus more on the more severe mental illnesses, and biological psychiatry has again moved into ascendancy. Szasz's challenging but nonetheless polarizing division (1961) of psychiatric disorders as either brain diseases or "problems in living" has helped to relegate the "functional" (i.e., nonorganic) disorders to the ever-growing and confusing therapeutic marketplace. I do not mean to disparage these shifting points of view, as it is clear that advances in psychiatry come from the intensive study of a particular approach with its particular point of view or methodology. Freud could thus best elucidate the unconscious by the psychoanalytic method, which minimized external stimuli, while the social psychiatrist best notes patterns of interpersonal relationships "in the field," while minimizing endopsychic phenomena. The biologically oriented psychiatrist follows an experimental model while trying to locate the critical variables causing illness. Sooner or later it does become necessary to integrate these advances with one another for the benefit of the patient-consumer. Haven's recent sensitive appreciation of these varying "approaches to the mind" (1973) has much in common with the view put forth in the present volume. As he states in his preface, "the extraordinary advances [in psychiatry] concern methods of investigating human nature more than they do theories of human nature" (p. vii). Havens describes four basic schools of psychiatric thought — the three logical types already noted plus a fourth rooted in the modern philosophical movement of existentialism, a point of view Havens is himself identified with. The four schools are (1) the descriptive-objective, (2) the psychoanalytic, (3) the inter-personal, and (4) the existential. Havens points out how exquisitely each of these approaches to patients gives us a different slant on the human condition. He feels these different views are capable of integration, hence the subtitle to his book, "Movement of the Psychiatric Schools from Sects Toward Science." And indeed psychiatry has refined these perspectives so that we could have a rather full picture of the individual-identified patient when these varying approaches are blended.

THE FAMILY SYSTEMS POINT OF VIEW

As if things were not complicated enough, we now turn to the paradigm shift posed by the family systems approach. All the psychiatric approaches discussed thus far share the view that the sine qua non, the final common pathway, following the medical model, of psychiatric causation is an identified patient. Sickness can result from hereditary factors, acute or chronic stress, a traumatic childhood, an underlying personality disorder, ennui, excessive use of alcohol, psychotic parents, social and economic conditions or some complex combination of these. The individual patient identified by himself or delegated by others is then treated by chemotherapy, psychotherapy, group therapy, milieu therapy, hospitalization or some combination of these. Even when family therapy is added to this list, it is usually introduced in the psychiatric setting as a modality for the treatment of an identified patient. *This is the Basic Paradigm of Psychiatry.* It is the family systems viewpoint that the family should be the unit of study *and* treatment. *The family is thus the patient.* This chapter and book discuss this point of view, which has been emerging over the past few decades and which reflects such a paradigmatic shift. It is a point of view qualitatively different from the others and therefore not easily assimilated into our regular way of seeing and doing things. For example, at the same time this chapter was written, the *American Journal of Psychiatry* ran a lead article on an "Overview of the Psycho-therapies" (Karasu 1977) that attempted to categorize over fifty psychotherapeutic schools. This extraordinary catalog of mid-twentieth century psychotherapies, while confirming Rieff's views of our age as subsuming the *Triumph of the Therapeutic* (1966), also reflects the basic paradigm at hand in that the overview focused only upon "modalities that are essentially dyadic in nature" (p. 852). The nondyadic therapies would have complicated the overview and were thus intentionally overlooked.

Another difficulty in using this clinical approach is the continued failure of insurance companies to incorporate family treatment unless an individual patient is designated. In my experience, if the diagnosis of marital maladjustment is noted on an insurance claim form as most accurately reflecting a presenting situation, it is usually returned with a request for a more individually oriented diagnosis. (See chapter 9 for a fuller discussion of the difficulties posed by the family paradigm.)

So also, most clinic record keeping and fee collection systems are thrown into confusion by family therapy unless an individual patient is specifically registered as the patient. In the family clinic of the psychiatric outpatient department of the Albert Einstein College of Medicine each adult member of the family registers individually, thus insuring a more thorough evaluation of each member as well as more readily permitting treatment of the family as a system. Copies of family treatment summaries are then placed in each person's chart.

In a revealing footnote to his discussion of the interpersonal school Havens gives credit to Adelaide Johnson (1969) who developed a fresh method of investigation that has become one of the precursors of the family system's viewpoint. She was one of those early investigators who treated separately though collaboratively different family members and began to notice ongoing pathological systemlike interaction rather than a patient passively affected by a surrounding pathological family. Havens apologizes for slighting her work but found it "considerably more difficult to use on a clinical basis" (p. 344). *That is just the point about the family systems view*. It does not fit our usual way of working in psychiatry.

WHAT'S THE MATTER WITH "WHAT'S THE MATTER WITH HAMLET?"?

In no work of literature is this paradigm problem more dramatically illustrated than in Shakespeare's *Hamlet*, proving again the inexhaustibility of meaning in and relevance of this play. The following discussion will not again attempt to analyze or reinterpret *Hamlet* but rather to note schematically the fact that the internal structure of the play and the subsequent limitless and fascinating diagnosing and delving into the motivations of Hamlet illustrate the central paradigm. Lidz (1975), who most recently tackled afresh the problem of Hamlet, put it this way, "*Hamlet*, in particular, attracts the psychiatrist because it is a play that directly challenges his professional acumen. He can join the characters in the play in seeking the cause of his antic behavior." While still reflecting the old paradigm in seeking for the cause of Hamlet's behavior, Lidz's study, more than any previous, recognizes and contributes to the development of the new paradigm. Thus we ask the meta-question, What, after all, is the matter with "What's the Matter with Hamlet?"

Put in the most simple terms the plot involves Prince Hamlet's overburdening task of avenging the murder of his father by his uncle who has also seduced and married his mother. Under the weight of this task Hamlet acts in such a way that he is deemed mad. Theories of why Hamlet acts or is mad are put forth by Horatio, Polonius, Gertrude, Rosencrantz and Guildenstern, Claudius, Hamlet himself, and subsequently by literary critic after critic, as well as psychologists, psychiatrists, and psychoanalysts since the seventeenth century. Most theories are partially correct, as are the differing "approaches to the mind" noted in the introduction to this chapter. And yet each theory represents at the same time the point of view or bias of the particular observer or theorist. The questions rarely asked by Shakespeare, the characters of the play, critics, or psychologists are: Why could Claudius not control his urge to kill his brother? What led Gertrude into an adulterous and hasty incestuous marriage to her brother-in-law? What was the nature of the family system that allowed the enactment of the oedipal crime?

Shakespeare did not ask such questions because he was portrayng and exploring the emergence of a more modern man in whom the external interpersonal battlefields become internalized to a marked degree. Hamlet is at war with himself and broods over whether it is better "To be or not to be?" As Eissler (1971) correctly notes:

> Medieval man would never have understood Hamlet. Ever since man's obligation to take spiritual authority for granted has become subject of doubt, and he has had to fall back on his own resources, as the only guide by which to decide what is right and what is wrong, this problem has become an unsettling one for him. [p. 198]

In prescientific times man felt himself inextricably caught up in a world where tragedy was everyone's (unconscious) fate, made barely intelligible and obscured by wish-fulfilling systems of religious belief. Where Oedipus blindly and unconsciously killed his father, Hamlet, by way of contrast, emerges with a heightened level of consciousness that bespeaks a greater awareness of self and with it the hope (illusory though it may be) of climbing out of the darkness. This is part of the enormous attraction of Hamlet and his special place in Western literature. He appears on the edge of self-determination, on the edge of climbing out of a malignant family system that cannot look at itself.[1] He is perhaps the first truly "analyzable" character in Western literature. Long before the emergence of psychoanalysis he was the object of more "analysis" than any other character in literature.

Thus, in addition to reflecting the basic psychiatric paradigm, Hamlet also illustrates a cultural paradigmatic shift especially prominent in Elizabethan England. Auerbach's study of the

---

1. While this chapter will not specifically analyze the interaction of the characters, it is worth noting at this point that the inability of the other characters to look at themselves is especially illustrated in their tendency to spy upon others. Claudius and Polonius have a veritable CIA in Rosencrantz, Guildenstern, and Reynaldo, whom they send to keep a close eye on Hamlet and Laertes.

"representation of reality in Western literature" (1953) puts it this way:

> In Elizabethan tragedy and specifically in Shakespeare, the hero's character is depicted in greater and more varied detail than in antique tragedy, and participates more actively in shaping the individual's fate ... One might say that the idea of destiny in Elizabethan tragedy is both more broadly conceived and more closely linked to the individual's character than it is in antique tragedy. In the latter, fate means nothing but the given tragic complex, the present network of events in which a particular person is enmeshed at a particular moment.... (Greek tragedy) can hardly be compared with the multiplicity of subject matter, the freedom of invention and presentation which distinquish the Elizabethan and the modern drama, generally. What with the variety of subject matter and the considerable freedom of movement of the Elizabethan theatre, we are in each instance given the particular atmosphere, the situation, and the prehistory of the characters. The course of events on the stage is not rigidly restricted to the course of events of the tragic confict but covers conversations, scenes, characters, which the action as such does not necessarily require. Thus we are given a great deal of "supplementary information" about the principal personages; we are enabled to form an idea of their normal lives and particularly characters apart from the complication in which they are caught at the moment. [pp. 319-320]

The tragedy of the House of Atreus has become the tragedy of Hamlet. The individualism (of Western civilizations) set in motion since the Middle Ages has continued unabated to the present day. There are now expressions of concern that this "rugged individualism" is one of the underlying factors whereby collectivities such as the family unit have suffered. Individual psychoanalytic treatment, a treatment rarely practiced in collective or preindustrial societies, characterizes this trend. Man (woman) is the measure of all things and he or she is in psychoanalysis treated in relative isolation from his/her surroundings. Explored further in the next chapter, the emergence of family therapy is in part a reaction to this emphasis on individualism which has left man with a diminished sense of communal attachments. It is as well a recognition that many emotional disturbances are completely part of a familial drama more like a Greek than a Shakespearean tragedy.

WHAT IS THE MATTER WITH HAMLET?

In the Beginning: Grief

Hamlet, at the start of the play, is clearly grief stricken, a "diagnosis" pretty much universally agreed upon. His open expression of grief over the untimely loss of his father nonetheless poses a threat to his mother and stepfather. Gertrude's first words in the play are a plea to her son:

cast thy nighted color off
Do not for ever with thy vailed lids
Seek for thy noble father in the dust. [I.ii. 72-75]

What of her grief at the loss of her husband? Does she seek to extend her own denial to her son so that she need not mourn? Or, if she had been complicitous in her husband's death, she clearly seeks to obliterate Hamlet's grief as a reminder of her guilt. Claudius, whose guilt is undeniable, follows suit by chiding Hamlet:

Tis sweet and commendable in your nature, Hamlet
To give these mourning duties to your father;
But you must know, your father lost a father;
That father lost, lost his. ... [I.ii. 92-95]

With an extraordinary degree of psychological and philosophical detachment Claudius speaks of "your father lost *a father"* when he is in fact talking about *his own father.* Hamlet's rage is further kindled as he soon learns that his uncle's callousness is part of the hypocritical concealment of his crime.

Before Hamlet begins to act mad, Horatio, with an extraordinary prescience, anticipates that the confrontation of Hamlet with the Ghost might drive him mad. He warns Hamlet not to follow the Ghost. It is the same warning we shall later see in *Salome* (see chapter 10) as the guards try to keep her from the fateful meeting with John the Baptist, the representation of her dead father. Horatio:

> What if it tempt you toward the flood, my lord
> Or to the dreadful summit of the cliff.
> That beetles o'er his base into the sea
> There assume some other form
> Which might deprive your sovereignty of reason
> And draw you into madness? Think of it.
> The very place puts toys of desperation,
> Without more motive, into every brain
> That looks so many fathoms to the sea
> And hears it roar beneath. [I.iv. 76-85]

The universal imagery connecting madness with the sea and depths of every man's unconscious will not deter Hamlet as he picks up the sea imagery, plunges in and says of the Ghost.

> It waves me still.
> Go on, I'll follow thee. [I.iv. 86-87]

Marcellus then forbodingly closes the scene with his famous line that shifts from the fear for Hamlet to concerns for the nation:

> Something is rotten in the State of Denmark. [I.iv. 100]

A paradigm shift to be sure. Shakespeare is here comfortable with all levels simultaneously as he interweaves the intrapsychic threads with the rank and corrupt tapestry of the external world.

The ordinary citizen, Marcellus, is aware that the recent, sudden death of the king and the queen's hasty marriage to his brother indicates some national disturbance just as American citizens sensed something rotten in the state when the Watergate dam broke. In Elizabethan England the destiny of the nation and the royal family were so intertwined that Marcellus might as easily have said there is something rotten in our royal family. But as we shall see, the focus will shift from the rotten state of Hamlet's family to his madness.

From Grief to Madness

After learning of the circumstances of his father's death and agreeing to set things right, Hamlet becomes unsettled and begins the behavior that has been the basis of endless speculation and theorizing. The differing theories of his madness begin to emerge, each partially correct but determined by the point of view of the observer, thus preventing them from seeing their own part in the drama.

1. Polonius, as a widower, is even more jealous than the ordinary father when his only daughter becomes romantically involved. His fatherly warnings and prohibitions against returning Hamlet's affections are reinforced by Laertes and given to Ophelia before Hamlet's change of behavior. Polonius naturally sees Hamlet's behavior as a reaction to unrequited love.

> *Polonius:* This is the very ecstacy of love,
> Whose violent property fordoes itself
> And leads the will to desperate undertakings
> As oft as any passion under heaven
> That does afflict our natures. I am sorry.
> What, have you given him any hard words of late?
> *Ophelia:* No, my good lord; but as you did command,
> I did repel his letters and denied
> His access to me.
> *Polonius:* That hath made him mad. [II.i. 113-122]

2. Gertrude, who has lost her husband and remarried his brother, sees those facts plain and simple as the cause of her son's distemper:

I doubt it is no other but the main,
His father's death and our o'erhasty marriage. [II.ii. 59-60]

3. Rosencrantz, when Hamlet reveals that he feels imprisoned in Denmark as "there is nothing good or bad but thinking makes it so," offers his causative theory. It is ambition.

Why then your ambition makes it one. 'Tis too
Narrow for your mind. [II.ii. 268-269]

4. Hamlet replies that it is "bad dreams," to which
5. Guildenstern repeats Rosencrantz's earlier theory

Which dreams indeed are ambition for the very
Substance of the ambitions is merely the shadow
of a dream.

6. Hamlet in the next act sarcastically parrots back to Rosencrantz the ambition theory.

Rosencrantz: Good my lord, what is your cause of distemper? [III.ii. 345]
Hamlet: Sir, I lack advancement. [III.ii. 348]

7. Claudius, even before he is caught in the mousetrap scene, is appropriately suspicious of his stepson's behavior and disbelieves Polonius' theory.

Love, his affections do not that way tend;
Nor what he spake, though it lacked from a little,
Was not like madness. There's something in his soul
o'er which his melancholy sits on brood;
And I do doubt the hatch and the disclose
Will be some danger; which for to prevent,

I have in quick determination
Thus set it down; he shall with speed to England
For the demand of our neglected tribute.
Haply the seas, and countries different,
With variable objects, shall expel
This something settled matter in his heart,
Whereon his brain still beating puts him thus
From the fashion of himself.
. . . .
Madness in great ones must not unwatched go. [III.i. 172-185, 199]

Claudius does not advance a theory but recognizes in Hamlet's madness, regardless of diagnosis, a danger to himself and chooses a solution comparable to hospitalization by planning to send him to England. How many young adults in the early stages of mental illness are first hospitalized when they begin to express and act upon matricidal or patricidal impulses.

8. In the final scene even Hamlet uses the idea of his madness to absolve himself of responsibility for Polonius' murder. In greeting Laertes before the fateful duel he says:

Give me your pardon, sir, I have done you wrong;
But pardon't, as you are a gentleman.
This presence knows,
And you must needs have heard, how I am punished
With sore distraction. What I have done
That might your nature, honor, and exception
Roughly awake, I here proclaim was madness.
Was't Hamlet wronged Laertes? Never Hamlet.
If Hamlet from himself be ta'en away,
And when he's not himself does wrong Laertes
Then Hamlet does it not, Hamlet denies it.
Who does it, then ? His madness. [V.ii. 226-238]

Never has an insanity defense from a divided self been so eloquently uttered.

Thus through displacements or projections of their own preoccupations and points of view, the characters in the play put forth loss, anger, ambition, motives of revenge, and the irreducible taint of madness itself, as partially correct causes of Hamlet's disorder. These theories in turn defend each of them against any further awareness of their own conflicts. Polonius does not want to examine his anxiety and jealousy over the possible loss of the only woman in his life, Gertrude need not look further into the implications of her hasty remarriage. Claudius can psychopathically attempt to eliminate the anticipated retaliation for the murder of his brother, and finally Hamlet himself can deny his murderous impulses, all by focusing upon *his madness*.

Furness's *New Variorum Edition* as well as Holland's *Psychoanalysis and Shakespeare* abstract and review many more psychological theories about Hamlet that have been put forth over four centuries. These plus all the theories of literary critics will not be reviewed here except again to note that they *all* reflect the basic paradigm that stands in contrast to the family systems paradigm regarding mental illness.

IMPLICATIONS FOR THEORY AND PRACTICE

The field of family therapy introduces a paradigmatic shift in our already divergent views of mental illness. Mental illness, however its causes are viewed, has been seen as manifested by an individual patient. The family systems view suggests that the individual's illness is an epiphenomenon reflecting an underlying familial disorder. The family system paradigm is still so new that no generally agreed-upon descriptive vocabulary or typology of familites has yet emerged (see Wertheim 1973, Reiss 1971). Also the radical conceptual shift involved in the new paradigm cannot easily be integrated into traditional clinical practice. How then are we to proceed? First, we must recognize that these paradigms are but ways of looking at and organizing clinical data and thus serve a heuristic purpose. The paradigms are not mutually exclusive. Emotional disturbances are both individual and social, intrapsychic and interpersonal. There are no purely individual or purely family disorders. The new paradigm will, we hope, counterbalance the excessive emphasis of the basic paradigm upon the individual. What is necessary is a theory that combines our rather extensive understanding of individual functioning with a family system level of explanation.

Psychoanalysis remains the most comprehensive psychological theory of individual development; though it has also become in practice the most individually oriented of all the psychological approaches, its theory is so grounded in family experiences that it could be expanded to include the observation and treatment of families from a psychoanalytic point of view. This is further explored in chapters 5 and 6 where the works of Freud and other psychoanalytic writers on the family are reviewed.

The psychoanalytic point of view regarding Hamlet quite naturally begins with the Oedipus complex. Without going into the already extensive psychoanalytic writings on Hamlet (see Eissler 1971, Wertham 1941, Lidz 1975, Sharpe 1929, Holland 1966) there is general agreement that Hamlet's internal oedipal conflict was complicated by a family situation that *in reality* directly mirrored his unconscious fantasies. Although, as we mentioned earlier, his conflicts were fairly well internalized, he was also embroiled in a rather severe ongoing pathological family system marked by denial, externalization, projection, and acting out.

Geleerd's discussion (1961) of the role of reality factors that contribute to neurosis in adolescents is most relevant here:

> I draw attention to the traumata which are not primarily staged by the adolescent but *are part of real life* [italics mine] and happen to be a repetition of infantile traumata or fantasies. These traumata intensify the neurosis ... one might say they "fixate" the infantile neurosis. [p. 403]

Hamlet's dilemma could not be better summarized. Psychoanalysis has, however, for complex reasons discussed in chapter 6, chosen not to deal directly with such traumatic external realities except to acknowledge that psychoanalytic treatment is usually not indicated at such times (A. Freud 1968). Yet such traumatic external realities are more a part of everyday family life than we have cared to recognize. In fact the increasing privacy of family life in the industrial era has contributed to the increasingly idiosyncratic methods of child rearing unmonitored by the wider social system (Laslett 1973). These aspects of family life can be studied and treated far more often than has been done up until the present time. The modern family, itself more variable, is probably creating greater variability and individuality (as well as aberrancy) in its offspring than ever before. There are some who feel that the recent greater incidence of narcissistic disorders are a reflection of this increase in familial disturbances.

Hamlet can serve here to illustrate the possible therapeutic options in such situations where both internal and external factors are so prominent. Should a patient present himself for help because of symptoms of anxiety or depression stirred up by his life situation, individual treatment is usually appropriate, especially if the person is aware of the need to change aspects of himself. If however, externalization predominates and family members see one another as the cause of their difficulties or complain of rebellious behavior and seek hospitalization for their disturbed relative (as Claudius might have done in the modern era), a recommendation that the family come for exploratory sessions is indicated. As Langsley et al. (1968) recently demonstrated, hospitalization can in a high perccentage of such cases be averted (see chapter 9 for further discusson of the indications for individual and family therapy).

The decision to treat the individual or the family should be determined by the specific clinical situation. Up until 1950 the basic psychiatric paradigm precluded such a choice and dictated treatment only of the individual. Since 1950 the possibility of treating a family conjointly was introduced, and we turn now to T.S. Eliot's *The Cocktail Party*, which illustrates the emergence of this modality and the questions it raises.

REFERENCES

Auerbach, E. (1953). *Mimesis: The Representation of Reality in Western Literature.* Trans. W.R. Trask. Princeton, New Jersey: Princeton University Press, 1968.

Eissler, K.R. (1971). *Discourse on Hamlet and* Hamlet. New York: International Universities Press.

Freud, A. (1968). Indications and contra-indications for child analysis. *Psychoanalytic Study of the Child* 23:37-46.

Furness, H. (1877). *A New Variorum Edition of Shakespeare.* New York: Dover, 1963.

Geleerd, E.R. (1961). Some aspects of ego vicissitudes in adolescence. *Journal of the American Psychoanalytic Association* 9:394-404.

Havens, L. (1973). *Approaches to the Mind.* Boston: Little, Brown.

Holland, N. (1966). *Psychoanalysis and Shakespeare.* New York: McGraw-Hill.

Johnson, A. (1969). *Experience, Affect, and Behavior.* Chicago: University of Chicago Press.

Karasu, B. (1977). Psychotherapies: an overview. *American Journal of Psychiatry* 134:851-863.

Langsley, D., et al. (1968). *The Treatment of Families in Crisis.* New York: Grune and Stratton.

Laslett, B. (1973). The family as a public and a private institution: an historical perspective. *Journal of Marriage and the Family* 35:480-492.

Lidz, T. (1975). *Hamlet's Enemy.* New York: Basic Books.

Reiss, D. (1971). Varieties of consensual experience: III. contrast between families of normals, delinquents and schizophrenics. *Journal of Nervous and Mental Disorders* 152:73-95.

Rieff, P. (1966). *The Triumph of the Therapeutic.* New York: Harper and Row.

Shakespeare, W. *Hamlet,* New York: Washington Square Press, 1958.

Sharpe, E.F. (1929). The impatience of Hamlet. *International Journal of Psycho-Analysis* 10:270-279.

Simon, B. and Ducey, C. (1975). Ancient Greece and Rome. In *World History of Psychiatry*, Ed. J.G. Howells. New York: Brunner-Mazel.

Stoppard, T. (1967). *Rosencrantz and Guildenstern Are Dead*. New York: Grove Press.

Szasz, T. (1961). *The Myth of Mental Illness*. New York: Harper-Row.

Wertham, F. (1941). The matricidal impulse: critique of Freud's interpretation of Hamlet. *Journal of Criminal Psychopathology* 2:455.

Wertheim, E. (1973). Family unit therapy: the science and typology of family systems. *Family Process* 12:371-376.

Chapter Two

THE EMERGENCE OF
FAMILY THERAPY

In 1949 T.S. Eliot wrote *The Cocktail Party,* an English drawing room comedy about a psychiatrist's treatment of a married couple and one of their friends, a member of their "network." The family therapy movement in psychiatry in which the therapist is the healer of couples, families, and other natural groups began during the decade that followed (Bowen 1966, p. 345).[1]

This chapter will discuss the coincidence of this literary event and the therapeutic innovation of family therapy from two vantage points: (1) How do we understand the emergence of the family therapy movement in mid-twentieth-century America? This discussion will rely heavily upon a number of Talcott Parsons's formulations, particularly as represented in his article "Mental Illness and 'Spiritual Malaise': The Role of the Psychiatrist and of the Minister of Religion" (1964). (2) For the psychiatrist, what theoretical and technical issues are raised by the

---

1. That a poet anticipated the paradigm shift discussed in the previous chapter has a parallel in Freud's crediting Schopenhauer as a forerunner of the discovery of psychoanalysis (Freud 1917).

treatment of the family rather than the individual, as described in Eliot's play?

HISTORY AND SOCIOLOGY

Structural Changes

The anthropological, sociological, and historical literature on the family as an institution is voluminous. Debates about its definition, universality, complexity, structure, function, and relation to the wider social system and to "personality" have long occupied the social sciences.

Phillipe Aries (1962) in *Centuries of Childhood* called attention to the significant shift in Western society's awareness of "the family" as something apart from other groups. Where it had once been synonymous with society, "the family" began to hold society at a distance, to push it back beyond a steadily extending zone of private life (p. 398).[2] This shift occurred slowly since the Middle Ages, when the boundaries of the household and the social order were diffuse. The process of differentiation from an extended kinship system exemplified in the medieval household to today's nuclear family is a shift of overwhelming significance.

Within the earlier, relatively undifferentiated social system, "childhood" was also a less differentiated part of the life cycle. Where today's child, with its prolonged dependency, experiences a discontinuous socialization process (Benedict 1956), the medieval child was viewed as a little adult who was apprenticed out of his family by the age of seven.

Aries sees the specialized function of the modern family as predominantly socialization. He views this as the basis of its power rather than, as many observers say, its weakness. This formulation lies at the heart of Talcott Parsons's analysis of recent social changes affecting the narrower functions of the family.

---

2. Laslett (1973) has more recently and convincingly illustrated this shift to the privacy of the family.

Parsons has noted that, in more primitive social systems, the kinship structure dominates other subsystems, so that few structures are independent of it. In the modern state the nonkinship units such as the political structure, large business firms, universities, churches, and professional associations have not only become free of kinship ties but also assumed positions of power beyond the social influence of the family. Inevitably, this process involves a loss of function of the family as it was. It loses economic, political, and educational functions, for example. The family is now primarily involved with the socialization of children and the stabilization of adult personalities. Together with this more concentrated function of the family unit, the emergence of the primacy and privacy of the nuclear family is one of its most salient features. Parsons (1955) views this shift as the source of significant strain upon the individual.

> In particular, the nuclear family's spouses are thrown upon each other, and their ties with members of their own families of orientation, notably parents and adult siblings, are correspondingly weakened. . . . The consequence of this may be stated as the fact that the family of procreation, and in particular the marriage pair, are in a "structurally unsupported" situation. Neither party has any other adult kin on whom they have a right to "lean for support" in a sense closely comparable to the position of the spouse. [pp. 19-20]

It is just this strain that Parsons links to the growth of the mental health professions in America. The unprecedented salience of the nuclear family in the most industrialized nation in the world developed along with an enormous vogue for treating human problems from the point of view of mental health. "It is the 'American method' to attempt to solve problems in foci of strain by calling in scientifically expert aid. In industry we take this for granted: in human relations it is just coming to the fore" (p. 25).

Value Changes: The Role of Religion

The changes in family structure just noted have been accompanied by a significant disruption in the area of beliefs and values. *Spiritual malaise, anomie,* and *the culture of unbelief* are some terms that have come to represent aspects of the modern era. It is to this area that the religious system, which has undergone a narrowing of functions similar to the family, focuses in its attempt to establish meaning. A characteristic feature of religions today is the varied attempts to reinterpret the traditional belief systems to fit the modern times.

The religious system addresses itself to questions of "ultimate concern," in the sense of Tillich (1952), and commitment to the wider cultural tradition. In Eliot's view (1948) "any religion, while it lasts, and on its own level gives an apparent meaning to life, provides the framework for a culture, and protects the mass of humanity from boredom and despair" (p. 106).

The religious system is here seen as analytically distinct from "the family system" in that it concerns itself with a different aspect or phase of individual development. Where religion in the widest sense integrates the individual into his postadolescent world, the family is responsible for the organization of personality structure, especially in the formative years. Psychiatry is viewed here in a general sense as a "corrective" for problems in this socialization process, and it is a part of what is called the "health or medical system."

In less-differentiated societies, the health and religious sectors are fused. The saving (healing) of souls is particularly central in the development of Christianity. The confessional has long been noted for its therapeutic aspect. Despite these areas of overlap, religion has focused more on the collective, whether viewed as a congregation or parish, while the mental health professions until very recently have generally focused on the troubled individual with psychotherapy based upon a dyadic model.

Within this context Talcott Parsons (1964) predicted a new profession emerging within the religious sector that would address itself to the spiritual malaise experienced by individuals.

A spiritual counselor loosely tied to the church would act as an interpreter and intermediary for the parishioner who could speak freely of his disenchantment with the prevailing religious beliefs without fear of reproof by his particular sect. He thus predicted a professional group whose relation to religion on the one hand, and the parishioner on the other, would be analogous to the relation of the mental health professions to the family and the patient (p. 321).

What Parsons did not anticipate was the evolution of the phenomenon of social psychiatry with its focus of concern the community and its promise of well being for larger numbers of people. Part of the social psychiatry movement (which may be characterized as a shift of emphasis from the individual to larger units) is the evolution of family therapy with its particular focus on that natural group which is intermediate between the individual and the wider social system. This development of social psychiatry is undoubtedly due not only to the strains alluded to above but also to the degree to which "science" and its applications have come to replace religion as a source of ultimate meaning in the modern era (Kramer 1968). This chapter examines the confusion that now exists in respect to the roles of the various mental health professions and religious leaders and introduces some of the family therapy concepts that Eliot intuited.

THE PLAY

It is significant that all seven of the principal characters have no ongoing relations with blood relatives. The decreased influence of the extended kinship system and the isolation of the nuclear family are here explicit. Edward and Lavinia Chamberlayne are an upper-middle-class English couple in the middle of their years. They are without apparent kin except for a sick aunt who is fabricated in the first scene to explain Lavinia's absence from their cocktail party. Lavinia has left Edward for the first time in their five-year marriage. Also present at the party is Alex, a bachelor of means with connections throughout the world. A

benevolent avuncular figure, he has returned from one of his trips
to the East. His counterpart, Julia Shuttlethwaite is a well-
situated, chatty, auntlike intruder, who hides her interest in all
the goings on of this social network behind a pose of
scatterbrained forgetfulness. Edward's and Lavinia's childless
marriage has been marked by both opposition and inseparability
since their honeymoon at Peacehaven, a site chosen only after
characteristic battle:

> *Lavinia*: When we were planning our honeymoon,
> I couldn't make you say where you wanted to go...
> *Edward*: But I wanted *you* to make that decision.
> *Lavinia*: But how could I tell where I wanted to go
> Unless you suggested some other place first? [p. 338]

Stabilization of their marriage has been achieved through
extramarital affairs between Edward and Celia Copplestone, a
young romantic poetess, and between Lavinia and Peter Quilpe, a
young novelist aspiring to a career in the cinema. Both Celia and
Peter are at the party.

With such a secretive menage there is little wonder their
conversation takes on an awkward and absurd quality (about
tigers and champagne mouthwash). The form and title of the
play, *The Cocktail Party* is Eliot's way of highlighting the
communicative and moral breakdown of the modern era.

It is hinted that Peter's dreams of a career in America and his
defection from Lavinia has threatened the delicate balance.
Lavinia has consulted with a Dr. Henry Harcourt-Reilly, who
arrives at the party as an unidentified and apparently uninvited
guest.

Dr. Reilly, aided by Alex and Julia, guides this group to the
final scene two years later when we find that Lavinia and Edward
are reconciled. They are once again giving a cocktail party. Alex
brings the horrid news of Celia's crucifixion as a misionary. Peter,
pursuing his career in America, has returned to do some
"shooting" in England. The unorthodox therapy that preceded
this ending illustrates some of the changing concepts and

techniques introduced by the shift from treating the "individual"
to treating "the family."

FAMILY THEORY AS REFLECTED IN THE COCKTAIL PARTY

The Family as the Unit

The shift in the unit of study from the individual to the family,
whether conceived of as "a system" governed by rules (Jackson
1965), or as a group of persons with interlocking intrapsychic
conflicts (Ackerman 1956), represents a conceptual revolution in
psychiatry.

Just prior to the conjoint consultation in the second act,
Edward asks for asylum. Dr. Reilly notes this request as serving
two functions: (1) "escape from himself" and (2) "to get the better
of his wife" (p. 345). Here is an understanding of the danger of
hospitalization of an "individual" as a pathological resolution of
interpersonal difficulties prophetic in that such alternatives to
hospitalization as, for example, day hospitals that keep the
families intact were first introduced in the 1950s (Wood 1960,
Zwerling and Wilder 1962).

> *Reilly:* And there are also patients
> For whom a sanatorium is the worst place possible.
> We must first find out what is wrong with you
> Before we decide what to do with you. [p. 348]

He goes on to state an extraordinary rationale for conjoint family
therapy just before introducing Edward's wife to the session.

> But before I treat a patient like yourself
> I need to know a great deal more about him,
> Than the patient himself can always tell me.
> *Indeed, it is often the case that my patients*
> *Are only pieces of a total situation*

Which I have to explore. The single patient
Who is ill by himself, is rather the exception.
[p. 350, italics mine]

Dr. Reilly is here following a caveat of Freud written in 1905 (p. 18). Where Freud gathered the pieces of the total situation from his patient, the family therapist seeks such data by direct observation. The departure from the rules of the confidential doctor-patient relationship is here as radical as when Freud departed from the model of professional conduct of his time. The ethics of that time precluded the frank revelation of sexual fantasies (Freud 195, pp. 7-14). Dr. Reilly's behavior is met by comparable resistance.

> *Edward*: What do you mean? Who is this other patient?
> I consider this very unprofessional conduct —
> I will not discuss my case before another patient. [p. 350]
> *Lavinia*: Well, Sir Henry!
> I said I would come to talk about my husband:
> I didn't say I was prepared to meet him.
> *Edward*: And I did not expect to meet *you*, Lavinia.
> I call this a very dishonourable trick.
> *Reilly*: Honesty before honour, Mr. Chamberlayne.
> [p. 351]

With this rule characteristic of many family therapists, the joint session begins. This rule is comparable to that which Freud enjoined upon the individual patient, that is to withhold no conscious thoughts.

After exposing the mutual marital infidelities, Dr. Reilly points out what unites them. Edward's problem is his inability to love anyone. During his wife's brief departure, he realized he did not love Celia but, in fact, wanted the return of his wife without whom he felt vacant. With Peter's defection Lavinia was faced with her inner feelings of being unlovable. They were thus confronted with:

> *Reilly*: .... How much you have in common. The same isolation.
> A man who finds himself incapable of loving
> And a woman who finds that no man can love her [p. 355]
> *You* [Lavinia] could always say: He could not love any woman;
> *You* [Edward] could always say: No man could love her.
> ....
> And so could avoid understanding each other. [p. 356]

This "traded dissociation" (Wynne 1965, pp. 297-300) serving as an "interpersonal defense" (Boszormenyi-Nagy 1965) against painful self-awareness was the bond that united them. They could not live together, and they could not live apart. This elucidation of the interlocking dynamics represents a conceptual bridge between the intrapsychic and interpersonal models of psychology. Within psychoanalysis this kind of interlocking pathology was first described by Johnson and Szurek (1952), who in the 1940s noted the acting out by children of their parents' forbidden impulses. This insight evolved out of the study of both parent and child concurrently, though not conjointly. The shift from treating the individual to treating the "family" has profound implications for the physician's role: where does the physician's responsibility rest, and whose agent is he, the individual's, the family's or society's? (Grosser and Paul, 1965).

Object Relations

The theories of family therapy are still in the process of development. Boszormenyi-Nagy (1965), Laing (1967), and Brodey (1961) have tried to extend the psychoanalytic object relations theory from the intrapsychic into the interpersonal frame of reference. In this connection, W. Brodey's discussion of image relationship has direct relevance to Edward's description of his wife's impact on him:

We had not been alone again for fifteen minutes
Before I felt, and still more acutely —
Indeed, acutely, perhaps, for the first time,
The whole oppression, the unreality
Of the role she had always imposed upon me
With the obstinate, unconscious, sub-human strength
That some women have. Without her, it was vacancy.
When I thought she had left me, I began to dissolve,
To cease to exist. That was what she had done to me!
I cannot live with her — that is now intolerable;
I cannot live without her, for she has made me incapable
Of having any existence of my own. [pp. 348-349]

Brodey defines an image relationship as one in which a person (A) tries to maintain accurate prediction of the other's (B) behavior. A's inner image of B takes precedence over any unexpected behavior of B. The emphasis is on changing reality to fit with expectation rather than expectation to fit reality. Rigidity prevails. Brodey defines a narcissistic relationship as one in which two people make image relationships each to the other and each acting within this relationship to validate the image-derived expectation. He views acute psychosis as the attempt of one member to break out of this system (p. 22).

In a sense Lavinia's departure and Edward's "breakdown" were attempts to break out of their stagnant relationship into a newer equilibrium.

Of interest here is Eliot's comments in an essay written in 1948:

It is human, when we do not understand another human being and, cannot ignore him, to exert an unconscious pressure on that person to turn him into something that we can understand: many husbands and wives exert this pressure on each other. The effect on the person so influenced is liable to be the repression and distortion, rather than the improvement, of the personality: and no man is good enough to have the right to make another over in his own image. [pp. 138-139]

Systems: Homeostasis

Extending the above view of equilibrium between Edward and Lavinia, we turn to the wider network. As mentioned earlier, the marital relationship had stabilized through extramarital relations, Edward with Celia and Lavinia with Peter, forming two interlocking triangles. The centrality of triangles in family theory has been stressed by Bowen (1966) and by Haley (1967). When the equilibrium of this system was threatened by Peter's disengagement from Lavinia, Lavinia sought the aid of Dr. Reilly. This highlights two theoretical issues (from a systems point of view) related to the concept of homeostasis (Jackson 1957).

1. A family group establishes a degree of homeostasis that is altered when any one member of the group changes his behavior or leaves the group. Clinical psychiatry has long taken note of the importance of such "precipitating events" in the decompensation of an individual (as, for example, in a mother's depression when her last child begins school or the sexual acting out of a parent when a son or daughter reaches adolescence). At such periods related to developmental phases, families are strained, and extrafamilial assistance is often required. As mentioned in the first section, the increasing isolation of the nuclear family from its extended kinship network has left the family without its traditional sources of support at these times.

2. Homeostasis is also affected by the introduction of a new member. A therapist is such a "new member." Whether in individual therapy or family therapy, he is a potential "change agent." Whether that change is effected by free association and insight or by more active environmental manipulation is not the issue here. The outsider (expert) uses his unique position as one not "caught in the system." In psychoanalysis the therapist avoids complementing the transference of the patient's past patterned system of object relations, and in family therapy the therapist avoids induction into the family's present patterned styles of relating and communicating. This role of the therapist-stranger is immediately evident in the opening scene of *The Cocktail Party*.

TECHNIQUES AND ROLE OF THE THERAPIST

The technique of the therapist is intimately bound up with his role. The most striking aspect of Dr. Reilly's behavior at the opening of the play is his appearance at the Chamberlayne home as an uninvited guest. He hides his identity during this "home visit" (Behrens and Ackerman 1956) and when the other guests have departed, is invited by Edward to remain.

> Don't go yet.
> I very much want to talk to somebody;
> And it's easier to talk to a person you don't know.
> The fact is, that Lavinia has left me. [p. 304]

His circle had become so complex that Edward could confide in no one, and he reaches out to the stranger. No sooner has he begun than the unidentified guest takes charge and prepares a drink for his host with the following instructions:

> Let me prepare it for you, if I may...
> Strong ... but sip it slowly ... and drink it sitting down.
> Breathe deeply, and adopt a relaxed position. [p. 304]

With this bit of gestalt therapy as preparation he suggests to Edward that he may be better off without his wife. This unexpected suggestion is met with considerable opposition.

> This is not what I expected
> I only wanted to relieve my mind.
> By telling someone what I'd been concealing.
> ....
> I think your speculations rather offensive. [pp. 305-306]

Somewhat in contrast to the approach of the individual therapist, the family therapist is often called upon to "move quickly" and gain entrance into the family. Dr. Reilly has handled this first phase of any family therapy by literally entering the home and taking charge. When Edward objects, the guest will not accept no.

And I knew that all you wanted was the luxury
Of an intimate disclosure to a stranger.
Let me, therefore, remain the stranger
But let me tell you, that to approach the stranger
Is to invite the unexpected, release a new force,
Or let the genie out of the bottle
It is to start a train of events
Beyond your control. So let me continue. [p. 306]

Just as the mother-infant symbiotic equilibrium is often disturbed by strangers, "new" relationships tend to threaten and change older sets of relations.

The Paradoxical Prescription (Watzlawick et al. 1967)

Left by his wife and left with his own ambivalence, Edward feels bereft. Dr. Reilly prescribes that Edward accept the separation and "do nothing." He thus suggests that Edward, no longer knowing himself due to his overinvolvement with Lavinia, learn who "he is" in her absence. Edward can deal with this suggestion by following it or opposing it. In either case he must do something (even if he does nothing). Watzlawick et al. (1967) have described such "maneuvers," which bring patients back into "control" of their symptoms or condition, as paradoxical prescriptions. The prescription, in fact, produces the very opposite of its manifest content.

Edward: .... the effect of all his argument
Was to make me see that I wanted her back. [p. 322]

More recently this "strategic" approach to family therapy has been more fully developed by Palazzoli and her group (1978).

Working Toward Self-Differentiation

Self-differentiation forms the core of Murray Bowen's theory and practice of family psychotherapy (1966). It is a central theme in Eliot's play. Dr. Reilly's suggestion that Edward learn "who he is" elicits Edward's desire for his wife's return:

> And I *must* get her back, to find out what has happened
> During the five years that we've been married.
> I must find out who she is, to find out who I am. [p. 308]

Her departure has had the effect of making Edward feel lost in the dark.[3] Dr. Reilly's efforts are clearly directed toward differentiating each person from what Bowen (1966, p. 347) describes as emotional "stuck togetherness."

A related idea that the self is largely defined by "others" is an idea emphasized in the writings of R. D. Laing (1962). To be taken out of one's usual life situation is to lose oneself or to be disoriented. Psychoanalytic theory views such phenomena as manifestations of poor self-object differentiation (see chapter 6).

The departure of Lavinia has encouraged the hopes of Celia who moves to consolidate her relationship with Edward. Startled when Edward announces that the effect of Dr. Reilly's arguments was to make him want his wife back, Celia no longer recognizes her paramour.

> *Celia:* . . . . I see another person
> I see you as a person whom I never saw before.
> The man I saw before, he was only a projection — [p. 327]

Celia must also differentiate in response to Edward's "new self." The circle is reverberating with change and the shock of new recognitions, giving substance to the observation of Bowen (1966) that "the family is a system in that a change in one part of the system is followed by compensatory changes in other parts of the system" (p. 351). As the hidden relationships of self-deception and

3. The allusion to being lost in the dark, together with his meeting himself as a "middle aged man" (p. 325), are undoubtedly borrowed from Dante's *Divine Comedy;* Dr. Reilly, like Virgil, guides the Chamberlaynes out of the dark wood but cannot provide the final vision of Beatrice. For Dante and Eliot this is the function of faith and religion.

intrigue become manifest, the emergence of new self-discovery is
required. Celia and Edward depart with a toast to their
"guardians," expressing their wish for protection in their new
state of separateness.

When Edward and Lavinia find each other together again, they
struggle and talk of expectations of change.

> *Lavinia*: .... I shall treat you very differently
> In future.
> ....
> *Edward*: I may not have known what life I wanted,
> But it wasn't the life you chose for me.
> You wanted your husband to be successful,
> You wanted me to supply a public background
> For your kind of public life. You wished to be a hostess
> For whom my career would be a support.
> Well, I tried to be accommodating. But in future,
> I shall behave, I assure you, very differently. [p. 339]

They quarrel over who has changed, but change they must.

> *Edward*: So here we are again. Back in the trap,
> With only one difference, perhaps — we can fight each other,
> Instead of each taking his corner of the cage. [p. 341]

The first act ends with the hint of the possibility of a new
equilibrium. The stage is set for the confrontation with Dr. Reilly
several weeks later.

The Omnipotence of the Therapist

At the end of the first act all the principals, including Lavinia,
reconvene in response to telegrams sent mysteriously by Dr.
Reilly. Lavinia, bewildered, only feels

.... that yesterday
I started some machine, that goes on working,
And I cannot stop it; no it's not like a machine —
Or if it's a machine, someone else is running it. [p. 336]

The imagery of "machinery" suggesting a *deus ex machina* implies both the power and the impersonality of the therapist. Dr. Reilly has manipulated events in preparation for his later consultations with Lavinia, Edward, and Celia.

Following the second act consultation with Edward and Lavinia noted above and having sent them off to make the best of their circumstances and to "seek their salvation with diligence," Dr. Reilly sees Celia to whom he offers the alternative of sainthood:

There *is* another way, if you have the courage.
The first I could describe in familiar terms
Because you have seen it, as we have seen it,
Illustrated, more or less, in lives of those about us.
The second is unknown, and so requires faith — [p. 364]

And Celia is on her way to the missionary work that ends in her death at the hands of aborigines. As with the Chamberlaynes, Dr. Reilly ends this meeting with the blessing:

Go in peace, my daughter.
Work out your salvation with diligence. [p. 366]

These religious overtones contribute to the ambiguity of Dr. Reilly's role. Alec Guinness, who played the role of Reilly, insisted in an interview that there was a "misunderstanding" if the role were viewed as that of a "psychiatrist." Rather, he said it was that of a "mental-spiritual advisor and guide in a definitely religious sense" (Zolotow 1950).

Although Guinness, Eliot, and the play's director wished to separate the medical and religious roles, the text is ambiguous. Reilly is identified as a doctor, he has a nurse and he charges fees, etc. His medical role shifts into obvious religious modes. Julia reminds him of the limitations of his medical profession when he expresses uncertainty in work with such as Celia:

Julia: You must accept your limitations. [p. 368]

Earlier Edward has expressed his feeling that his condition was beyond the reach of medicine:

It would need someone greater than the greatest doctor
To cure *this* illness. [p. 323][4]

Julia and Alex, we discover, are assistants to Dr. Reilly, whether viewed as part of the "mental health team" or in the play's terms as 'guardians,'[5] and they, together with Dr. Reilly, conclude the multiple consultations with "libations."

Eliot was criticized for portraying Reilly as a kind of omnipotent, Godlike figure who decides the course of other people's lives. Eliot's reply was that Dr. Reilly "only in a way, assists nature" (Hailer 1950), hinting that the power of leaders is only apparent and largely deceptive, deeply dependent on the context or the rest of the "system." This insight into the dependence of the individual upon his context is a major contribution of the general systems theory, which serves as a basis for much of the newer, nondyadic therapies.

The power and charisma of many family therapists, whether attributable to their behavior or to transference or both remain problematical in terms of technique. Much of what is written by or about the pioneers in the field demonstrate quite active direction of the family. Two recent interesting examples of this

4. This statement about the limitations of the physician in this context is reminiscent of the observation of Lady Macbeth's doctor that: "More needs she the divine than the physician." (*Macbeth* V. i.69) and Macbeth's: "Canst thou minister to a mind diseased?" (V. iii. 40)
5. The concept of guardian was probably taken from Plato's *Republic*. Interestingly the guardians were not to have families so they could devote themselves fully to the ruling of the community (city-state).

directorial mode can be seen in (1) Malcolm's *New Yorker* essay "The One-Way Screen" (1978), which describes the work of Minuchin and (2) Napier's and Whitaker's excellent and unique introduction to the field, *The Family Crucible* (1978).

This problem is compounded by the use of the one-way screen, which is a double-edged sword in the field of therapy. For the first time the therapeutic process can be studied and taught firsthand as other professions are, with student-apprentice and teacher seeing one another work. Psychotherapy is unique among the professions in its reliance upon the spoken and written transmission of its methods rather than direct observation. Freud rarely wrote about technique. Two dangers, however, are that much therapy does require a context of privacy and, all too often, an inevitable theatrical element intrudes when therapy goes public. A family and therapist being viewed by others creates an atmosphere that tends to call for direction, as in the theater. Therapeutic "activism" is thus fostered. There are many families that require and benefit from such public exposure and feedback. This may be a welcome undoing of the extreme "privatization" of so many families in the modern era that we discussed earlier. Many families also require and benefit from such an active role on the part of the therapist. But there are as many or more where such activity interferes with the family members overcoming their own resistances to change. In *The Family Crucible* the authors accept the role of symbolic surrogate parents to the families they treat. This makes their fictionalized but believable account of one family's treatment quite dramatic and readable, but at the same time it raises the questions of when and where the interventions they employ are warranted (see chapter 8; see also chapter 5, p. 97, for Freud's comment on the indications for therapeutic activities).

ELIOT'S RELIGIOUS CONCERN

The relation of the healer or the martyr to the rest of the community is a major preoccupation of Eliot's. He is most concerned in this play with the salvation of the community of ordinary people exemplified by Edward and Lavinia, the cocktail party givers. He feels there is an organic relation between the ordinary and the exceptional ways of life. Celia's crucifixion has the function of cementing the ordinary lives of those about her. Concretely, her departure eased the reconciliation of Edward and Lavinia. In a more religious sense her sacrifice gives symbolic legitimacy to the cultural ideals of her society. The Chamberlaynes and Peter are drawn closer together by Celia's death.

This cosmology is analogous to the family-psychiatry view of the patient's necessary organic relation (as sick one, scapegoat, or vehicle for acting out) to his family. It is to this relationship that the family therapy field, standing between the individual orientation of medical psychiatry and the social focus of community psychiatry, turns its attention. Where Eliot felt the necessity for a few to suffer for the many, family therapy questions the necessity of such sacrifice and attempts to alter family systems to avert such outcomes (Vogel and Bell 1960).

Eliot's religious concerns are relevant to the introductory section of this chapter. It is the structural differentiation of modern society that Eliot associates with the breakdown in moral and social conventions. He hoped to counter this with a restoration of a "Christian Society" (1939). He also sought to return the theatre to its religious origins, especially in restoring poetic drama. He felt a religious attitude to human life was necessary for the writing of true poetic drama (Jones 1965, p. 22).

Religion and Psychiatry

Religious and psychiatric practitioners have long been preoccupied with the relations between them and have struggled to delineate their differentiated roles (Larson 1968, Preston 1955). In this chapter we have alluded to the confusing and overlapping boundaries of religion and psychiatry without spelling out explicitly the dilemmas faced by their practitioners. It is a thesis of this chapter that the very indeterminateness of the boundaries makes such an explication all but impossible.

The profound changes at all levels of modern society leave in their wake the need for reintegration at cultural, social, and individual levels. The relative failure of traditional structures in responding to these changes has paralleled society's turning to "science" for answers to questions of morality and values.[6] M. Kramer (1968) concluded his very relevant discussion of these issues with the following paragraph:

> Science, in the figures of Copernicus, Darwin, and Freud, has destroyed the meaning and purpose of man which has been rooted in traditional religion. This was achieved inadvertently by destroying some of the crucial evidential base on which this view rested. The behavioral sciences have struggled with the meaninglessness of man and have been plagued by the problem. The repeated discovery of man's need for meaning and purpose in life has tempted the behavioral scientist to meet this need by providing a meaning. Too often, it seems to me, the behavioral scientist has confused his scientific role with his personal philosophy and provided moral answers in the guise of scientific ones. It is this confusion of science and morality that is one of the more serious moral implications of the scientific revolution. [pp. 451-452]

CONCLUSION

Just as the discoveries of Freud influenced and were influenced by the Victorian era, the recent burgeoning field of family psychotherapy reflects society's attempt to deal with unprecedented changes, especially in the structure and function of the family. *The Cocktail Party*, portraying the psychiatrist as the new high priest of the social order, reflects some of the dilemmas of professionals who attempt to grapple with these changes. The

---

6. There has also been a reversion in some sectors of society to the occult and mystical, as well as a revivalistic return to "fundamentalist" beliefs.

portrayal of a psychiatrist behaving in an "unethical" and "unorthodox" manner by treating the family network has led us into a discussion of recent theoretical and technical innovations in the field of psychiatry and some aspects of the relation between religion and psychiatry.

With the birth of family therapy a host of problems and questions thus necessarily arose and remain to the present day. Are there definable stages in the development of families comparable to the stages of individual development? If so, how are we to characterize abnormal or healthy family development? Can a typology of families be developed that addresses itself to such a clinical focus? The next two chapters touch upon these issues. The concept of the family life cycle and its relation to the individual life cycle are raised in a discussion of Edward Albee's *Who's Afraid of Virginia Woolf?*, a play about another marital couple who, like Edward and Lavinia, are childless.

Then in chapter 4 we turn to another Eliot play, *The Family Reunion*, for a discussion of the abnormal individual and *familial* developmental disturbances found in psychiatry's most troublesome and still unsolved clinical problem, schizophrenia.

REFERENCES

Ackerman, N.W. (1956). Interlocking pathology in family relationships, In *Changing Concepts in Psychoanalytic Medicine*, ed. S. Rado and G.E. Daniels. New York: Grune and Stratton.

Aries, P. (1962). *Centuries of Childhood, A Social History of Family Life*. New York: Vintage Books.

Behrens, M.L., and Ackerman, N.W. (1956). The home visit as an aid in family diagnosis and therapy. *Social Casework* 37:11-19.

Benedict, R. (1956). Continuities and discontinuities in cultural conditioning. In *Personality in Nature, Society, and Culture*, ed. C. Kluckohn, H. Murray, and D. Schneider. New York: Knopf.

Bowen, M. (1966). The use of family theory in clinical practice. *Comprehensive Psychiatry* 7: 345-374. Reprinted in *Family Therapy in Clinical Practice*. New York: Jason Aronson, 1978.

Boszormenyi-Nagy, I. (1965). Intensive family therapy as process. In *Intensive Family Therapy*, ed. I. Boszormenyi-Nagy and J. Framo. New York: Harper and Row.

Brodey, W.M. (1961). Image, object, and narcissistic relationships. *American Journal of Orthopsychiatry*. 31:69-73.

Eliot, T.S. (1939). *The Idea of a Christian Society*. Published in *Christianity and Culture*. New York: Harcourt, Brace and World.

———(1948). *Notes Toward the Definition of Culture*. Published in *Christianity and Culture*. New York: Harcourt, Brace and World.

———(1952). *The Complete Poems and Plays (1909-1950)*. New York: Harcourt, Brace and World.

Freud, S. (1905). Fragment of an analysis of a case of hysteria. *Standard Edition* 7.

———(1917). A difficulty in the path of psychoanalysis. *Standard Edition* 17:143-144.

Grosser, G.S., and Paul, N.L. (1964). Ethical issues in family group therapy. *American Journal of Orthopsychiatry*. 34:875-884.

Hailer, F. (1950). Interview with T.S. Eliot. *New York Times* April 16, 1950, II, 1:5.

Haley, J. (1967). Toward a theory of pathological systems. In *Family Therapy and Disturbed Families*, ed. G. Zuk and I. Boszormenyi-Nagy. Palo Alto: Science and Behavior Books.

Jackson, D. (1957). The question of family homeostasis. *Psychiatric Quarterly Supplement* 31:79-90.

———(1965). The study of the family. *Family Process* 4:1-20.

Johnson, A., and Szurok, S.A. (1952). The genesis of antisocial acting out in children and adults. *Psychoanalytic Quarterly* 21:323-343.

Jones, D.E. (1965). *The Plays of T.S. Eliot*. Toronto: University of Toronto Press.

Kramer, M. (1968). The behavioral and moral implications of the scientific revolution for psychiatry. *Comprehensive Psychiatry* 9:440-452.

Laing, R.D. (1962) *The Self and Others*. Chicago: Quadrangle Press.

————(1967). Individual and family structure. In *The Predicament of the Family*, ed. P. Lomas. London: Hogarth Press.

Larson, R.F. (1968). The clergyman's role in the therapeutic process: disagreement between clergymen and psychiatrists. *Psychiatry* 31:250-263.

Laslett, B. (1973). The family as a public and private institution: an historical perspective. *Journal of Marriage and the Family* 35:480-492.

Malcolm, J. (1978). The one-way screen. *New Yorker*, May 15, 1978.

Napier, A., and Whitaker, C. (1978). *The Family Crucible*. New York: Harper and Row.

Palazzoli, M.S., et al. (1978). *Paradox and Counterparadox*. New York: Jason Aronson.

Parsons, T. (1955). The American family: its relation to personality and to social structure. In *Family Socialization and Interaction Process*, ed. T. Parsons, R.F. Bales, et al. Glencoe, Ill.: Free Press.

————(1964). Mental illness and "spiritual malaise": the role of the psychiatrist and of the minister of religion. In *Social Structure and Personality*. New York: Free Press.

Preston, R.A. (1955). Landmarks in the relations of psychiatry and religion. *Bulletin of the Menninger Clinic* 19:191-198.

Shakespeare, W. *Macbeth*. Baltimore: Penguin Books, 1956.

Tillich, P. (1952). *The Courage to Be*. New Haven: Yale University Press.

Vogel, E., and Bell, N. (1960). The emotionally disturbed child as a family scapegoat. *Psychoanalysis and Psychoanalytic Review* 47:21-42.

Watzlawick, P., Beavin, J., and Jackson, D. (1967). *Pragmatics of Human Communication*. New York: W.W. Norton.

Wood, E. (1960). Interpersonal aspects of psychiatric hospitalization, I. the admission. *Archives of General Psychiatry* 3:632-641.

Wynne, L.C. (1965). Some indications and contraindications for exploratory family therapy. In *Intensive Family Therapy*, ed. I. Boszormenyi-Nagy and J. Framo. New York: Harper and Row.

Zolotow, M. (1950). Interview with Alec Guinness. *New York Times*, February 26, 1950, II, 3:2.

Zwerling, I., and Wilder, J. (1962). Day hospital treatment for acutely psychotic patients. In *Current Psychiatric Therapies*, Part IV, ed. J. Masserman. New York: Grune and Stratton.

Chapter Three

CHILDLESSNESS AND THE FAMILY LIFE CYCLE

At the moment of conception, life shakes hands with death.
— Edward Munch

I finally feel my wife and I are able to be models for our child
(about to be born).
— Analysand toward end of analysis

In psychology the concept of the individual life cycle (ILC) with its developmental tasks and sequences, as most elaborated by Erikson (1950), has become part of our conventional scientific wisdom. In the emerging family systems approaches the importance of the family life cycle (FLC) has recently received greater attention (Zilbach 1968, Duvall 1962, Rhodes 1977). Haley's book *Uncommon Therapy* (1973), for example, is organized around the concept of the family life cycle. He notes how frequently emotional disorders correspond to critical stages in the family's development.

At the Albert Einstein College of Medicine family therapy

training program, a seven-stage family life cycle sequence has been included in a family diagnostic evaluation form. It has here been expanded to eight stages. An integration of the individual life cycle and such a family life cycle has yet to be attempted. Erikson did this indirectly, in noting, for example, the importance of basic trust for such later stages as the establishment of intimacy when a new family unit is formed (1950, pp. 230-231). Below the two sets of stages are listed, and a diagrammatic integration is then introduced in which the FLC sequence is placed in contiguity with Erikson's eight stages.

Erikson's eight stages of the Individual Life Cycle (ILC)	*Eight stages of the Family Life Cycle (FLC)*
I Trust vs. Distrust	4. Family with infant 0-2½
II Autonomy vs. Shame	5. Family with preschool child
III Initiative vs. Guilt	6. Family with school-aged child
IV Industry vs. Inferiority	7. Family with adolescents
V Identity vs. Role Diffusion	1. Courtship
VI Intimacy vs. Isolation	2. Marriage
VII Generativity vs. Stagnation	3. Pregnancy
VIII Integrity vs. Despair	8. Family with children launched (Grandparenthood)

The stages of family development here presented are somewhat arbitrary but reflect the sense that the family unit organizes itself differently over the years largely around the stages of development of its children. By way of caution, this chronological sequence of FLC stages serves a primarily heuristic purpose. The present high rate of divorce and remarriage contributes to many modern families not fitting easily into this schema. They usually can be represented as a "combination" of these stages. There are also the many recent "alternatives" to the traditional family unit that further makes this categorization hard to apply universally. This points to the more general problem of the absence and perhaps impossibility of any acceptable typology of families. The behavioral sciences have yet to evolve typologies that do justice to the developmental, structural, ethnic, and most clinically relevant, the functional dimensions of families.[1] The present model is a statistically "normative"one that, however, makes no assumptions about the health or normality of individuals or families. Varying degrees of health and pathology can be noted in families at any stage of their evolution. Also, it is possible for a family that does not go from stage 2 to 3, for example, to be a healthy family if the generative impulse has some outlet other than direct child rearing. The question of what constitutes health in a family, value loaded as that is, is even more complex than the question of what constitutes individual psychological health. Only very recently has the question of what constitutes a healthy family been reviewed and addressed more systematically (Lewis et al. 1976). Also in this discussion there is no attempt to discuss the impact or influence of the wider culture or of subcultures upon these unfolding sequences. Different cultures and subcultures place varying importance on each of the individual and family stages. The present schema certainly reflects our heightened cultural focus upon childhood and youth as well as psychology's reliance on the Freudian emphasis on child development. Five of the eight individual stages of Erikson deal with the first quarter of the average life span.[2]

In the attempt to diagram an integration of the individual and family life cycles, I wished to include the cyclical or phasic interdependence of individuals forming families which in turn produce the next generation of individuals. This overlapping of

1. A note on family typology: While no satisfactory typology of families exists Howells (1971) has reviewed various typologies that have appeared in the literature. Wertheim (1973) has more recently constructed a typology deductively, but there have been as yet no attempts to apply it clinically or in research. Reiss (1971), on the other hand, has inductively derived a typology of families that corresonds in some respects to Wertheim's.

2. For an extended discussion of the life cycle at different periods of history see Aries' *Centuries of Childhood*, Chapter 1, "The Ages of Life" (1962). Interestingly, there has been a greater interest recently in adult development which views that previously neglected stage as now crisis ridden (e.g., Gould 1972, Levinson 1978; see also Vailliant 1977 whose follow-up study of pre-World War II Harvard students demonstrated a less crisis-ridden but nonetheless variable unfolding of personality development in the third, fourth and fifth decades of life).

the two cycles over time suggested the following spiral shape. Certain difficulties then emerged in integrating these cycles that turned out to reflect some of the inherent dilemmas or points of strain for the individual and the family in our culture. These cycles at their end stages (VIII and 8) could not easily be integrated with one another. Individuals toward the end of their lives tend in our more mobile and highly differentiated social system to have family ties attentuated. These senior citizens, as we have euphemistically come to call them, frequently live alone, and there is evidence that many of these individuals, cut off from their families in the later years, are more prone to the despair that Erikson describes as the unfortunate outcome of that stage of development.

At the family level the relatively isolated nuclear family has a more discrete beginning, middle, and end phase than the earlier extended family structure. The well-functioning modern family is thus paradoxically more self-dissolving than its earlier counterpart. So it *also* tends to drop out in the final stage.[3]

In the following diagram these discontinuities are represented by shading to indicate the relative "phasing out" of "the individual" and "the family" at their end stages.

3. There has been a great deal of controversy recently around the question of the alleged newness of the nuclear family (see Laslett 1972) and its recent brittleness (see Quitt 1976). While acknowledging that the evolution of the so-called extended family to the nuclear family is more complex than previously appreciated, that the family has changed markedly in its functioning, largely in response to wider economic and technological changes, is undeniable. These changes have profound effects on personality formation in children and later personality stabilization of adults. Barbara Laslett, to take but one dimension, has demonstrated the movement of families toward an increasingly private rather than public structure (see Laslett 1973). Such a change she argues has the effect of decreasing the wider social control of behavior while conversely increasing its variability. I would argue that her hypothesis also helps explain the recent rise to prominence of the mental health professions. For it is the mental health professions' task to treat the ever-increasing variability (i.e., pathology, abnormality) resulting from the family's altered relation to the wider social system. Edward Shorter's recent book *The Making of the Modern Family* (1975) is the most thorough review of these changes.

Erikson's Stages of Individual Development
Correlated with Eight Stages of the Family Life Cycle

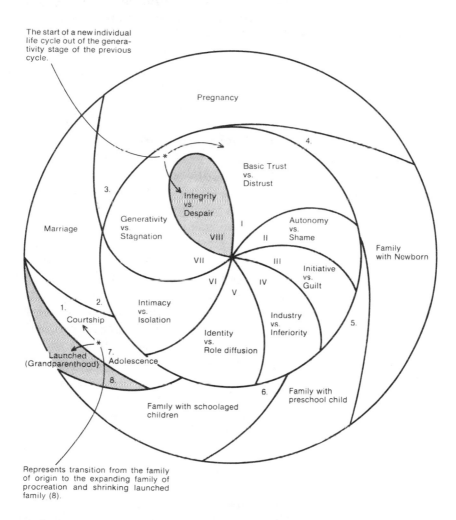

The start of a new individual life cycle out of the generativity stage of the previous cycle.

Pregnancy

Basic Trust vs. Distrust

Integrity vs. Despair

Generativity vs. Stagnation

Autonomy vs. Shame

Marriage

Family with Newborn

Intimacy vs. Isolation

Initiative vs. Guilt

Courtship

Industry vs. Inferiority

Identity vs. Role diffusion

Launched (Grandparenthood)

Adolescence

Family with preschool child

Family with schoolaged children

Represents transition from the family of origin to the expanding family of procreation and shrinking launched family (8).

In the individual life cycle schema of Erikson the assumption is made that the problems of each stage of development are colored by the way in which the earlier stages of development have been experienced. In the present context this assumption is extended to the family life cycle in that the modes of traversing the difficulties and tasks of its phases have their precursors in the earlier individual life cycles of each parent. As children go through the varying phases of development, there is a complex interplay of the parents' partial and complex recapitulation of their own development in the next generation. This view of the generational transmission of emotional disturbance has been most articulated by Bowen (1966) and Nagy and Spark (1973). There are also numerous illustrations in the psychoanalytic literature of this phenomenon, which will be noted in chapters 5 and 6. This perspective has led some family therapists to extend their therapeutic intervention to the families of origin of, for example, a married couple, even if they are living at great distances from these families (Framo, 1976, Napier and Whitaker 1978).

The schema presented here is highly condensed and does not imply a simple and direct one-to-one correspondence of the two cycles. The overlapping, for example, of the family with a newborn (FLC #4) stage and the Basic Trust stage (ILC #I) merely notes the central importance of these stages to one another. The parents of a newborn must also deal with other life cycle issues in one way or another. It is just that the presence of a newborn in the home especially touches upon conflicts in the parents around the issues of basic trust. If that stage has been successfully traversed by the parents the likelihood of difficulty in those individual and family stages is lessened.

Similarly when a child, for example, has a school phobia, it is not uncommon to find a comparable conflict in one of the parents around that stage in their own development. This again does not imply that a school phobia does not have earlier developmental precursors in parent and child (as for example problems with separation-individuation). Most disturbances at any stage except in unusual reactive situations (e.g., the unexpected death of a family member) result in part from such earlier conflicts. It is just that the most immediate forces in the development of symptoms frequently frow from the contemporaneous family context. It is such a view that places importance on the evaluation of and intervention in that context *before* embarking upon individual treatment where intrapsychic factors are then seen to be more determinative of continuing pathology.[4]

Returning to these interweaving family and individual life cycles, where does one find a point of entry? The biological conception of the first child is in some ways the family's most critical stage. This stage is instinctually rooted in biology and assures the preservation of the species. It also actualizes the parents' childhood wish of displacing and/or identifying with their own parents by having a baby. This wish, repressed in childhood, when enacted in derivative form in adulthood extends (from stage 2 to stage 4) the family structure quantitatively and qualitatively while simultaneously beginning a new individual life cycle. Its importance in the FLC is perhaps comparable in significance to the separation-individuation process (stages I and II of Erikson) in the individual cycle. A child who has not successfully individuated self from object struggles with developmental arrest, just as a married couple that does not actualize a generative impulse (which need not be limited to biological offspring) also struggles with developmental arrest and stagnation. While this FLC stage is most commonly defined by the addition of a new member, the separation-individuation process is facilitated by the presence of another person besides the maternal object, usually, though not necessarily, the father (Abelin 1971). The adage two's company and three's a crowd with its romantic connotation probably has its roots in this early stage of individual and family development. Either the arrival of a sibling and/or the presence of the father disturbs the mother-infant symbiotic tie while simultaneously facilitating individual development.

While usually the source of joy and celebration, the arrival of a

4. This shift toward seeing the family first was noted in chapter 2, on *The Cocktail Party*, where Dr. Harcourt-Reilly proceeded to break with conventional psychiatric practice by interviewing husband and wife together. And we shall see subsequently, in chapter 5, on Freud's writings on marriage and the family, that in the Dora case he also asserted the critical role of the patient's family. It took fifty years for this awareness to be translated into the change in therapeutic intervention reflected by family therapy.

newborn is nonetheless also accompanied by anxiety and usually unacknowledged or repressed anger. The responsibilities of parenthood must be met, and the intimate marital relationship, fantasied or otherwise, is to varying degrees attenuated. That the arrival of a newborn is attended by rather significant amounts of stress can be noted in its association with overt mental illness. Postpartum illnesses most frequently encountered in the mother have been described on occasion in other family members (Asch 1974). Lomas (1967) clinically noted in his family-oriented paper on postpartum illness the critical role of the home atmosphere, which is at times particularly unreceptive to a newcomer. The stressfulness of this stage is also suggested by its accompanied high rate of separation and divorce.

While most married couples may experience the arrival of a newborn as a normative stress, all too often an already strained marriage will attempt consciously or unconsciously to achieve a firmer equilibrium by having a child. Depending on the specific psychodynamics involved, this may immediately fail with an ending of the marriage or it may establish a new homeostasis that works with complications for each member's psychological development. In such an instance the above adage might be reversed. Two's a crowd and three's company. This is especially true in families with a schizophrenic offspring. In families with a young schizophrenic offspring the parents are often at a loss for words when asked to imagine what their lives would be like without their child. The history often includes the parents never having taken a vacation without their child or children. Family therapists have seen case after case in treatment where assisting parents in taking a weekend together without their schizophrenic offspring for the first time in years, has the following sequelae. Having left their son or daughter with relatives, they then call home to see "if everything is all right," thus setting in motion a premature ending of their time together. As we shall note in the next chapter on T.S. Eliot's *The Family Reunion* (about schizophrenia and the family) such separation means the loss of a symbiotic bond with its accompanying fear of death and disintegration. This fear was dramatized in *The Family Reunion*, by the actual death of the mother upon the individuation and departure of her son.

The equilibrating third person or activity that helps diminish the threat of object loss and/or deflects the hostility that endangering a dyadic relationship, may be a child, an extramarital partner, a parent, overwork, alcohol, or drugs. The family systems approaches, especially the work of Bowen (1978), has emphasized the pathogenic impact of such tendencies toward "triangling" in a person or activity.

With this brief discussion of the relationship of the individual and family life cycles as background, we turn to Edward Albee's *Who's Afraid of Virginia Woolf?* This epochal drama portrays a married couple unable to make the transition from stage 2 to 3 except through the creation of a triangle via a secretly shared fantasied child. The play is about their difficulty in creating generational continuity given their own traumatic pasts. From the opening scene, in dramatic structure and content, the play deals with this impasse. Their ambivalence toward one another, extended to the unexpected guest, the newcomer, the child and to some degree the next generation, resolves itself in childlessness.

THE PLAY

Imagine how we might view the cast of characters if they were to be seen clinically. In the initial diagnostic evaluation of a family seeking help we usually note the biographical data identifying each family member.

The Players

Martha:	A large, boisterous woman, 52, looking somewhat younger. Ample but not fleshy.
George:	Her husband, 46. Thin; hair going gray.
Honey:	26, a petite blonde girl, rather plain.
Nick:	30, her husband. Blond, well put-together, good looking.

The Scene

The living room of a house on the campus of a small New England college.

We are apparently confronted with two childless couples. We note that Martha is older than her husband, and within minutes of the play's opening that detail is to take on greater significance. After demanding one drink after another Martha adds the aggressive demand that George "give your Mommy a big sloppy kiss." Defining herself albeit mockingly as mother to George, she then asks him for affection. In more technical terms she introduces a generational boundary into the marriage while simultaneously confusing that boundary with a contradictory communication. It is not unlike parents who, when kissing their children goodnight, ask that they be kissed goodnight.

The other couple, we note, are young enough to be Martha and George's children, and they are in fact soon alluded to as "kids" when they arrive as guests. That Nick and Honey are substitute children is further illustrated in George mistaking Nick's age as twenty-one, the age of their soon-to-be-revealed fantasied son. They are also *new* to the campus, quasi-orphans who at the last campus in Kansas "had to make our way all by ourselves ..." (p. 27). Martha has invited them for drinks at 2:00 A.M., after a party given by her father, the president of the college. Two o'clock in the morning is a peculiar time for the arrival of guests. The only other newcomers known to put in an appearance at such an hour are newborns, not yet acquainted with the culturally appropriate times for arrivals and departures. Birth and death, marking the two ends of the individual life cycle, continue as universally unscheduled arrivals and departures.

But what of children, we query? George and Martha might have checked with one another and answered in the negative. They would be unwilling at first to reveal their fantasied son who has grown up with them and whose twenty-first birthday was the next day. Nick and Honey plan to have children "when we're more settled." The play, after the arrival of Honey and Nick, is a long early morning's journey into day during which each person's vulnerabilities and secrets are uncovered in not-so-funny games titled "Humiliate the Host," "Hump the Hostess," and "Bringing Up Baby." At the end the imaginary son is given up, leaving George and Martha alone, "just the two of us."

The setting is on a college campus, our society's traditional transitional stage between youth and adulthood. The college is in a town called New Carthage. More of that detail later.

The Newcomer and the Formation of a Triangle

The first lines of a novel, as often the first utterance in a psychotherapeutic session, foreshadows what is to follow. The opening of the play starts at once with the electrifying, murderous dueling of Martha and George. They are coming home after another of Martha's father's parties for the faculty.

(Set in darkness. Crash against front door. Martha's laughter heard. Front door opens, lights are switched on. Martha enters, followed by George)

Martha: Jesus. . . .
George: . . . Shhhhhhh. . . .
Martha: . . . H. Christ. . . .
George: For God's sake, Martha, it's two o'clock in the . . . .
[p. 3]

The stage directions call for a crash against the door as the couple goes from darkness into light, all images suggestive of the birth delivery. Martha then invokes the product of a virgin birth, the savior of mankind. This opens a play about a fantasied child created to save a sadomasochistic marriage as Christ was "born to save mankind." We never do learn what she is exclaiming about. The exclamation is merely a cue for George to shush her and begin another cycle of their characteristic vitriolic battling. This characteristic battling has already become an informal diagnostic category. In clinical settings it is not uncommon for a case

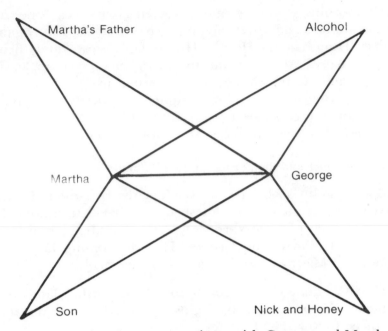

presentation to invoke a comparison with George and Martha.[5]

As mentioned in the beginning to this chapter the family systems approaches have pointed to the need for such a triangle or triangles to stabilize the escalating violence. For George and Martha there are several triangles that deflect these feelings:

1. There is Martha's father, the college president to whom Martha compares George unfavorably and upon whom they are both dependent.

5. A couple consulting me for marital dissatisfaction described their never having fought in thirteen years of marriage. They feared that expression of their negative feelings might turn into battling "like that in *Who's Afraid of Virginia Woolf?*" They each came from families where parents fought considerably. Their fear of repeating their parents' difficulties was reinforced by rather marked obsessive-compulsive character structures. When the wife ever so gently revealed some of her emotional vulnerability, her husband in the next session expressed the feeling that she had taken quite a beating the last time, and he feared it was now his turn to "take a beating," as it were. They were thus in their emotional isolation warding off an overt sadomasochistic interaction that is the stamp of Albee's play.

2. Alcohol does not contain their rages but serves to trigger even greater levels of fighting. Steinglass and his associates (1976) have recently described the intricate patterns of a couple's interaction which alcohol elicits and participates in. In their work alcoholism is viewed less as a specific medical illness than as part of an interpersonal process.

3. The creation of an imaginary child helped stabilize twenty-one years of their twenty-three-year marriage. At the time of the play he is "away at college."

4. His place is taken during the course of the play by the guests, Nick and Honey. They then share in the triangling process with alcohol, which in turn serves to reveal aspects of their own troubled relationship.

Families of Origin

What earlier life experience and family structures are here repeated or transformed, requiring this pathological triangling? What do we learn of Martha's and George's parents? Are there any siblings? Siblings often help defuse the more intense involvement of only children in the primary family triangle. Martha and George are apparently only children. Martha "grew up with daddy," who is described by George as a patriarchal figure in the college where he demands and expects his staff to "cling to the walls of this place, like the ivy" (p. 41). When they die the staff are buried on campus to fertilize the grounds while the old man defies the life cycle and never dies. George fantasizes that he must already be two-hundred years old. On the other hand, Martha's mother died "early." We are not told at what age, but the implication is that Martha was motherless. Her motherlessness is reinforced by the added detail that her father remarried, for money, an old lady with warts. She died soon after. Martha idealized her father and planned to marry a faculty member who would ultimately succeed him. George could not live up to this idealized image, hence the debunking of him and the hoped-for compensation via the fantasied son. Martha, in having a fantasied

child, could control the mother-child relationship that was
disrupted in her own development.

George, we learn, killed both of his parents accidentally. He
killed his mother with a shotgun during early adolescence. Then
at sixteen he killed his father in a car accident, when he was
learning to drive. "He swerved the car, to avoid a porcupine, and
drove straight into a large tree" (p. 95).

At the end of the play when George directs the death of their
fantasy son he adds with a chuckle that he was killed "on a
country road, with his learner's permit in his pocket, he swerved,
to avoid a porcupine, and drove straight into a [. . . .] large tree" (p.
231). In having a fantasied child, George has spared himself the
actualization of his fear of a repetition of the death of the father
(himself) at the hands of the son. It is relevant here that he finally
does away with their son just as Nick, the surrogate son, has gone
off to hump Martha.

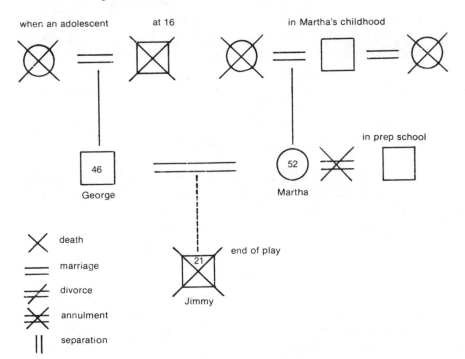

In the family diagnostic evaluation form mentioned earlier space is left to outline the genealogy of the family, a procedure pioneered by Bowen. For George and Martha it would look like this.

The Imaginary Child

In addition to George's and Martha's fighting for control of one another, the control of the parent-child relationship was the grounds for many of Martha's and George's battles as each felt the other was the more destructive parent of their child.

> *George* [describes Martha]: [. ...] climbing all over the poor bastard, trying to break the bathroom door down to wash him in the tub when he's sixteen, dragging strangers into the house at all hours. ... [p. 215]

> *Martha*: And as he grew ... and as he grew ... oh! so wise! ... he walked evenly between us [. ...] and these hands, still, to hold us off a bit, for mutual protection, to protect us all from George's ... weakness ... and my ... necessary greater strength ... to protect himself ... and *us*. [pp. 221-222]

> *George* [after mockingly describing how Martha had had a disappointing husband, a father who cared little for her]: [. ...] has a son who fought her every inch of the way, [. ...] who didn't want to be used as a goddamn club whenever Martha didn't get things like she wanted them! [p. 225]

> *Martha*: [. ...] A son who was so ashamed of his father he asked me once if [...] he was not our child; who could not tolerate the shabby failure his father had become [. ...] Who writes letters only to me! [pp. 225 226]

> *George*: Oh, so you think! To me! At my office!

They go on and on projecting onto the son each of their narcissistic concerns. The defense of projective identification in family interrelations has been most fully studied and described by Zinner and Shapiro (1972) in studies at the NIMH of borderline adolescents and their families. The defense allows a person to ward off painful affects, impulses, and memories by externalizing and reenacting them with significant others. The projective defense is, of course, central to the development of phobias. The play's title is, in fact, a condensation of the childhood counter-phobic limerick, "Who's afraid of the big bad wolf?" and Virginia Woolf, the noted writer, who committed suicide in her later years and was herself childless.

Just as keeping the son's existence secret protected the projective defense by denying any corrective reality, the killing of the son stripped the defense and turned Martha and George back upon themselves.

> *George*: It will be better. [. . . .]
> *Martha*: Just . . . us?
> *George*: Yes. [. . . .]
> (Puts his hand gently on her shoulder; she puts her head back and he sings to her, very softly)
> Who's afraid of Virginia Woolf?
> Virginia Woolf
> Virginia Woolf,
>
> *Martha*: I . . . am . . . George . . . . [pp. 240-241]

When such externalizing defenses are given up in either individual or family therapy, patients come to acknowledge the depression and vulnerability they had been warding off.

Nick and Honey

We learn little of Nick's and Honey's earlier histories, other than that they were childhood playmates, apparently also without siblings, who played at the game of doctor when they were eight and six. Their later courtship is dramatically recounted and serves as further graphic indication of the play's focus on the inability to conceive. Their wedding was precipitated by an hysterical pregnancy and followed by subsequent abortions or miscarriages. Their young marriage thus parallels George's and Martha's. Honey's imaginary pregnancy forced a marriage, while George and Martha created an imaginary child to keep their marriage going. Honey's wish for a child is later reiterated four times while George and Martha reminisce about the raising of their son. The theme of aberrant reproduction is further developed and interwoven in the generational bantering between George and Nick early in the play. Nick, a biologist, is seen by George as part of the threatening younger generation in the academic world. George fears the eclipse of his discipline, history, by the new army of scientists whom he imagines will replace the traditional reproductive process with the extrauterine procedure of cloning. This experimental method of genetically reproducing offspring identical with the (one) parent is metaphorically equatable with George's and Martha's self-centered projections "out of their heads" and onto their imaginary child.

New Carthage

Albee's choice of New Carthage as the setting for Martha's and George's warring suggests parallels to old Carthage. According to legend, Carthage, a major ancient warring city and rival to Rome, was founded by Dido, who had been driven from her own home. Her later childless, tragic romance with the Trojan prince Aeneas is celebrated in Virgil's *Aeneid*. Aeneas, the son of Venus, also a homeless wanderer after the defeat of Troy, ended up in Carthage, where he and Dido became lovers. When Aeneas was reminded by Jupiter of his mission to found the kingdom that was to become Rome, Aeneas left Carthage and Dido killed herself upon a funeral pyre.

Some centuries later, after Carthage was finally destroyed in a war with Rome in 146 B.C., the Romans are said to have salted the earth so that nothing would grow there. The theme of homelessness, childlessness, and sterility is thus reinforced by Albee's choice of New Carthage.

THE SUCCESS OF *WHO'S AFRAID OF VIRGINIA WOOLF?*: SOCIOLOGICAL AND PSYCHOANALYTIC CONSIDERATIONS.

In chapter 2, on T.S. Eliot's *The Cocktail Party*, we discussed the emergence of the family therapy movement as a response to the increasing isolation and instability of the modern family.[6] In creating, in 1949, the first family therapist in literature, Eliot anticipated the arrival of this particular healer onto the therapeutic stage.

During the three decades since then, when the instability of the family has become even more manifest, the United States's most successful playwright wrote his most celebrated play. Albee's *Who's Afraid of Virginia Woolf?* portrays a husband and wife, themselves products of traumatic childhoods, clawing at one another and unable to create a viable next generation. This play portraying two destructive and sterile marriages has become a milestone in American drama comparable to Miller's *Death of a Salesman*. Its popularity reflects our culture's preoccupation with the troubled institution of the family and concerns about its survival.

While one can argue that all great literature and drama beginning with the Bible elaborates the perrenial conflicts of individual and family life, the particular theme of childlessness/ parentlessness that pervades Albee's play taps an underlying cultural anxiety about the survival of the family unit no longer able to effectively raise the next generation. In Albee's play this is dramatized in the inability to have children at ail. For all the conflict in the biblical family of Adam and Eve the subsequent generations were swollen with offspring. Oedipus, despite his

---

6. Another impetus to the family therapy movement stemmed from psychiatry's attempt to unravel the still-baffling mystery of schizophrenia. In the fifties the study of families with a schizophrenic member led researchers and clinicians to begin to recognize the "system properties" of the family unit. But the energy of the family therapy movement comes from the almost epidemiclike instability of the family and the mental health professions' inability to treat all the individual casualties of that instability.

tragic fate, nonetheless fathered a further generation, troubled though it was.

While the play manifestly reflects contemporary concerns about the family, its power to grip audiences as it has done requires a more psychological exploration. Unconscious/preconscious fantasies and conflicts must help to explain its popular appeal.

Two psychoanalytically oriented papers about Albee's play have appeared in the literature. Avery (1973) chose to emphasize the dynamics of the sadomasochistic relationship, utilizing the object relations theory of Guntrip. Avery views the inseparability and perseverance of George and Martha as serving "one of man's deepest conflicts — his need for loving attachment and his dread of loss" (p. 347). The sadomasochistic coloring of the attachment is summarized by Avery as the need to "retain an object relationship with the internalized primitive parental objects" (p. 359). In Avery's study, which emphasizes the need to ward off feelings of loss and abandonment, he adds the biographical detail of Albee's own adoption as probably contributing to the artistic working out of this conflict.

Blum (1969), while making no such inference and not mentioning Albee's adoption, develops the point of view drawn directly from the play that an adoption fantasy, as an elaboration of the universal family romance, "is the hidden underlying theme which gives cohesive unity to the play" (p. 902). Blum's detailed and convincing analysis in terms of the family romance from an intrapsychic and ILC point of view reflects the FLC view put forth in this paper. The family romance fantasy stems from the child's inevitable disappointment with his parents. Preoedipal and oedipal ambivalent feelings toward the parents seek resolution by the fantasy of adoption. The real biological parents are fantasied to be of royalty or nobility. So, for Blum, the structure of the play with its two sets of parental couples represented by history and biology resonates with the child's uncertainty as to who its "real" biological vs. experienced historical parents are.

Viewed from the family life cycle perspective, the conflict is manifested not by the wish of the child to reject its parents, but by the parents' need to reject the child by remaining childless. The creation and later destruction of a mythic child is here viewed as a pathological resolution of the generativity vs. stagnation polarity in the individual life cycle with a corresponding impasse at the pregnancy stage of the family life cycle. The tendency for marital couples to create pathological triangles to reduce their dyadic tensions was noted and related to their own earlier family life experiences.

Blum's discussion of the play as a variation of the family romance points to a frequent misunderstanding or ambiguity within psychoanalytic theory. That ambiguity relates to the relative importance of reality vs. fantasy in the development of emotional disturbances. While psychoanalysis has always recognized the importance of the environment, there has been a tendency to place greater emphasis upon the role of internal drives, fantasies, and wishes. This is due, in part, to psychoanalytic methodology that generates such data (see chapter 6). It is also due to the fact that the patients treated by psychoanalysis tend to be those on the healthier end of the continuum of patients. Psychopathology in these patients is determined less by external traumatization than by internal unconscious conflicts.[7] Weighing such internal and external determinants, difficult as that is, would be facilitated by more direct observation of children and their families.

The family romance and its relation to adoption illustrates this difficulty, for in adoption the family romance is *actualized*. It is one thing to deny one's parentage by a fantasy of noble ancestry and quite another to be given up for adoption. The same point is made in chapter 1, on Hamlet, whose oedipal wishes have received greater emphasis than the fact that his mother and uncle *realized* his incestuous and murderous wishes. No doubt the more reality conforms with the unconscious fantasy life the more we speak of traumatization. No longer does an unpleasant fantasy

7. F. Pine (1977) has most recently stated this differently in stressing the importance, for patients undergoing psychoanalytic treatment, of "a reasonable stability of their core attachments from infancy and early childhood."

need to be repressed or otherwise defended against, a painful reality must be integrated by the ego. One method of dealing with such a "trauma" is through the reelaboration or distortion by further fantasies and by often-repeated action. Unacceptable reality is thus reshaped into a structure of fantasy and illusion. This tension between illusion and reality, so central to the artistic endeavor generally, is especially pronounced in Albee's play as we wonder, for example, if the child is real or not. The reworking of traumata in the life of the artist is given a slightly different emphasis by Phyllis Greenacre (1957), who has emphasized the constitutional component of the artist's "greater than average sensitivity to sensory stimulation." In this context she (1958), also demonstrated the important role of the family romance in the development of the artist.

When the artist successfully transcends his personal experience in the artistic product he expresses for the reader or audience powerful preconscious or unconscious fantasies or conflicts. In Albee's play the rejection by parents of children reverses the ubiquitous family romance fantasy of adoption giving the play its power. In portraying two childless marital couples so turned in upon themselves and an imaginary child, the play also portrays the family at a quasi dead end at a time when the family as an institution has come under great strain and criticism.

REFERENCES

Abelin, E.L. (1971). The role of the father in the separation-individuation process. In *Essays in Honor of Margaret S. Mahler*, ed. J.B. McDevitt and C.F. Settlage. New York: International Universities Press.

Albee, E. (1969). *Who's Afraid of Virginia Woolf?* New York: Atheneum.

Anthony, E.J., and Benedek, T. (1970). *Parenthood: Its Psychology and Psychopathology*. Boston: Little, Brown.

Aries, P. (1962). *Centuries of Childhood: A Social History of Family Life*. New York: Vintage Books.

Asch, S.S., and Rubin, L.J. (1974). Post-partum reactions: some unrecognized variations. *American Journal of Psychiatry* 131:870-874.

Avery, N.C. (1973). The exorcism of a tabooed wish: an analysis of *Who's Afraid of Virginia Woolf? Seminars in Psychiatry* vol. 5:347-357.

Blum, H.P. (1969). A psychoanalytic view of *Who's Afraid of Virginia Woolf? Journal of the American Psychoanalytic Association* vol. 17: 888-903.

Boszormenyi-Nagy, I., and Spark, G. (1973). *Invisible Loyalties: Reciprocity in Intergenerational Family Therapy*. New York: Harper and Row.

Bowen, M. (1978). *Family Therapy in Clinical Practice*. New York: Jason Aronson.

Duvall, F. (1962). *Family Development*. New York: J.B. Lippincott.

Erikson, E. (1950). *Childhood and Society*. New York: W.W. Norton.

Framo, J. (1976). Family of origin as a therapeutic resource for adults in marital and family therapy: You can and should go home again. *Family Process* 15: 193-210.

Freud, S. (1905). A case of hysteria. *Standard Edition* 7.

Gould, R. (1972). The phases of adult life: a study in developmental psychology. *American Journal of Psychiatry* 129:521-531.

Greenacre, P. (1957). The childhood of the artist: libidinal phase development and giftedness. *Psychoanalytic Study of the Child* 12:47-72.

———(1958). The family romance of the artist. *Psychoanalytic Study of the Child* 13: 9-43.

Haley, J. (1973). *Uncommon Therapy*. New York: W.W. Norton.

Howells, J.G. (1971). *Theory and Practice of Family Psychiatry*. New York: Brunner-Mazel.

Laslett, B. (1973). The family as a public and private institution: an historical perspective. *Journal of Marriage and the Family*. 35:480-492.

Laslett, P., ed. (1972). *Household and Family in Past Time*. New York: Cambridge University Press.

Levinson, D. (1978). *The Seasons of a Man's Life*. New York: Knopf.

Lewis, J. et al. (1976). *No Single Thread, Psychological Health in Family Systems*. New York: Brunner-Mazel.

Lomas, P., ed (1967). In *The Predicament of the Family*: The significance of post-partum breakdown. London: Hogarth Press.

Napier, A., and Whitaker, C. (1978). *The Family Crucible*. New York: Harper and Row.

Pine, F. (1977). On therapeutic change: perspectives from a parent-child model. In *Psychoanalysis and Contemporary Science*, vol. 5. New York: International Universities Press.

Quitt, M.H. (1976). The contemporary "crisis" of the American family: the perspective of a family historian and psycho-historian. *Journal of Psychohistory*, vol. 4, no. 1.

Reiss, D. (1971). Varieties of consensual experience: III contrast between families of normals, delinquents and schizophrenics. *Journal of Nervous and Mental Diseases* 152:73-95.

Rhodes, S. (1977). A developmental approach to the life cycle of the family. *Social Casework* 57:301-310.

Shorter, E. (1975). *The Making of the Modern Family*. New York: Basic Books.

Speck, R , and Attneave, C. (1973). *Family Networks*. New York: Pantheon.

Steinglass, P. (1976). Experimenting with family treatment approaches to alcoholism 1950-1975, a review. *Family Process*, vol. 15: 97-123.

Valliant, G. (1977). *Adaptation to Life*. Boston: Little, Brown.

Wertheim, E. (1973). Family unit therapy, the science and typology of family systems. *Family Process*, 12:361-376.

Zilbach, J. (1968). Family Developments. In *Modern Psychoanalysis*, ed. J. Marmor. New York: Basic Books.

Zinner, J., and Shapiro, R. (1972). Projective identification as a mode of perception and behavior in family of adolescents. *International Journal of Psychoanalysis*, vol. 53:523-529.

Chapter Four

SCHIZOPHRENIA AND
THE FAMILY

In the last chapter we examined the relationship of the individual and family life cycles in *Who's Afraid of Virginia Woolf?*, a play in which a continuing interplay of these cycles was precluded by the impasse of childlessness. We noted in that chapter that the birth of the first child represented the most critical stage in a family's development, profoundly and irreversibly altering the family's structure. Simultaneously the baby is enveloped in a brief phase of symbiosis, soon to be followed by the separation-individuation process, which Mahler, Pine, and Bergman have called "the psychological birth of the human infant" (1975). Severe disturbances in this early stage of development have been implicated in the development of the schizophrenic disorders. We turn now to T.S. Eliot's *The Family Reunion,* a play portraying a "schizophrenic" man and his family. It illustrates some clinical insights of both individual psychiatry and family psychiatry.

PLOT SUMMARY

We are told in the play that thirty-five or forty years before the action begins, Lord Monchensey and Lady Amy were unhappily married and childless. Amy became pregnant with her first son, Harry, only after her youngest sister, Agatha, came to live with them. The pregnancy precipitated Lord Monchensey's plans to murder his wife. Agatha, who had become his mistress, interceded for the sake of the unborn child, whom she afterward felt to be partly her own. After two more sons were born, Lord Monchensey left his family and died soon after. Amy raised her sons with the aid of servants and relatives, after "adopting" Mary, the orphaned daughter of a cousin.

Amy had hoped and designed that Harry and Mary would wed and remain on the family estate. Instead, against his mother's wishes, Harry married a depressed and dependent woman in a ceremony that excluded his family except for his Aunt Agatha. While on a transatlantic voyage a year before the play begins, his wife drowns. Harry is not sure if he pushed her or fantasied that he had pushed her overboard. The play opens as Amy, feeling her own death to be near, summons her family to a reunion on her birthday with the hope that Harry would take charge of Wishwood, the family estate.

In the play's two acts, which precede and follow Amy's birthday dinner, Harry, helped by Mary and Agatha, is able to leave his family again. This time he goes without the menacing furies (hallucinations) that had been pursuing him since he had left home eight years previously. His mother dies upon his departure.

THE SCHIZOPHRENOGENIC MOTHER AND THE SKEWED FAMILY

The concept of the "schizophrenogenic mother" was first briefly described by Frieda Fromm-Reichmann (1948).

The schizophrenic is painfully distrustful and resentful of

other people, due to the severe early warp and rejection he encountered in important people of his infancy and childhood, as a rule mainly in a schizophrenogenic mother. [p. 265]

The concept with its etiological (and somewhat blaming) implication stimulated considerable clinical research, which has been reviewed and contributed to by Cheek (1964). As in the early work of Johnson and Szurek (1952) on the influence of parents in the acting out of their children, the concept facilitated a shift in emphasis from a model weighted on intrapsychic factors in understanding mental illness to a more interpersonal one. It helped investigators study parents directly and ultimately, by the fifties, helped them study and treat the entire family as a group.

The clinical literature has, in addition to its etiological emphasis, on rare occasions given a fuller account of the schizophrenic's mother. Searles (1958) for example, in his paper on the relationship between the schizophrenic and his mother, has contributed a more sympathetic view of this vilified woman. The characterization of Amy in *The Family Reunion* is "classical" in its demonic aspects, but it also provides more insight into her "schizophrenogenesis." Amy's opening speech expresses her depression, her fear of death, and her longing for warmth:

> I have nothing to do, but watch the days draw out,
> Now that I sit in the house from October to June,
> And the swallow comes too soon and the spring will be over
> And the cuckoo will be gone before I am out again.
> O sun, that was once so warm, O light that was taken for
> > granted
> When I was young and strong, and sun and light unsought
> > for
> And the night unfeared and the day expected
> And clocks could be trusted, tomorrow assured
> And time would not stop in the dark! [p. 225]

We see moments later that this fear of death is rooted in her dread of separation. She sees herself, her family, and her home as inextricably bound together.

> If you want to know why I never leave Wishwood
> That is the reason. I keep Wishwood alive
> To keep the family alive, to keep them together,
> To keep me alive, and I live to keep them.
> You none of you understand how old you are.
> And death will come to you as a mild surprise,
> A momentary shudder in a vacant room. [p. 227]

This underlying, pervasive fear of separation makes her exert a formidable control over family affairs. The theme of her all-powerful dominance is first expressed by the other family members who as a chorus speak of being puppets of Amy as they assemble for her birthday.

> Why do we feel embarrassed, impatient, fretful, ill at ease,
> Assembled like amateur actors who have not been assigned
>   their parts?
> Like amateur actors in a dream when the curtain rises, to
>   find themselves dressed for a different play, or having
>   rehearsed the wrong parts.
>   . . . .
> Yet we are here at Amy's command, to play an unread part in
>   some monstrous farce, ridiculous in some nightmare
>   pantomime. [p. 231]

Expressing his sense of Amy's omnipresence, Harry, upon his return, is immediately obsessed with being looked at. The source of this haunting feeling of being observed later emerges as Mary and Harry reminisce about their childhoods.

> *Harry*: Why were we not happy?
> *Mary*: Well, it all seemed to be imposed upon us;
> Even the nice things were laid out ready,
> And the treats were always so carefully prepared;

There was never any time to invent our own enjoyments.
But perhaps it was all designed for you, not for us.
   Harry: No, it didn't seem like that. I was part of the design
As well as you. But what was the design?
It never came off. But do you remember
   Mary: The hollow tree in what we called the wilderness
   Harry: Down near the river. That was the block house
From which we fought the Indians. Arthur and John.
   Mary: It was the cave where we met by moonlight
To raise the evil spirits.
   Harry: Arthur and John.
Of course we were punished for being out at night
After being put to bed. But at least they never knew
Where we had been.
   Mary: They never found the secret.
   Harry: Not then. But later, coming back from school
For the holidays, after the formal reception
And the family festivities, I made my escape
As soon as I could, and slipped down to the river
To find the old hiding place. The wilderness was gone,
The tree had been felled, and a neat summer-house
Had been erected, 'to please the children.'
It's absurd that one's only memory of freedom
Should be a hollow tree in a wood by the river. [p. 248]

Ever under the watchful eye of Amy, they can recall but one memory of privacy. Harry explains to the family doctor why he can have no self apart from his mother and her feelings.

Everything has always been referred back to mother.
When we were children, before we went to school,
The rule of conduct was simply pleasing mother;
Misconduct was simply being unkind to mother;
What was wrong was whatever made her suffer,
And whatever made her happy was what was virtuous —
Though never very happy, I remember. That was why
We all felt like failures, before we had begun. [pp. 258-259]

Fromm-Reichmann (1948) emphasizes the importance of nonverbal aspects of child rearing.

> The Schizophrenic, since his childhood days, has been suspiciously aware of the fact that words are used not only to convey but also to veil actual communications. Consequently, he has learned to gather information about people in general, ... from their inadvertent communications through changes in gesture, attitude, and posture, inflections of voice or expressive movements. [p. 273]

It is clear that Harry has sensed the force of this nonverbal communication when he tells Dr. Warburton about his mother's power over the children.

> I think that the things that are taken for granted
> At home, make a deeper impression upon children
> Than what they are told. [p. 259]

These seemingly inevitable cues are illustrated in his memory of the day his father died.

> I remember the silence, and the hushed excitement
> And the low conversation of triumphant aunts.
> It is the conversations not overheard,
> Not intended to be heard, with the sidewise looks
> That bring death into the heart of a child.
> That was the day he died. Of course. [p. 260]

Harry must have hoped that his father might serve as a buffer in his relationship with his mother. On the night he was told of his father's death, he gave up all hope:

> ... When she kissed me,
> I felt the trap close. [p. 261]

The absence of the father in this family created more of a vacuum within which Amy's need to control was all the greater.

In Lidz's studies of the families of schizophrenics (1960, 1963) he noted the repeated presence of seriously disturbed marital relationships. He divided these into two basic types, which he called schismatic and skewed. The schismatic family was characterized by an open schism between the parents and repeated threats of separation. The skewed family was one with a semblance of harmony due to the acceptance by one spouse of the serious psychopathology of the dominant partner.

> In all ... the fathers were particularly ineffectual, assuming little responsibility for family leadership other than earning a livelihood. They were either weak, ineffectual men who went along with wives who were schizophrenic or at least questionably so, or they were disturbed men who could maintain an outward form of capability and strength because of the support of a masochistic wife. [1960, p. 605]

The Monchensey family appears to be a hybrid of these types. The marriage was schismatic while it lasted. However, upon the husband's departure it became "skewed," not only by his absence but also by the other family members' acceptance of Amy's behavior.

Some insight into the reason for this appears in Amy's bitter statement to her sister. "I *would* have sons, if I could not have a husband" (p. 282). She reveals the interchangeability of husband and son. This generation reversal, together with her wish to keep Harry in an infantile state, suggests the kind of contradictory demands made upon schizophrenics. While Amy wants Harry to return and take charge of Wishwood, she nevertheless longs to turn back the clock.

> ...I wanted...
> ...nothing except to remind him
> Of the years when he had been a happy boy at Wishwood;
> For his future success. [p. 283]

Agatha, who has some distance from the family system,

responds to this plea for a denial of reality by exposing its
relational intent of controlling Harry's life.

Success is relative
It is what we can make of the mess we have made of things,
It is what he can make, not what you would make for him.
[p. 283]

UNDIFFERENTIATION: THE RUBBER-FENCE PHENOMENON

The insistence that Harry must make his own life, that he must
separate and differentiate from his family, is a central theme of the
play. This theme is directly linked with the play's focus on the
powerful mother-child relationship. It is the separation and
differentiation from the state of fusion with the mother that
psychoanalysts (see Mahler 1952) and many family therapists
(e.g., Bowen 1968, Slipp 1973) have described as the primary if not
major source of difficulty in schizophrenia.

The play underscores the vital need for separation with its
emphasis on life's first separation, birth. Amy's birthday is the
occasion for the family reunion. The warm sun she longs for in
the opening speech is a kind of wish to return to a state of union
with her own mother. These hopes are now displaced and
centered on her first-born son. This is in accord with Searles's
hypothesis (1965) that:

the well-known symbiotic relatedness ... is fostered by a
transference to this child on the mother's part of feelings and
attitudes originally operative in a symbiotic relationship
which obtained between herself as a small child and her own
mother. [p. 225]

The symbiosis is repeated in the next generation when Harry
marries a woman who will not leave him alone. Harry says he has
pushed her overboard:

You would never imagine anyone could sink so quickly.
I had always supposed, wherever I went
That she would be with me; whatever I did
That she was unkillable. [p. 235]

Later Downing, his chauffeur, relates:

          Always [they were together], Sir.
That was just my complaint against my Lady.
It's my opinion that man and wife
Shouldn't see too much of each other, Sir.
Quite the contrary of the usual opinion,
I dare say. She wouldn't leave him alone.
. . . .
She wouldn't leave him out of her sight. [p. 241]

Harry tried to free himself from this fusion by pushing her overboard only to discover his need to resolve the underlying tie to his mother.

Nothing is more threatening to symbiotic fusion than change. Preventing change in order to perpetuate their undifferentiation is one of his mother's persistent aims.

Amy: Nothing is changed, Agatha, at Wishwood.
Everything is kept the same as when he left it,
Except the old pony, and the mongrel setter
Which I had to have destroyed.
Nothing has been changed. I have seen to that. [p. 228]

Amy: We are very glad to have you back, Harry.
. . . .
You will find everybody here, and everything the same.
. . . .
Your room is all ready for you. Nothing has been changed.
[pp. 232-233]

Mary: Your mother insisted
On everything being kept the same as when you left it.
[p. 246]

Ivy: You are quite right, Gerald, the one thing that matters
Is not to let her see that anyone is worried.
We must carry on as if nothing had happened ... [pp. 266-
267]

Harry sensed early on this campaign to arrest his development.
Dr. Warburton remembers his childhood illnesses:

And we had such a time to keep you in bed.
You didn't like being ill in the holdiays.

To which Violet adds:

It was always the same with your minor ailments
And children's epidemics: you would never stay in bed
Because you were convinced that you would never get well.
[p. 255]

We can imagine Harry fighting at this early age for his life. His
fear of never getting well expresses the anxiety of his defenseless-
ness in the face of his mother's control.

Reliance on symbiosis and prevention of change, translated
into family terms, reflects a belief in the self-sufficiency of the
family as a unit isolated from the wider society. Denying contact
with the wider world means that developmental milestones like
marriage are disequilibrating and tend to be discouraged.

Amy hoped that Harry would stay in the family by marrying
Mary, her designee and second cousin. This insulation of the
family has been described by Wynne, et al. (1958) as the "rubber
fence phenomenon":

The normal pattern or organization of family roles and
relations constitutes a differentiated subsystem of society
rather than a self-sufficient, complete social system.
When there is a continual effort in family relations to
maintain pseudomutuality, the family members try to act as
if the family could be a truly self-sufficient social system with

a completely encircling boundary. Schizophrenic family members, in failing to articulate a differentiation of family member from family role structure, tend to shift and obscure the idea of the family boundaries. The unstable, but continuous boundary, with no recognizable openings, surrounding the schizophrenic family system, stretches to include that which can be interpreted as complementary and contracts to extrude that which is interpreted as non-complementary. This continuous but elastic boundary we have called the rubber fence. [p. 211]

Such families are deeply threatened by a new marriage, which can be approved only if the prospective family member can be encircled. So early in the play we learn Amy's view of Harry's wife.

I am very glad that none of you ever met her.
....
She never would have been one of the family,
She never wished to be one of the family,
She only wished to keep him to herself
To satisfy her vanity. [p. 230]

Then later when talking to Gerald about Harry's distraught state, Amy "prefers to believe that a few days at Wishwood among his own family, is all that he needs" (p. 237). Amy will permit an outsider, Dr. Warburton, to speak with Harry only because he is an "old friend of the family."

Family secrets become especially important in such families, not because they really are secrets, but because they serve as a rationale for keeping family members together. In this sense a schizophrenic's family is a kind of secret society demanding complete loyalty and placing a pressure on the family members who, in the play, speak as an uneasy, undifferentiated chorus:

Why should we stand here like guilty conspirators, wait-
    ing for some revelation
When the hidden shall be exposed, and the newsboy shall
    shout in the street?

When the private shall be made public, the common
  photographer
Flashlight for the picture papers....
    ....
Why do we all behave as if the door might suddenly open,
  the curtain be drawn
The cellar make some dreadful disclosure, the roof disap-
  pear ... [pp. 242-243]

The metaphor of the open door or the disappearing roof at a family level, is analogous to Freud's concept of the lifting of repression at the individual level. The family secrets serve to protect the unity of the family, as the defense of repression hopes to control the instincts and thereby the integrity of the ego. How often have schizophrenics revealed the family secrets during the acute state of their illnesses, thereby blowing the lid off both in terms of family organization and individual personality organization.

That individual and family organization are thus conceptually and existentially interlocked is grappled with in a paper by Laing (1967). He sees "the family" as a synthesis of the internalization of each of its member's experience of "the family." He concludes that "the 'family' is united by the reciprocal internalization by each of each other's internalization" (p. 111). It is this coinherence in more undifferentiated families that leads to the blurring of boundaries between individual and family, reflecting in another way the rubber-fence phenomenon.

The recent innovation of "network therapy" may owe it's alleged effectiveness in the treatment of families of schizophrenics to the resultant widening of the family circle. The network counters the centripetal fusing force, which leaves individual and family undifferentiated.

When Harry finally is ready to leave home, Mary, still sharing in the family fear of separation, tries to extract from his chauffeur and servant a "promise never to leave his Lordship." Downing replies:

After all these years that I've been with him

I think I understand his Lordship better than anybody;
And I have a kind of feeling that his Lordship won't need me
Very long now. I can't give you any reasons. [p. 288]

Downing here acknowledges that Harry has begun the process
of growth and differentiation.

DIFFERENTIATION AND GROWTH

How do we understand Harry's recovery? It emerges from two
more solid relationships characterized by mutuality in contrast to
the engulfing relationship with his mother. The first is with his
childhood playmate, Mary; the second is with his Aunt Agatha.
    In the first act as Harry and Mary share memories of childhood,
they move closer together. Mary reaches out to him and tries to
understand him.

Harry: You do not know,
You cannot know, You cannot understand.
    Mary: I think I could understand, but you would have to
be patient
With me, and with people who have not had your
experience. [p. 250]

Harry insists that she cannot understand him. He begins to drive
her away, and then with obvious ambivalence asks her to stay:

No, no don't go. Please don't leave me
Just at this moment. I feel it is important.
Something should have come of this conversation. [p. 250]

As they then move closer, Harry, who had felt there is no way out
of his "no exit" existence, senses a ray of hope:

You bring me news
Of a door that opens at the end of a corridor,

Sunlight and singing; when I had felt sure
That every corridor only led to another,
Or to a blank wall; that I kept moving
Only so as not to stay still. [p. 252]

Just at this moment Harry is overwhelmed by such intimacy and
reprojects the image of his ever watchful mother, in the form of
hallucinations.

Don't look at me like that! Stop! Try to stop it!
I am going. Oh, why, now? Come out!
Come out! Where are you? Let me see you,
Since I know you are there, I know you are spying on me.
Why do you play with me, why do you let me go,
Only to surround me? — When I remember them
They leave me alone: when I forget them
Only for an instant of inattention
They are roused again, the sleepless hunters
That will not let me sleep. [pp. 252-253]

In this state of panic Harry, in speaking — to his hallucinations
— begins to differentiate a new emerging self from the self of his
childhood.

Come out!
(The curtains part, revealing the Eumenides in the window
embrasure.)
Why do you show yourselves now for the first time?
When I knew her, I was not the same person.
I was not any person. Nothing that I did
Has to do with me. The accident of a dreaming moment,
Of a dreaming age, when I was someone else
Thinking of something else, puts me among you.
I tell you, it is not me you are looking at
Not me you are grinning at, not me your confidential looks
Incriminate, but that other person, if person,
You thought I was: let your necrophily
Feed upon that carcase. [p. 253]

So at the moment of being touched by Mary, Harry feels himself more trapped by his inner world, but he gives a hint that he wishes to shed a former self.

From the outset of the play Agatha is the most differentiated from the family. She is less involved in the need to keep the family as unchanging. Early in the play in response to Amy's insistence that nothing is changed at Wishwood, Agatha predicts that Harry will have changed.

> .... I mean that at Wishwood he will find another Harry.
> The man who returns will have to meet
> The boy who left. Round by the stables,
> In the coach-house, in the orchard,
> In the plantation, down the corridor
> That led to the nursery, round the corner
> Of the new wing, he will have to face him —
> And it will not be a very *jolly* corner. [p. 229]

It is Agatha who reveals to Harry the "hidden" secrets surrounding his birth. He discovers that Agatha had become his father's mistress, had prevented the murder of his mother, and had longed to have him as her own son. She is a "mother" who unlike his biological mother can allow him to separate and grow, and he exclaims in relief:

> Look, I do not know why,
> I feel happy for a moment, as if I had come home.
> It is quite irrational, but now
> I feel quite happy, as if happiness
> Did not consist in getting rid of what can't be got rid of
> But in a different vision....
> ....
> .... Now I see
> I might even become fonder of my mother —
> More compassionate at least — by understanding.
> But she would not like that. Now I see
> I have been wounded in a war of phantoms.
> Not by human beings — they have no more power than I.

The things I thought were real are shadows, and the real
Are what I thought were private shadows. O that awful
  privacy
Of the insane mind! [p. 275-276]

He is finally freed from the "knotted cord" that ties him to
Wishwood and his illness. With the assistance of both Mary, who
tries to reach him and Agatha, a surrogate mother, Harry
experiences a kind of rebirth and is able to leave home without
being haunted by his pursuing hallucinations. That his recovery
necessitated his mother's death is a reflection of what Eliot
expressed more explicitly in *The Cocktail Party* (see chapter 2)
when Dr. Reilly insists on seeing the family:

Indeed, it is often the case that my patients
Are only pieces of a total situation
Which I have to explore. The single patient
Who is ill by himself, is rather the exception. [p. 350]

What the limits of that "total situation" are is the central question
asked in the family therapy paradigm.

WHAT IS SCHIZOPHRENIA?

In times past Harry would have been deemed possessed or
demented. More recently he would be labeled schizophrenic. All
these views have in common that "madness" enters, originates in,
or is equated with an individual's mind or personality.

The recent innovation of family psychiatry establishes another
vantage point from which individual illness may be viewed.
Using the medical idiom, we describe Harry's "illness" as the
"symptom" of a pathological family process one of the central
aspects of which is a persistent symbiotic bond structured and
reinforced by a set of family myths (Ferreira 1963) and programs of
behavior (Ferber and Beels 1970). In his own discussion of the
play, Eliot criticized its ambiguity as to whether it would be

viewed as the tragedy of the mother or the salvation of the son (1961, p. 90). This is a query at an individual level of analysis. Viewed from a family frame of reference, the play is a tragedy of the Monchensey family or of any family if the death of one family member must follow upon the separation and growth of another. But more important, the tragedy is not in Amy's death but in the lives of each of the family members to the degree that he is inextricably bound to the family. The ambiguity is, in fact, an indication of how well Eliot perceived an essential underlying dynamic in abnormal human development, namely the complex interrelationship between two almost fused individuals.

What then is schizophrenia? This chapter has discussed the central theme of *The Family Reunion* as that of the developmental phase of separation and differentiation from an undifferentiated state. When this phase is unsuccessfully negotiated in parent and child in a family without sufficient countering differentiating forces, an atypical person results. Often such a person is labeled schizophrenic because the family needs to stabilize an increasingly unstable family system. This stabilization is analogous to Freud's discussion of sympton formation on an individual level. A family system achieves some relief when the focus of its tensions is hospitalized. The patient is separated from the family but at the same time further tied to them by virtue of his "illness" and subsequent dependency. The impulse to retain and the defense of extrusion are here united in the hospitalization, which like a symptom may then become fixed and subject to secondary gain. In a family system the secondary gain is shared by all and leads to what has been termed family collusion. The dangers of thus diagnosing a young person as schizophrenic when he is trying unsuccessfully to break away from an undifferentiated family has been discussed by Haley (1967).

Schizophrenia is viewed here not as an illness but rather as a label that is part of a dynamic process involving interlocking genetic, psychological, social and cultural factors. The genetic predisposition that is a part of the process has been discussed by Wender (1967), who has also discussed the limitations of such significant single etiological factors (1967). We might say, in conclusion that Harry's recovery from "schizophrenia" was facilitated by corrective interpersonal experiences and, in part, by his never having been labeled and treated as such.

REFERENCES

Bowen, M. (1966). The use of family theory in clinical practice. *Comprehensive Psychiatry* 7:354-374.

Cheek, F. (1964). The "schizophrenic mother" in word and deed. *Family Process* 3:155-177.

Eliot, T.S. (1961). *On Poetry and Poets*. New York: Noonday Press.

———(1952). *The Complete Poems and Plays*. New York: Harcourt, Brace and World.

Ferber, A.S., and Beels, C.C. (1970). Changing family behavior programs. *International Psychiatry Clinics* 7, No. 4.

Ferreira, A.J. (1963). Family myth and homeostasis. *Archives of General Psychiatry* 9:457-463.

Fleck, S., Lidz, T., and Cornelison, A. (1963). Comparison of parent-child relationships of male and female schizophrenic patients. *Archives of General Psychiatry.* 8:1-7.

Fromm-Reichmann, F. (1948). Notes on the development of treatment of schizophrenics by psychoanalytic psychotherapy. *Psychiatry* 11: 263-273.

Haley, J. (1967). The doctor as part of the schizophrenic interchange. *International Journal of Psychiatry* 4:534-542.

Johnson, A., and Szurek, S.A. (1952). The genesis of anti-social acting out in children and adults. *Psychoanalytic Quarterly* 21:323-343.

Laing, R.D. (1967). Individual and family structure. In *The Predicament of the Family*, ed. P. Lomas. London: Hogarth Press.

Lidz, T., Cornelison, A.R., Fleck, S., and Terry, D. (1957). Schism and skew in the families of schizophrenics. In *A Modern Introduction to the Family*, ed. N. Bell and F. Vogel. Glencoe, Ill.: The Free Press, 1960. Appeared as The intrafamilial environment of schizophrenic patients: II. marital schism and marital skew. *American Journal of Psychiatry* 114:241-248.

Mahler, M.S. (1952). On child psychosis and schizophrenia: autistic and symbiotic infantile psychoses. *Psychoanalytic Study of the Child* 7:286-305.

Mahler, M.S., Pine, F., and Bergman, A. (1975). *The Psychological Birth of the Human Infant.* New York: Basic Books.

Searles, H. (1958). Positive feelings in the relationship between the schizophrenic and his mother. In *Collected Papers on Schizophrenia and Related Subjects.* New York: International Universities Press, 1965.

Slipp, S. (1973). The symbiotic survival pattern: A relational theory of schizophrenia. *Family Process* 12:377-398.

Speck, R., and Rueveni, U. (1969). Network therapy — a developing concept. *Family Process* 8:182-191.

Wender, P. (1967). On necessary and sufficient conditions in psychiatric explanations. *Archives of General Psychiatry* 16:41-47.

———(1969). The role of genetics in the etiology of the schizophrenias. *American Journal of Orthopsychiatry* 39:447-458.

Wynne, L.C., Ryckoff, I.M., Day, J., and Hirsch, S.I. (1958). Pseudo-mutuality in the family relations of schizophrenics. *Psychiatry* 21:205-220.

Part II

THE LITERATURE OF INDIVIDUAL AND FAMILY INTERACTION

Chapter Five

FREUD ON MARRIAGE
AND THE FAMILY

In the four preceding studies of dramatic literature individual psychology and the family systems theories have been juxtaposed as differing paradigms with theories and modes of practice essentially unintegrated with one another. The next three chapters will introduce some of the technical literature with a view toward integrating these disparate clinical approaches. In this chapter we turn to Freud's writings on marriage and the family. Though psychoanalysis became the quintessential individual treatment and the most compelling and comprehensive theory of a person's psyche, Freud's observations on the family, made in passing, have a fresh and modern ring to them and serve as a relevant starting point.

Psychoanalysis penetrated the depths of the mind by a rigorous application of the psychoanalytic method, the data base of which was relatively free of any direct observation of a person's social field. While psychoanalytic theory has been evolving and changing over the years, there still has been reluctance to utilize data obtained by nonanalytic methods. The major exception to this has been the more recent investigations of mother-infant interaction as well as observations made in the preschool nursery. On the other hand, newly emerging family systems theories have, using quite different data, tended to ignore man's intrapsychic life, while beginning to describe their own compelling insights regarding man's interpersonal behavior.

I believe that a major impediment to the meaningful integration of these "sciences" lies in the differing applications of their theories. Psychoanalysis evolved out of an intensive effort to understand and treat *the individual.* As an applied science it is devoted to the fullest development of an individual's potential; its goal is naturally individualistic, reflecting the heightened individualistic values of our culture at the turn of the century.

The family systems theories are emerging at a time when the malfunctioning of the family in postindustrial society has become glaringly apparent. As an applied science its general goal has been the improved functioning of the family unit. Hence the emphasis upon communication and the contextual forces impinging upon all of us. If psychoanalysis was a psychology of the inner-directed, achievement-oriented, super-ego-dominated Oedipus, the newer therapies including the family modality represent a social psychology of the outer-directed, consumer-oriented ego-and-id-dominated Narcissus. Psychoanalysis has responded to this shift by recently (Kernberg 1975) also turning attention to the understanding and treatment of the now ubiquitous narcissistic disorders. This, while the family therapies have tried to reduce these dysfunctional, narcissistic trends by promoting more direct and less distorted communications within the family unit.

What is intriguing in all of this is that psychoanalysis is nonetheless for all its emphasis on intrapsychic forces a theory grounded in "the family." As a theory of the development of man's psychic structure it turns to the interplay of a child's endowment and his primary family experiences. The potential refinement and elaboration of psychoanalytic theory by the introduction of the findings of family studies would seem a natural and welcome development. Psychoanalysis as a theory is far broader in scope than its very limited application as a therapy.

Its further development ought not to be limited by data gathered only by the psychoanalytic method, and its application need not be limited to the practice of psychoanalysis. In fact, the application of psychoanalytic theory to marital and family therapy promises to be of benefit in those clinical situations that today rarely come to the attention of the psychoanalyst but instead are treated by an ever-expanding array of ad hoc therapies. In its wish to retain the purity of its method, psychoanalysis reduced the possibility of psychoanalytic treatment for potentially analyzable patients whose presenting interpersonal disturbances mask a neurotic character structure. Some patients after a period of psychoanalytically oriented family therapy recognize the benefits to be derived from a personal psychoanalysis (see chapter 9).

In the preparation of this chapter, I utilized the recently published *Index* of Freud's *Standard Edition*. There were about thirty references to the family and eleven references to marriage in the *Index*. To demonstrate Freud's primary interest in intra-psychic forces, I initially chose memory as a contrasting subject, as it represented the cornerstone of Freud's (and Breuer's) early model of psychological illness. After all, "hysterics suffered from reminiscences." There were approximately 250 references to the subject of memory. This was, perhaps, a skewed comparison, for there are other subjects that might refer indirectly to marriage and the family, for example, the specific family members. There were 350 references to fathers and fatherhood. Many would expect the references to mothers and motherhood to outnumber these. There were about 200 citations on mothers. This almost two-to-one ratio reflects the centrality in Freud's writings of the oedipal stage of development, especially as seen in the child's relation to the father. The interest in the preoedipal mother/infant relationship only came into focus in the years after Freud's death and was most recently summarized by Mahler, Pine, and Bergman (1975). As a matter of fact in the Cumulative Index of the *Psychoanalytic Quarterly* (1932-1966) the ratio of father to mother references is reversed. There are no references to sons or daughters, eleven to brothers and sisters in the Index of the *Standard Edition*, while *boys* and *girls*, the terms Freud used for sons and daughters, each have about 125 references. There are also about 600 references to childhood and children, a testimony to the preoccupation of psychoanalysis with child development. In this sense Freud can be seen as the scientist who helped crystallize an evolving cultural preoccupation described by Aries (1962) and de Mause (1974) of the relatively recent "discovery of childhood." Child rearing, once practiced without much thought, has today become somewhat of an obsession. We are more aware of children than ever before, while paradoxically and simultaneously we are turning away from caring for them or so our media (*Newsweek*, September 22, 1975) and many social scientists (Bronfenbrenner 1970) are telling us. While child development thus stands out as one of the pillars of the psychoanalytic structure, it is eclipsed in this Index survey by the topic which Freud considered his most outstanding contribution, that is the discovery of the unconscious and its elucidation through dream interpretation. There are over 2,000 citations related to dreams and dreaming!

As noted above, Freud's central interest in depth psychology precluded an extensive study of marriage and the family. Nonetheless a review of his writings on these subjects affords an interesting journey in itself and prepares the ground for a subsequent discussion of the interrelation of psychoanalytic theory and the newly emerging developments in family theory, therapy, and research.

PRE- AND EARLY PSYCHOANALYTIC PHASE
(1888-1905)

Shortly after studying with Charcot, Freud wrote a review of hysteria for a medical encyclopedia, in which he reiterated Charcot's view that at bottom hysteria was a hereditary disorder. The emphasis on heredity, however, did not lead to therapeutic nihilism, for in the section on management he advocated actively dealing with the immediate contemporaneous familial factors. His description of the family's aggravating if not etiological role has a modern "family systems" ring to it.

The first condition for a successful intervention is as a rule removal of the patient from his regular conditions and his isolation from the circle in which the outbreak occurred. . . . As a rule an hysterical man or woman is not the only neurotic of the family circle. The alarm or tender concern of parents or relatives only increases the patient's excitement or his inclination, where there is a physical change in him, to produce more intense symptoms. If, for example, an attack has come on at a particular hour several times in succession, it will be expected by the patient's mother regularly at the same time; she will ask the child anxiously whether he is already feeling bad and so make it certain that the dreaded event will occur. Only in the rarest instances can one succeed in inducing relatives to look on at the child's hysterical attacks quite calmly and with apparent indifference; as a rule the family's place must be taken by a period in a medical establishment, and to this the relatives usually offer greater resistance than do the patients themselves. [1888, pp. 54-55]

In this prepsychoanalytic phase Freud (1893) was experimenting with hypnosis and reported a successful treatment in the home of a woman who was unable to feed her newborn infant. Following Freud's hypnotic suggestion, the patient ventilated anger toward her own mother for not feeding her properly. This treatment resolved for the time being the patient's symptoms. I noted in a previous publication (1974) how Freud in this early case began to explore the "inner" forces at work in his patients and necessarily paid less attention to external forces. Rather than pointing to the interpersonal difficulties she had with her family, Freud noted that she had "ideas running counter to her intentions." This was an early version of the soon-to-be-described concepts of the unconscious, ambivalence, and intrapsychic forces in general.

The same year saw the publication of Freud's and Breuer's (1893) Preliminary Communication in which they put forth the view that hysteria resulted from traumatic experiences. Shortly thereafter, Freud (1896, pp. 189-221) postulated that these traumatic experiences were of a sexual nature that ultimately led back to repressed memories of childhood sexual experiences. The cause of this baffling illness was about to be laid at the feet of corrupting parents, older siblings, and those other notorious Viennese child seducers, the nursemaids and tutors.

Crude and faulty as this theory seems to us today, it began questioning the narrower medical formulation of the day, which shed no light on this common malady. In fact one could view the medical model here as cloaking the hidden, unspoken, patriarchal family dramas of his patients. Women, who made up the bulk of sufferers, wreaked havoc in their families and made the medical practitioners of the day appear impotent and helpless. Freud's case histories were soon to sound more like novels than medical cases, thus giving rebirth to a psychosocial model of mental illness. These case histories would have read like simpleminded novels with villains and victims had Freud within another year not critically reexamined his seduction theory. He was to write his friend Fliess: "I will confide in you at once the great secret that has been slowly dawning on me in the last few months. I no longer believe in my neurotica" (1897, Letter 69, p. 259). Further clinical investigation together with his self-analysis had led him to question the universality of these childhood sexual seductions. In a manner that was to become characteristic of him, Freud made a virtue of this obstacle. Rather than discarding this data, he asked why so many of his patients were clinging so tenaciously to these ideas. Here a giant leap forward was made in psychology. The discovery of the universal presence of incestuous fantasies and of infantile sexual wishes succumbing to repression created a new theory of inner psychological dramas that was to replace the external family seduction theory that had such a short life in Freud's thought. So the theory of hysteria had undergone two rapid transformations. A mysterious hereditary medical illness with no discernible physical pathology was seen first as a reaction to a familial drama and subsequently as a manifestation of the repressed sexual conflicts of the patient in question. The questions remained, and remain, if these conflicts are universal how is it that everyone does not fall ill, and what is the mechanism of the choice of neurosis. Freud was of course to insist that the line between illness and health was a fine one and that people were ever moving from health to illness and back again. But one can still ask further when are these transitions made and at what particular times.

The Dora case, which came during this phase of psychoanalytic theory, illustrates dramatically the shift in Freud's thinking indicated above (1905). Although the case was written to demonstrate the validity of his recently published *Interpretation of Dreams* the clinical case contains one of the most elegant family descriptions in clinical psychiatry. It includes the by now oft quoted caveat, "that we are obliged to pay attention in our case histories to the purely human and social circumstances of our patients. Above all our interest will be directed towards their family circumstances" (1905, p. 18). The case contains a fairly detailed picture of the parental sexual intrigues, which included an attempt to get eighteen-year-old Dora into a modified wife-swapping arrangement with Dora as a stand-in for her mother. Dora's hysterical reaction to this context brought her into treatment with Freud in 1900. This was but three years after discarding his sexual seduction theory. Though not ostensibly taking sides in this family difficulty, he proceeded to try to get Dora to recognize her own unconscious participation in the menage. As Erikson noted (1968, pp. 251-252), she would hear of no such thing and fled treatment. Subsequently she led a rather severe neurotic life as noted in Deutsch's follow-up report (1957).

PSYCHOANALYTIC PHASE (1905-1939)

Freud on Marriage and the Role of Women

Following the 1888 discussion of the family's role in hysteria, the first allusion to marriage and the family appears "perhaps appropriately" in his book on *Jokes and the Unconscious* (1905a pp. 110-111). In this book he notes the abundance of jokes about the institution of marriage. Society's collective ambivalence toward this once sacred institution is evident in the myriad of jokes aimed at it. Since the turn of the century with the reduction in the functions of religion and the family, psychotherapy and the mental health professions, as Parsons (1964) has noted, have assumed an ever-increasing importance. In this connection Philip Reiff (1966) has, in fact, termed our age the *Triumph of the Therapeutic*. In this quasi "transferential" way the psychotherapies have joined the institution of marriage and the family as an object of ridicule and humor. Rarely does a popular magazine not include some cartoon about the patient/client and his Freudian or transactional therapist.

Part of mankind's undercurrent of hostility toward marriage and the family stems from the child's ambivalent attitude toward his parents. Another stems, according to Freud, from the restrictions that society places upon the sexual drive through, among other mechanisms, the institution of monogamous marriage. This point of view citing the opposition of the interests of civilization and the individual needs, most elaborated in his 1930 *Civilization and Its Discontents*, was already explicated in a rarely read paper titled, "Civilized Sexual Morality and Modern Nervous Illness" (1908, pp. 179-204). It contains a devastating critique of marriage at the turn of the century and includes a remarkable indictment of society's suppression of women. This article seems to have gone unnoticed by the many recent feminists who accuse Freud of being an uncritical proponent of Viennese society. The pertinent parts of this section go on for some ten pages and only parts of it are quoted here at some length.

This brings us to the question whether sexual intercourse in legal marriage can offer full compensation for the restrictions imposed before marriage. There is such an abundance of material supporting a reply in the negative that we can give only the briefest summary of it. It must above all be borne in mind that our cultural sexual morality restricts sexual intercourse even in marriage itself, since it imposes on married couples the necessity of contenting themselves, as a rule, with a very few procreative acts. As a

consequence of this consideration, satisfying sexual intercourse in marriage takes place only for a few years. . . . After
these three, four, or five years, the marriage becomes a failure
in so far as it has promised the satisfaction of sexual needs.
For all the devices hitherto invented for preventing conception impair sexual enjoyment, hurts the fine suscepti-
bilities of both partners and even actually cause illness. Fear
of the consequences of sexual intercourse first brings the
married couple's physical affection to an end; and then as a
remoter result, it usually puts a stop as well to the mental
sympathy between them, which should have been the
successor to their original passionate love. The spiritual
disillusionment and bodily deprivation to which most
marriages are thus doomed puts both partners back in the
state they were in before their marriage, except for being the
poorer by the loss of an illusion, and they must once more
have recourse to their fortitude in mastering and deflecting
their sexual instinct. [p. 194]

The harmful results which the strict demand for abstinence
before marriage produces in women's natures are quite
especially apparent. It is clear that education is far from
underestimating the task of suppressing a girl's sensuality
till her marriage, for it makes use of the most drastic
measures. Not only does it forbid sexual intercourse and set a
high premium on the preservation of female chastity, but it
also protects the young woman from temptation as she
grows up, by keeping her ignorant of all the facts of the part
she is to play and by not tolerating any impulse of love in her
which cannot lead to marriage. The result is that when the
girl's parental authorities suddenly allow her to fall in love,
she is unequal to this psychical achievement and enters
marriage uncertain of her own feelings. In consequence of
this artificial retardation in her function of love, she has
nothing but disappointments to offer the man who has saved
up all his desire for her. In her mental feelings she is still
attached to her parents, whose authority has brought about
the suppression of her sexuality; and in her physical

behavior she shows herself frigid, which deprives the man of any high degree of sexual enjoyment. [pp. 197-198]

Their upbringing forbids their concerning themselves intellectually with sexual problems though they nevertheless feel extremely curious about them, and frightens them by condemning such curiousity as unwomanly and a sign of a sinful disposition. In this way they are scared away from any form of thinking, and knowledge loses its value for them. The prohibition of thought extends beyond the sexual field. I think that the undoubted intellectual inferiority of so many women can be traced back to the inhibition of thought necessitated by sexual suppression. [pp. 198-199]

Some pages later there is an interesting view put forth of the general effect of this state of the marital union upon the children of such marriages.

A neurotic wife who is unsatisfied by her husband is, as a mother, over tender and over anxious towards her child, onto whom she transfers her need for love; and she awakens it to sexual precocity. The bad relations between its parents moreover, excite its emotional life and cause it to feel love and hatred to an intense degree while it is still at a very tender age. Its strict upbringing, which tolerates no activity of the sexual life that has been aroused so early, lends support to the suppressing force and this conflict at such an age contains everything necessary for bringing about lifelong nervous illness. [p. 202]

The introduction of more adequate contraception and the emergence of the women's liberation movement have greatly altered this bleak picture of marriage at the turn of the century. The changes of the recent decades have produced a quite different picture with quite different problems. The instability of modern marriage has replaced its earlier chronic disharmony. The clinical sequelae of this development is staggering as we see more and more problems of developmental deficit amidst familial fragmentation.

Freud on the Relation of Parents to Children

The preceding very brief paragraph describing the potential impact of marital disturbances upon children is a somewhat more sophisticated return of the old seduction theory abandoned in 1896. During the decade following the publication of the *Interpretation of Dreams* (1900-1910), Freud made many relevant observations about parenting. Though the thrust of the *Three Essays on Sexuality* (1905b) was the discovery of sexual impulses in children independent of external parental influence, there are some remarkable descriptions of the impact of mothers upon children, which are a prelude to the more recent and more systematic researches into mother-infant interaction. In noting that the adolescent in his finding a sexual object is in some sense "refinding" the love of his childhood, Freud (1905b, pp. 223-224) recapitulates the importance of the original love relation.

A child's intercourse with anyone responsible for his care affords him an unending source of sexual excitation and satisfaction from his erotogenic zones. This is especially so since the person in charge of him, who after all, is as a rule his mother, herself, regards him with feelings that are derived from her own sexual life: She strokes him, kisses him, rocks him, and quite clearly treats him as a substitute for a complete sexual object. A mother would probably be horrified if she were made aware that all her marks of affection were rousing her child's sexual instinct and preparing for its later intensity. She regards what she does as asexual, "pure" love, since, after all she carefully avoids applying more excitations to the child's genitals than are unavoidable in nursery care. As we know, however, the sexual instinct is not aroused only by direct excitation of the genital zone. What we call affection will unfailingly show its effects one day on the genital zones as well. Moreover, if the mother understood more of the high importance of the part played by the instincts in mental life as a whole — in all its ethical and psychical achievements — she would spare herself any self-reproaches even after her enlightenment. She is only fulfilling her task in teaching the child to love. After all, he is meant to grow up into a strong and capable person with vigorous sexual needs and to accomplish during his life all the things that human beings are urged to do by their instincts. It is true than an excess of parental affection does harm by causing precocious sexual maturity and also because, by spoiling the child, it makes him incapable in later life of temporarily doing without love or of being content with a smaller amount of it. One of the clearest indications that a child will later become neurotic is to be seen in an insatiable demand for his parents' affection. And on the other hand neuropathic parents, who are inclined as a rule to display excessive affection, are precisely those who are most likely by their caresses to arouse the child's disposition to neurotic illness.

A few pages later Freud again reviewed the importance of the child's relation to his parents in determining his later choice of sexual object in that "any disturbance of those [marital] relations will produce the gravest effects upon his [the child's] adult sexual life. Jealousy in a lover is never without an infantile root or at least an infantile reinforcement. If there are quarrels between the parents, or if their marriage is unhappy, the ground will be prepared in their children for the severest predisposition to a disturbance of sexual development or to a neurotic illness" (1905b, p. 228).

Totem and Taboo in addition to its speculations regarding the origins of the family, the incest taboo, and Oedipal guilt, also has cogent observations relevant to this exploration in a discussion of a mother's relation to her daughter, especially as it leads to the often encountered difficulties between mothers and sons-in-law (1913, p. 15).

A woman whose psychosexual needs should find satisfaction in her marriage and her family life is often threatened with the danger of being left unsatisfied, because her marriage relation has come to a premature end and because of the uneventfulness of her emotional life. A mother, as she grows older, saves herself from an unhappy marriage by putting herself in her children's place, by identifying herself with them; and this she does by making their emotional experiences her own. Parents are said to stay young with their children, and that is indeed one of the most precious psychological gains that parents derive from their children. Where a marriage is childless, the wife has lost one of the things which might be of most help to her in tolerating the resignation that her own marriage demands from her. A mother's sympathetic identification with her daughter can easily go so far that she herself falls in love with the man her daughter loves; and in glaring instances this may lead to severe forms of neurotic illness as a result of her violent mental struggles against this emotional situation. In any case, it very frequently happens that a mother-in-law is subject to an impulse to fall in love this way, and this impulse itself or an opposing trend are added to the tumult of conflicting forces in her mind.

Freud goes on to analyze the other side of that relational coin as the son's need to ward off the incestuous tie to the prospective mother-in-law, and he notes as anthropological evidence the frequent rules of avoidance between sons and mothers-in-law among people of other societies.

Still other forces in this constellation involve the father's feelings toward his daughter and prospective son-in-law. I am in this context reminded of a couple that consulted me because of their inability to go through with their wedding plans. The history included the prospective bride's father's objections to all his daughter's suitors except for the one in question who was, at the time, still married. He could thus keep his favorite daughter from marrying and through identification with the suitor vicariously gratify his incestuous tie to his daughter. She could perpetuate her tie to her father and suffer for it in a nine-year courtship, which included her fiance twice not following through on their wedding plans. The ubiquitous presence of such cross-generational working out of oedipal conflicts was discussed psychoanalytically in some detail by Rangell (1955) in an article titled, "The Role of the Parent in the Oedipus Complex."

These isolated references to parents' vicarious working out of their wishes and conflicts through their children is more fully described in Freud's paper appropriately titled, "On Narcissism," (1914, pp. 90-91).

The primary narcissism of children which we have assumed and which forms one of the postulates of our theories of the libido, is less easy to grasp by direct observation than to confirm by inference from elsewhere. If we look at the attitude of affectionate parents towards their children, we have to recognize that it is a revival and reproduction of their own narcissism, which they have long since abandoned. The trustworthy pointer constituted by overvaluation, which we have already recognized as a narcissistic stigma in the case of object-choice, dominates, as we all know, their emotional attitude. Thus they are under a compulsion to ascribe every perfection to the child — which sober observation would find no occasion to do — and to conceal and forget all his shortcomings. Moreover, they are inclined to suspend in the child's favor the operation of all the cultural acquisitions which their own narcissism has been forced to respect, and to renew on his behalf the claims to privileges which were long ago given up by themselves. The child shall have a better time than his parents; he shall not be subject to the necessities which they have recognized as paramount in life. Illness, death, renunciation of enjoyment, restrictions on his own will, shall not touch him; the laws of nature and of society shall be abrogated in his favor; he shall once more really be the center and core of creation, "His Majesty the Baby" as we once fancied ourselves. The child shall fulfill those wishful dreams of the parents which they never carried out — the boy shall become a great man and a hero in his father's place, and the girl shall marry a prince as a tardy compensation for her mother. At the most touchy point in the narcissistic system, the immortality of the ego, which is so hard pressed by reality, security is achieved by taking refuge in the child. Parental love, which is so moving and at bottom so childish, is nothing but the parents' narcissism born again, which, transformed into object-love, unmistakably reveals its former nature.

This passage calls to mind the later work of Johnson and Szurek (1952) and their work on the transfer of superego difficulties across the generations. The cross-generational transfer of impulsive trends and conflicts through the defense of projective-identification has most recently become the focus of study of Zinner and Shapiro (1972) in their psychoanalytically oriented investigations of borderline adolescents and their families.

Neurosis and Unhappy Marriage

In an address to the fifth International Psychoanalytic Congress Freud (1918) turned to the subject of technique with some discussion of the use of "active" methods in psychoanalytic treatment. In this talk he noted the tendency of patients to recover from their neuroses prematurely through the formation of substitutive satisfactions.

It is the analyst's task to detect these divergent paths and to require him everytime to abandon them, however harmless the activity which leads to satisfaction may be in itself. The half-recovered patient may also enter on less harmless paths — as when, for instance, if he is a man he seeks prematurely to attach himself to a woman. *It may be observed incidently, that unhappy marriage and physical infirmity are the two things that most often supersede a neurosis. They satisfy in particular the sense of guilt (need for punishment) which makes many patients cling so fast to their neuroses.* By a foolish choice in marriage, they punish themselves.... [1919, p. 163, italics mine]

That today's analytic work has moved from the treatment of symptom neuroses to character neuroses is a commonplace observation. These character neuroses present most frequently in the area of work difficulties and/or disturbances in object relations. The frequency of the latter are manifest in the extraordinary incidence of divorce and what Freud called unhappy marriages. It is frequently the unhappy marital partners who come to the psychotherapist and/or family therapist. At times the problem is one of developmental or situational stress and relieved by a time-limited period of individual or marital treatment. But the presence of a chronically unhappy marriage of blame and recriminations is often a curtain "superseding" individual and usually complementary neuroses.

CONCLUSION: IMPLICATIONS FOR TREATMENT

Though Freud from the very start and throughout his career noted the family psychopathology surrounding his patients, he viewed the family circle as an obstacle to the patient's treatment and wrote (1912, p. 120) "As regards the treatment of their relatives, I must confess myself utterly at a loss and I have in general little faith in any individual treatment of them."

In concluding the *Introductory Lectures* five years later, Freud (1917) spelled out more directly his views on the adverse effects of family members on psychoanalytic treatment. In addition to the internal resistances of patients to analysis, he added the other unfavorable "external conditions" created by the patient's family. In comparing psychoanalytic treatment with a surgical operation, he (1917, p. 459) asked how such operations could succeed "in the presence of all the members of the patient's family, who would stick their noses into the field of the operation and exclaim aloud at every incision." He further stated that:

No one who has any experience of the rifts which so often divide a family will, if he is an analyst, be surprised to find that the patient's closest relatives sometimes betray less interest in his recovery than in his remaining as he is. *When, as so often, neurosis is related to conflicts between members of a family,* the healthy party will not hesitate long in choosing between his own interest and the sick party's recovery.

This is an unfortunate depiction of the untreated relative as the "healthy party." When a healthy person's self-interest is countered by a sick relative's recovery, we would necessarily read "self-interest" today as "narcissistic." His brief case illustration (1917, p. 460) is telling in this regard in describing how a young female patient's phobic behavior was keeping her mother from carrying on an extramarital affair. When the mother discovered that her affair was being discussed in her daughter's analysis with Freud, she brought the "obnoxious treatment" to an end and had the patient treated in a sanatarium.

Freud was by 1916 taking on only patients who were *sui juris*, that is, persons not dependent on anyone else in the essential relations of their lives. This is not so easily done in practice. The obstacles Freud notes and that I would describe as resistances in family members can be understood and interpreted. Retaining for the moment the surgical model, I would view such interventions as illustrative of necessary preoperative care. Freud felt such conditions of the patient's milieu rendered the patient inoperable (i.e., unanalyzable).

Freud relied ultimately upon the analysis and resolution of the transference neuroses as the mechanism of relief of neurotic suffering. The analyst, as Freud (1940, pp. 175-176) noted toward the end of his life, was thus necessarily a successor to the parents.

If the patient puts the analyst in the place of his father (or mother), he is also giving him the power which his super-ego exercises over his ego since his parents were as we know, the origin of his super ego. The new super ego now has an opportunity for a sort of after-education of the neurotic; it can correct mistakes for which his parents were responsible in educating him. But at this point a warning must be given against misusing this new influence. However, much the analyst may be tempted to become a teacher, model and ideal for other people and to create men in his own image, he should not forget that that is not his task in the analytic relationship, and indeed he will be disloyal to his task if he allows himself to be led on by his inclinations. If he does, he will be repeating a mistake of the parents who crushed their independence by their influence and he will only be replacing the parents earlier dependence by a new one. In all his attempts at improving and educating the patient, the analyst should respect his individuality. The amount of influence which he may legitimately allow himself will be determined by the degree of developmental inhibition present in the patient. Some neurotics have remained so infantile that in analysis too they can only be treated as children.

This warning against the analyst's inappropriate use of his influence is one of the central values in psychoanalysis and a major reason for the insistence upon retaining the purity of the psychoanalytic method. To alloy the "pure gold of analysis" (1919, p. 168) was not only to tamper with the method but also to threaten the independence and individuality of the analysand. The role of this central value is critical in understanding the general reluctance to introduce "parameters" into classical psychoanalytic treatment. To go beyond such parameters and see and treat a family unit within the psychoanalytic framework was virtually unthinkable. Not much imagination is required to sense how much more "active intervention" a family in conflict might "demand." Nonetheless, such "demands" for nurturance, guidance, or justice can be pointed out and interpreted analytically just as is done in individual psychoanalytic treatment.

While I acknowledge the very basic difference between classical psychoanalysis and the psychoanalytically oriented psychotherapies, it has been my experience that an "analytic attitude" is not dependent solely upon the couch. It is a matter of degree, and though more difficult I have found it possible to maintain a neutral, nonjudgmental, analytic attitude in working with families. In the context of a developing therapeutic alliance, the analyst offers an observing ego in noting the defensive operations and resistance of family members along with intrafamilial "transferencelike phenomena." In such a psychoanalytically oriented therapy the mode of improvement is not via the resolution of a transference neurosis but in the reduction of externalizing defenses that in turn makes the internal conflicts that underlie the neurotic interaction more accessible.

Also the more recent advances in ego psychology stemming from the structural theory make it theoretically easier to think in terms of treating, either individually or conjointly, the family members whose interferences are reflective of disturbances in object relations (viewed intrapsychically as disturbances in self-object representations). These, in turn, defend against painful affects. Such preparatory therapy can lead either to patients becoming more accessible to analysis or to a time-limited therapy resolving the presenting difficulty. (See chapter 9.)

Classical psychoanalysis as a treatment continues to be accessible to only a small number of patients. Psychoanalysis's present state of difficulty stems in part from its realistic inability to deliver services to larger patient populations where internal as well as external conditions preclude psychoanalysis. The recent appearance of other modalities (ranging from chemotherapy to group, family, and community therapy) offer some promise in alleviating the vast amount of emotional disturbances in our society. These varying modalities now compete with one another rather than spelling out those clinical situations best handled by each modality, or combination of modalities, and rather than moving toward some integration of these differing levels of intervention and conceptualization.

The integration of family observations and psychoanalytic theory seems to me to flow naturally from the fact that psychoanalytic theory is a theory of individual development as it unfolds first and primarily within the family. An exploration of the interface between psychoanalytic theory and family theory and research will enrich each while in turn further guiding our therapeutic endeavors.

REFERENCES

Aries, P. (1962). *Centuries of Childhood.* New York: Vintage.

Bronfenbrenner, U. (1970). *Two Worlds of Childhood. New York: Russell Sage Foundation.*

Deutsch, F. *(1957). A footnote to Freud's "A fragment of an analysis of a case of hysteria." Psychoanalytic Quarterly* 26:156-167.

Erikson, E. (1968). *Identity, Youth, and Crisis.* New York: W.W. Norton.

Freud, S. (1888). Hysteria. Standard Edition 1:39-59.

_____(1893a). A case of successful treatment by hypnotism. *Standard Edition* 1.

_____and Breuer, J. (1893b). On the psychical mechanism of hysterical phenomena: preliminary communication. *Standard Edition* 2:3-17.

_____(1896). The aetiology of hysteria. *Standard Edition* 3:189-221.

_____(1897). Extracts from the Fliess papers. *Standard Edition* 1:175-280.

_____(1905a). Fragment of an analysis of a case of hysteria. *Standard Edition* 7:3-122.

_____(1905b). Jokes and their relation to the unconscious. *Standard Edition* 8.

_____(1905c). Three essays on the theory of sexuality. *Standard Edition* 7:125-243.

_____(1908). Civilized sexual morality and modern nervous illness. *Standard Edition* 9:179-204.

_____(1912). Recommendations to physicians practicing psychoanalysis. *Standard Edition* 12:111-120.

_____(1913). Totem and taboo. *Standard Edition* 13:1-161.

_____(1914). On narcissism: an introduction. *Standard Edition* 14:167-182.

_____(1917). Introductory lectures on psychoanalysis, part III, lecture 28: analytic therapy. *Standard Edition* 16:448-463.

_____(1919). Lines of advance in psychoanalytic therapy. *Standard Edition* 17:159-168.

———(1926). The question of lay analysis. *Standard Edition* 20:179-258.

———(1940). An outline of psychoanalysis. *Standard Edition* 23:172-173.

Johnson, A., and Szurek, S.A. (1952). The genesis of antisocial acting out in children and adults. *Psychoanalytic Quarterly* 21:323-343.

Kernberg, O. (1975). *Borderline Conditions and Pathological Narcissism.* New York: Jason Aronson.

Mahler, M., Pine, F., and Bergman, A. (1975). *The Psychological Birth of the Human Infant.* New York: Basic Books.

deMause, L., ed. (1975). *The History of Childhood.* New York: Harper and Row.

Newsweek (1975, Sept. 22). Who's raising the kids.

Parsons, T. (1964). Mental illness and spiritual malaise: the role of the psychiatrist and of the minister of religion. In *Social Structure and Personality.* New York: Free Press.

Rangell, L. (1955). The role of the parent in the Oedipus complex. *Bulletin of the Menninger Clinic* 19:9-15.

Rieff, P. (1966). *The Triumph of the Therapeutic.* New York: Harper and Row.

Sander, F. (1974). Freud's "A case of successful treatment by hypnotism: An uncommon therapy." *Family Process* 13:461-468.

Zinner, J. and Shapiro, R. (1972). Projective identification as a mode of perception and behavior in families of adolescents. *International Journal of Psychoanalysis* 53:523-529.

Chapter Six

RECENT PSYCHOANALYTIC VIEWS

The failure to focus upon the family setting in which the child's personality develops and which profoundly influences his intrapsychic life has seriously limited psychoanalytic theory and its application to therapy.
—Theodore Lidz, *Hamlet's Enemy*

Despite being in practice a most radical and intense treatment of the individual, psychoanalysis as a theory includes as comprehensive an appreciation of the role of the family in personality development as has yet been formulated. As noted in chapter 5, Freud and his followers, for complex reasons, minimized their contact with family members. Nonetheless there has been a tendency, over the past three decades or so, toward greater inclusion of directly observable familial factors in psychoanalytic writings. In recent years, for example, Lidz and his associates (1965) have studied the family members of schizophrenics while others have pioneered the treatment of the family itself from a psychoanalytic point of view. Of the eighty-seven books listed in Haley and Glick's annotated bibliography of the family therapy and research literature (1971) published between 1950-1970, thirteen were written by psychoanalysts and/or included some integration with psychoanalytic thinking. Most recently Steirlin (1977) published a compilation of his work under the title "Psychoanalysis and Family Therapy." While this indicates a fair amount of overlapping interest in the field, we are still far from any systematic integration of family observations and psychoanalytic theory.[1] Glick and Haley's bibliography also illustrates the recent logarithmic growth and interest in family therapy generally. Eleven of the above eighty-seven books were published in the 1950s, while the remaining seventy-six were published in the 1960s. The present decade has already eclipsed the previous one.

There is one book that deserves special comment because of its suggestive title and early publication date. Flugel's *Psychoanalytic Study of the Family* (1921) is a recapitulation of the psychoanalytic theory of that time looked at from the vantage point of the family as the crucible of personality formation. Its fourteenth chapter concerns the attitudes of parents to children and the reciprocity of neurotic interaction between parents and children. Another early psychoanalytic book, the title of which also points to the crucial importance of "the family" was Anna Freud's and Dorothy Burlingham's *Children Without Families* (1944). Faced during the Second World War with history's natural experiment of large numbers of homeless children, Miss Freud and her collaborators were able to apply and extend the psychoanalytic ideas of the day to the observations and care of those orphaned children and infants. Their studies ushered in the next phase of development of psychoanalytic theory, that being the study of child development through naturalistic observation as well as through the new settings of child analysis and child guidance clinics. While the title of their book implies the importance of the family, the focus of interest was the mother-infant relationship. A year later, in fact, the annual *Psychoanalytic Study of the Child* was to join the official psychoanalytic

1. Meissner's excellent beginning attempt, (1978) utilizing the analytic concept of transference, came to my attention after this chapter was completed.

journals in publishing much of the further developments in psychoanalytic theory.

The task of outlining the relevant psychoanalytic literature that pertains to family processes is a formidable and unwieldy one in as much as the bulk of psychoanalytic writings are indirectly, if not directly, about family life. In fact, many papers based on classical psychoanalytic methodology are nonetheless filled with insights into family interaction. To simplify the task, I have chosen to begin with the thirty or so volumes of the *Psychoanalytic Study of the Child* using the recently published *Abstracts and Index to Volumes 1-25* (1975). I chose those titles that indicated that the focus of interest was the interface of intrapsychic and interpersonal forces and especially those studies utilizing the direct observation of family interaction. I have organized this survey into groupings based upon the life cycle as well as certain other topical considerations as follows:

A. Life Cycle
   1. Mother-infant relationship
   2. Parent-child relationship and parenthood
   3. The adolescent and his family
   4. The marriage relationship
   5. The later years
B. Issues of therapeutic intervention
C. Metapsychology

Obviously some of these headings are minimally represented in The *Psychoanalytic Study of the Child,* and I have added various relevant psychoanalytic papers without, however, doing an exhaustive literature search. The *Chicago Psychoanalytic Literature Index* was a major source of references. Following this brief survey of psychoanalytic writings on the family, I shall review the contributions to an integration of psychoanalysis and family process made by those family therapists who began their work with an analytic orientation. Partly because of the unreceptivity of psychoanalysis to these pioneering practitioners and partly because they began to explore the family as a "system," free of the assumptions of psychoanalysis, their work was not generally published in the psychoanalytic journals. Their work will be discussed separately though the division is somewhat arbitrary.

PSYCHOANALYTIC WRITINGS AND THE FAMILY

A-1. Mother-Infant Relationship

As mentioned in the introductory comments the psychoanalytic interest in child development arose in the post-World War II years and found a home for its findings in the *Psychoanalytic Study of the Child*. It might have been more accurate to describe much of the material published in this annual as psychoanalytic studies of the mother and child. The title of the annual, in fact, sums up its individual orientation despite the increasing use of observations of dyadic behavior. In these postwar years Rene Spitz, Anna Freud and her coworkers, Ernst Kris, Albert Solnit, Samuel Ritvo and colleagues at the Yale Child Study Center, and Margaret Mahler and her associates have significantly added to our understanding of early child development. Mahler, after describing the infantile psychoses in two decades of research, mapped out the separation-individuation process, thereby beginning to flesh out Freud's schematic psychosexual stages of development. The recent observational studies of Roiphe and Galenson (1972) (also Galenson and Roiphe 1971, 1976) further extend and refine our understanding of these psychosexual stages.

Mahler's work has now been elegantly summarized in *The Psychological Birth of the Human Infant* (Mahler, Pine and Bergmann 1975). While insisting that they were studying the development of intrapsychic structures, the authors were, of course, utilizing observable data. They thus address head on one of the knottiest problems in psychoanalytic theory, that is, how to correlate the external world with the internal world. Not surprisingly the substance of their work was the study of that phase of individual development when psychological separateness, inner from outer, differentiation of self from other, begins. In their introduction the authors note the need to *infer* intrapsychic phenomena from observable data.

It was clear from the outset that the central phenomenon under study, the intrapsychic process of separation and individuation, was not susceptible to direct observation; but cues to intrapsychic process could come from observation of mother-child interaction.... [p. 23]

The fact that these inferences about intrapsychic processes also involved the preverbal period of development was especially a departure from traditional psychoanalytic methodology. The authors note that their "constructions" of this preverbal period have parallels to the "reconstructions" that take place in classical psychoanalytic work, while also emphasizing the shift from the auditory psychoanalytic instrument to a greater reliance upon visual cues.

Observation of interaction, especially of the mother and her child, depend on the viewing of motor, kinesthetic, and gestural phenomena of the entire body. This is so, as they point out, "because the motor and kinesthetic pathways are the principal expressive, defensive and discharge pathways available to the infant" (1975, p. 15).

This has relevance to those interested in the application of psychoanalytic theory to family therapy for visual observation of family interaction also takes on greater importance in relation to verbal productions. The disparity, for example, between the words of a family and its actions, has frequently been noted by many observers of families as one of those aspects of communication suggestive of family disturbance.

Also of relevance to and overlapping with family processes is the paramount importance infant research places on adaptation and object relations. Freud had prepared the way for these developments many years before in *The Ego and the Id* (1923) when he shifted from the topographical model of the unconscious, preconscious and conscious to the structural division of the mind into the three agencies of id, superego, and ego. The structural model with its emphasis on the ego as a mediator between the inner and the outer world brought the question of both adaptation (of the ego and the environmental matrix) and object relations (the ego's relation to important others) into the purview of psychoanalysis. Mahler and her associates point out the greater relative importance of the adaptational point of view in early infancy than, for example, the "dynamic point of view." The dynamic view with its emphasis on impulse and defense assumes that more structuralization of the personality has taken place.

The relevance of this observation for family-related work should be mentioned here, for it is because of developmental deficits in separation-individuation with its consequent maladaptation in object relations that so many families seek help these days. Families with interpersonal disturbances now seek help at least as frequently as individuals with more internalized neurotic conflicts and symptoms.

This is a most important factor in the present crisis of psychoanalysis. Since the Second World War psychoanalytic theory held a promise far beyond its capacity to fulfill. Almost all psychotherapy in the U.S. was dependent on this compelling body of thought, the thrust of which was the importance of intrapsychic forces and their individual treatment. Making the unconscious conflicts conscious, altering the intersystemic conflicts of ego, superego, and id by interpretations within the one-to-one therapeutic relationship was the predominant paradigmatic model. It, of course, assumed a degree of internalized conflict "relatively" independent of the environment, that applies to all too few patients. We have already noted in the previous chapter how Freud had taken on only patients *sui juris*, that is, patients relatively independent of others in the conduct of their lives. This necessarily addresses itself to the complex question of analyzability and underlines the internal strain of a prevalent and compelling theory that could be practically applied to so few cases. This contradiction has been handled awkwardly and empirically by introducing, in child guidance clinics, some form of ancillary treatment for the parents, ususally the mother. Also, since 1950, the greater therapeutic engagement of the family of adults and children gave rise to the family therapy movement (see chapter 2).

It is through these "inventions" arising out of the necessity of widening the scope of observation and treatment that psycho-analytic theory can continue to unfold. The family therapy movement has described the powerful, collusive, interdependent, systemlike forces at work in family interaction, which so often interfered with the analyzability or individual treatment of so many patients. This enmeshment (Minuchin 1974), or undif-ferentiation (Bowen 1966) are often interactional manifestations of the inadequate intrapsychic individuation and separation that has been the focus of Mahler's research. One might see the classical analytic method as a heroic attempt to help individuals free themselves from these enmeshments by treating them in isolation from their family. The continuation and extension of problems in separation and individuation make the adaptational point of view of great importance *throughout* the life cycle, as well as the increasingly important dynamic point of view. The continuing importance of "adaptation" throughout the life cycle is especially underlined by the title of Lidz's *The Family and Human Adaptation* (1963). (See especially Pine 1979 in this context.)

The extensive literature on the very early years has almost exclusively focused on the mother-infant relationship. As a result of greater direct observation of the mother-infant relationship a far more complex, subtle, and sophisticated picture of the interplay of the developing child's constitution or temperament and its environment has emerged. The earlier schematic formula-tion of the drive-based psychosexual stages of development have now been integrated with the more recent work on self-object differentiation and developmental ego psychology, making the controversy between the drive-versus-object-relations schools of psychoanalysis seem artificial.

And what of the father? The relative exclusion of the father from both research and treatment settings is quite striking and reflects a wider sociocultural exclusion of the father from the child rearing role (see Mitscherlich 1970). Industrialization with its separation of the work sphere from the home left the mother more exclusively with her offspring. Paradoxically this "modern development" is a reversion to the arrangement of the preagricultural hunting and gathering societies. While it is true that the mother's biological nurturing role crosses cultures and historical epochs, the extreme separation of mother and father in child rearing is a function of the differentiation of modern society, especially fueled by industrialization. A certain value bias overemphasizing and rationalizing the importance of the mother-infant relationship has played a part in psychoanalytic contributions. An example of such a bias is the Goldstein, Freud, and Solnit book, *Beyond the Best Interests of the Child* (1973). This book, which has had a considerable impact upon the courts, has advocated the maintenance of continuity of care for children in divorce suits usually supporting the claims of mothers in custody conflicts. Only recently have adherents of arrangements such as joint custody brought to light the bias of these writers, reminding us that up until this century custody of children, almost always (and usually unjustly) was given by the weight of cultural forces to the father (Roman and Haddad 1978). Fraiberg's recent contribution, *Every Child's Birthright* (1977), has similarly been criticized for presenting a cultural bias as scientifically valid propositions.

The study of the mother-infant relationship naturally generated data that by design did not note the role of the father. Only recently has the role of the father in the separation-individuation process begun to be described (Abelin 1971, 1975; Burlingham 1973), though his importance in the very early years has, as Abelin noted, been periodically acknowledged (Loewald 1951, Mahler and Gosliner 1955). Abelin, one of Mahler's associates, has included observations of the earliest role of the father in the separation-individuation process, again demonstrating the importance of the questions (hypotheses) formulated in determining the methodology used to generate data. In this way theory building and data gathering continually influence one another, at times expanding a science and at times through overly rigid boundaries stultifying it. In this way theory, as paradigmatic (i.e., organizing), often limits and holds back scientific advances. This insight is the core of Kuhn's now oft-cited *The Structure of Scientific Revolutions* (1962).

As Abelin describes the early triangulation in the child's development, he is careful to emphasize that the developmental unfolding of this complex inner structuralization is quite sensitive to the influence of parental attitudes. "It is often difficult to distinguish between the contribution made by the child and that made by the parents to the mutual relationship: we are always dealing with circular processes." (1975, p. 295). (See also Bibring et al. 1961, Boyer 1956, Jackson, E. et al. 1950, 1952, Jacobs 1949, Jessner et al. 1955, Pine and Furer 1963, Ritvo and Solnit 1958, Robertson 1962, Rubinfine 1962, Sandler et al. 1957, Spitz 1945, 1946, Greenacre 1960, Sperling 1949, 1950.) We now turn more specifically to the question of the relationship of an individual's biological endowment and his home environment.

A-2. The Parent-Child Relationship and Parenthood

The role of the environment (external reality) remains a most problematic one in psychoanalytic theory. I do not mean to imply either here or in other parts of this book that when I speak of psychoanalytic theory it represents a single, agreed-upon body of thought. There are within psychoanalysis quite divergent and changing views and significant differences of emphasis. In the present context Freud himself, as noted in the last chapter, radically reversed himself on the role of the family in the etiology of psychoneuroses when he gave up his seduction theory and discovered the role of infantile sexuality (see chapter 5). Many psychoanalysts may thus feel that what is stated here applies to an earlier phase of psychoanalysis while others argue that the observational data reviewed here have little relevance to the practice of classical psychoanalytic technique. While the environment, especially the child's early environment, has a centrally important place in psychoanalytic theory and therapy, there is simultaneously a tendency to de-emphasize it, especially the

direct study of it. When Rene Spitz, for example, carried out his
researches in early development, he seemed to apologize for
departing from the "usual psychoanalytic methods" (1950, p. 73).
There are many examples of the dislike of "environmentalism" in
psychoanalytic writings. Friend (1976), in the introduction to his
recent review of the role of family life in child development,
worried about the problem of how psychoanalysts might
influence civilization "and at the same time not be thought of as
environmentalists" (p. 373). I shall illustrate with one other
example because it touches upon our earlier discussion of *Hamlet*
(chapter 1). Eissler's comments regarding the environment of
Hamlet are characteristic of this tendency:

> In analyzing these environmental factors, I may have given
> the impression that I regard Hamlet's plight as merely the
> reflection of his father's ambivalence. *Such a trend of
> thought is now current in many quarters*; it holds that the
> psychopathology that is observed in an individual is merely
> a reflection of the psychopathology of his environment, or a
> reaction to the unwisdom of his elders. [1971, p. 71, italics
> mine]

While a psychoanalytic case report is inconceivable without a
summary of the patient's early environment (the genetic point of
view), psychoanalytic writers insist on not placing too much
emphasis upon it. Why is this so?

One reason is the wish to conserve the central discoveries of
psychoanalysis, that being of the role played by unconscious
forces and by infantile sexuality. These discoveries, which
emphasize innate and internal forces, corrected a simpler earlier
view of humans as but blank slates upon which the environment
is imprinted. These discoveries also added a dimension to the
study of man at a level quite different from what today is
represented by the psychological, sociological, and anthropological frames of reference. These latter disciplines tend toward an
"environmentalism" from which psychoanalysis correctly wishes
to distinguish and differentiate itself.

Secondly, the day-to-day practice of psychoanalysis naturally focuses on the patient's inner psychic reality and how he frequently misinterprets and distorts external reality. The analyst and patient are constantly examining how external reality is used for neurotic needs rather than focusing on that reality per se. External reality plays a major role in the early development of psychic structure, which, in turn, comes to reshape reality in its own way. Reality in psychoanalytic theory thus recedes in relative etiological importance as the individual moves from infancy to adulthood. In addition, attempts to intervene in a patient's external reality have generally been viewed as manipulative and thus at odds with the central goal of psychoanalysis, the greater autonomous mastery by the ego of both his internal conflicts and external realities. In fact, a favorable outcome in analytic therapy depends in part upon the degree to which the patient assumes responsibility for his/her life. This includes the integration of the drives and a minimization of the tendency to see one's troubles as externally determined. This result is facilitated by the analytic situation. The nondirectiveness of the analyst facilitates the expression of the patient's transference, fantasies, and drives, the analysis and working through of which becomes the vehicle of change. Winnicott (1960) stated this rather extremely in a paper minimizing the role of childhood trauma in the psychoanalytic setting.

> In psychoanalysis as we know it there is no trauma that is outside the individual's omnipotence. Changes come in an analysis when the traumatic factors enter the psychoanalytic material in the patient's own way, and within the patient's omnipotence. [p. 585]

This is another, somewhat extreme example of how even traumatic factors are deemphasized in the service of the analytic work. I am not in agreement with this view and find that it is helpful to a patient to know whether certain events in childhood did or did not occur. This should not interfere with the further analysis of why these traumas were repressed or rendered ambiguous. In any case it is when external reality continues to be "traumatic" or noxious in the present life of a patient that psychoanalysis is often contraindicated and other modalities recommended. Anna Freud (1968) reviewed this question in her paper on the indications and contraindication for child analysis, and her comments apply as well to adult patients. She noted that analysis is most clearly indicated where the patient's turmoil is a product of his inner world. When the threat, the attacker, or the seducer are real people or where the pathogenic influences are embodied in the parents, the chance for successful analysis is reduced (*Abstracts and Index*, p. 113). This question will be more fully discussed in the subsequent part on therapeutic intervention, but in this context I would add that Anna Freud's distinction while heuristically useful is not always easy to apply clinically.

For the neurotic, inner conflicts are usually enacted and reenacted through the repetition compulsion. He unconsciously chooses significant others to make his external reality painful all over again.

The problem clinically is that so often the patient's inner turmoil is then masked by a difficult external reality albeit of his own unconscious choosing. Such patients do not usually present themselves to the psychoanalyst but do frequently end in the family therapist's office. My experience in such situations has led me to do conjoint family therapy where these externalizing tendencies can be more directly confronted and the individual patient or patients then prepared for more intensive individual treatment.

E.J. Anthony and T. Benedek, the editors of an excellent collection, *Parenthood: Its Psychology and Psychopathology* (1970), offered a third explanation for psychoanalysts' failure to study the developmental situation from the parents' point of view. They noted the general tendency in man to take himself for granted and to study those who are "different and at a distance. . . . Child development has thus been carefully described whereas the psychology of parenthood has remained a grossly neglected topic of description and investigation" (p. xix).

Fourth, there is in psychoanalytic theory an implicit philosophical position that I would call pessimistic determinism. It places human nature with its universal and biologically rooted preoedipal and oedipal drives at the heart of man's perennial difficulties and suffering. This trend was recently restated by Kovel (1970) who so convincingly demonstrated the interweaving of these darker instinctual strands into the fabric of some of our pathological social and cultural institutions, in this instance, the institution of racism. What Kovel accomplished is an appreciation of the interplay of human nature and human institutions that transcends the sterile nature/nurture controversies that persist in the literature. We, in fact, wonder at the persistence of this nature/ nurture dichotomy in the behavioral sciences. Is it an extension of and intrusion into scientific work of the introjective, projective and splitting mechanisms of the separation-individuation phase of development. The world and self in the infant's blurry eyes are either good *or* bad and thus hopefully within the sphere of the infant's omnipotent control. Some of the early attempts at reality testing in the separation-individuation phase of development are thus seen to persist not only in the world of our dreams and of our artistic productions but also in our "scientific" reality testing as well. This "splitting" tendency of seeing human nature as good or evil, the environment as beneficent or menacing, of man as master of, the slave of, or in harmony with nature, are matters of "basic value orientations." F. Kluckohn (1953) first systematically studied how all cultures express and reflect such generalized views, giving its members a sense of their relationship to the world. The scientific community, while striving to be value-free, is nonetheless a subculture that cannot fully free itself from such value orientations. The scientific enterprise is itself an orientation that, for the most part, seeks to facilitate man's mastery over the environment and to be sure has profoundly altered, through its application, what we know of the preindustrial world.

Fifth and last, psychoanalysis, as a medically based, scientific psychology has also sought a relatively value-free and nonblaming position in regard to human behavior. In the medical and behavioral sciences etiology inevitably gets associated with blame. Cigarettes are blamed for lung cancer, maternal deprivation is blamed for depression. One influential example of this tendency was the introduction of the concept of the schizo-phrenoenic mother (Fromm-Reichman 1948). While capturing a partial clinical truth, the concept pointed a causal finger, thus doing a disservice to the mothers of individuals with this multidetermined disturbance (see chapter 4).

All these considerations contribute to the tendency for psycho-analysis to minimize the role of parental influences (nurture) in comparison with innate drive aspects (nature). Having discussed the hazards of describing interaction free of "environmentalism," we will now note some of the papers that overlap with the previous part on the important role of the mother-infant relationship, but begin to focus on parenting in general.

The view of "the psychological birth of the infant" as evolving out of a symbiotic state with the maternal object indicates the criticalness of the maternal role. The study of the mother-infant dyad has clarified a species-specific individuation process. As is necessary, however, when one intensively studies a particular process, other aspects tend to fade into the background. The absence of research on the role of the father, already mentioned in the last part, can be restated again. What is the impact upon the mother-infant dyad of the quality and intensity of the marital relationship? Clinically one observes, later in the life cycle, the continued symbiotic bond of a mother and her schizophrenic offspring reinforced by a severe marital disturbance as well as, for example, the father's often vicarious and primitive identification with the patient (see chapter 4).

The unfolding of the separation-individuation process is not limited to the interplay of the mother's personality and the child's endowment. Little understood, for example, is the impact of the internal and external pressures mothers feel in regard to combining careers with motherhood. Few women, or men for that matter, are unaffected by these changing cultural expectations. A culture as rapidly changing as ours creates an unstable environ-mental matrix that at this point has an immeasureable impact upon the psychological birth of the human infant.

As we move from the more species-specific psychophysiological separation-individuation process to the wider sociopsychological parenting process, the role of the father takes on a more prominent aspect. In the previous chapter we already noted how Freud had referred far more frequently to fathers and fatherhood than to motherhood. This reflected his greater interest in the child's oedipal stage of development than the preoedipal stages.

So in this part we have the classic paper by Johnson and Szurek (1952) on the transmission of unconscious impulses and conflicts from one generation to the next, Rangell's paper (1955) on how parents often work through their oedipal conflicts through their children, and Neubauer's paper (1960) on the oedipal development of the one-parent child. Weissman's paper (1963) on the effects of preoedipal paternal attitudes on development and character is especially interesting. In this paper he describes in detail two patients he treated in psychoanalysis in whom repetitive, pathological, preoedipal, father-son play had obvious and profound impacts upon later character formation. What is especially intriguing in the present context was the relatively rare occurrence of the analyst's observation of the very same childhood interplay *in his office.* The following quote is only an aside in this interesting paper, but it nicely illustrates the continuation into adulthood of pathological object relations first established in early childhood *observed in the analyst's office.*

> I once had the opportunity of seeing this interplay between the father and son in my office. Since L was not working, the father paid for the analysis. The father occasionally asked to see me, ostensibly to discuss the patient's progress, but actually in a determination to interfere with the analysis and to find out what he himself could do to cure the patient. On one such occasion the patient told me that he wished to be present ... At the meeting the patient began treating his father as if he were a child. He showed solicitude for his father's health, and examined his hands and scrutinized his face as if he could find signs of illness. The father was totally submissive, as if the young man's behavior were entirely proper and meaningful. But as the conference developed, the

father became increasingly arrogant, obstinate, and finally reduced his son to a state of immobility and silence. The design of the pre-oedipal play was enacted once more. [Weissman 1963, pp. 122-123]

Because of the nature of the psychoanalytic situation such direct observations of family interaction rarely occurs. As soon as the consulting door is opened to relatives, the panoply of familial interaction that Freud felt contaminated the surgical psychoanalytic field, gives rise to the raw data of family psychiatry. It is again a matter of goals and a point of view. The psychoanalyst tries to help the patient free himself through the dyadic analytic treatment from such neurotic entanglements, while the family therapist working with the interactional system tries to free each of the participants caught in such ongoing neurotic interaction. The question of which modality is appropriate to which clinical situation is a most relevant one and will be taken up in section B, on intervention.

The role of the father in child development is most intriguingly introduced by the famous case of Schreber. While Freud's analysis (1911) gave new insights into the role of regression, restitutive processes, and narcissism in psychosis, (i.e., what goes on internally in the psychotic), Niederland (1959), half a century later, brought to light the extraordinary writings of Schreber's father, which were to shed further light on this classic case. The fact that the father of the most famous psychotic patient in the history of psychiatry turned out to be a nineteenth century pedagogue, whose influence over child-rearing practices in Germany is comparable to Spock's in our era, is filled with irony. Niederland unearthed those writings that Freud apparently chose to ignore and noted the uncanny correspondence of Schreber's delusions and his father's chid rearing methods. Schatzman (1973) further elaborated on the implications of Niederland's discovery into a more interpersonal view of psychosis. Would Freud's brilliant insights into the inner workings of the mind have been blunted by the knowledge that Niederland discovered? This again touches upon a major theme running through this book. Human behavior is of an order of complexity that its study can only resemble that of the proverbial blind men and the elephant, except that in our behavioral sciences we blind men are now studying ourselves. In the study of ourselves the psychoanalytic method has served as a major route to the understanding of the unconscious, videotapes and films of family interaction allow for the elucidation of interpersonal patterns often out of our awareness, while biochemical assays of urine and blood trace the hormonal correlates of our affective states, and the list of ways we have of seeing ourselves goes on and on. We are far from integrating these differing levels and must continue to pursue them somewhat independently of one another. There are times, however, when these levels can begin to be correlated with one another. The interface between psychoanalytic theory and family processes is one of these potentially fruitful areas.

While child development has been the major preoccupation of psychoanalysis, T. Benedek (1959) not too long ago wrote an unusual article on parenthood as a phase of development itself worth studying. The idea of that paper, now expanded in a book edited by Anthony and Benedek (1970), brings together a most comprehensive set of psychoanalytic writings on the subject of parenthood. It shows a refreshing appreciation of the interpersonal world of parent and child that does not lose sight of the continuing intrapsychic developments of both the parent and child. (See also Buxbaum 1964, Coleman et al. 1953, Cavenar and Butts 1978, Friedlander 1949, Mead 1957, Parens 1975, Olden 1953.)

A-3. The Adolescent and His Family: The Second Individuation Process

In chapter 3 we noted that the most critical and irreversible stage of the family life cycle was the arrival of the first child. The infant within four months then enters its most critical phase, that of the separation-individuation process, an intrapsychic process that, as Mahler has stated, "reverberates throughout the life cycle. It is never finished" (1975, p. 3). The second most critical stage of the family life cycle is the launching of its children. The earlier critical phase, with its task of giving physical and psychological birth to a child, now is reactivated as the family must again give birth, physically, psychologically, and also sociologically to a young adult. Blos, who contributed extensively to our understanding of the intraphysic processes in adolescence, was obviously influenced by the work of Mahler when he called adolescence the "second individuation process," requiring the "shedding of family dependencies, the loosening of infantile object ties in order to become a member of the adult world" (1967, p. 163).

While intensive observational studies of infants have enriched our psychoanalytic understanding of the first individuation process, until quite recently and for reasons noted in the previous section, there have been no direct observations of this second individuation process. Stierlin (1974) as well as R.L. Shapiro and his colleagues, J. Zinner (1972, 1974), E.R. Shapiro (1975) and D.A. Berkowitz (1974) began studying and treating borderline adolescents and their families at the NIMH in the late 1950s and 1960s. While there is great similarity between Stierlin's observations and those of Shapiro and his colleagues, the latter has worked more directly within the framework of psychoanalytic theory, and their conceptualizations dovetail rather nicely with the work of Mahler, as well as the recent writings of Kohut (1971) and Kernberg (1975) on the borderline and narcissistic disorders. More than any other writers they have documented and begun to conceptualize the interweaving of intrapsychic and interpersonal processes. Their contribution is presently the most sophisticated and subtle attempt to integrate individual psychology and family processes. Because they carried out their work with families of borderline patients where there has been inadequate separation-individuation, they naturally observed more primitive levels of object relations along with more primitive individual mechanisms of defense. The defensive maneuver that is most regularly described in their observations was that of projective identification.

The classical mechanisms of defense reviewed by A. Freud (1936), for the most part naturally derive from the intrapsychic orientation of psychoanalytic drive theory. Defenses, by definition, defend against unacceptable unconscious impulses, affects, wishes, or fantasies. They protect the ego against instinctual demands and for the most part are intrapsychic in their operation, though they all have some interpersonal consequences. One defense mechanism, that of projection, as A. Freud notes, "disturbs our human relations (as) when we project our own jealousy and attribute to other people our own aggressive acts" (p. 133). She goes on to describe a complex variation of this defense, "altruistic surrender," which permits a person to find *in others* a "proxy in the outside world to serve as a repository for the self's own wishes" (p. 136). In this way gratification of a projected impulse is achieved. As drive theory becomes more integrated with object-relations theory, the concept of defense needs expansion to include its interpersonal ramifications. Perhaps it would be more accurate to speak of such ego activities as serving (1) defensive functions for the individual and (2) equilibrating, adaptive, or maladaptive functions for a family or group. To illustrate: a severely obsessive-compulsive twenty-four-year-old who for his previous ten years spent four to five hours daily in the bathroom carrying out rituals, was referred to me by his individual therapist, together with his family, who would encourage him to come out of the bathroom when "he was ready." The severity of his defenses of isolation, undoing, and obsessional thinking served as a repository for the parents' own obsessive-compulsive trends, as well as protecting them from an underlying separation anxiety that would emerge if their son gave up this bathroom fixation and could separate and individuate from the family. For a good part of the year the family would arrive thirty to forty minutes late for their sessions, despite the understanding that I would see whoever would arrive on time. The parents were also thus further able to sustain a sadomasochistic marital relation by whipping one another with the blame for their son's difficulty. One can only imagine the unconscious rage being defended against and enacted within this family by this young man's "defenses against his instinctual demands" and the parents' compliance with his demands. Such behavior, sometimes

called *acting out,* is especially prominent in more pathological
families and usually serves preoedipal aims originating in the
preverbal period of development. Just as a child in the
rapprochement crisis may defend against further separation by
regressive clinging and other manipulations of significant others,
families of borderline patients also defend against further
differentiation and separation by a host of interpersonal maneuvers. They, for example, limit self-object differentiation by a
defensive delineation of the other that tries to deny the realistic
parts of the other. This process first described by Melanie Klein
(1946) as projective identification has been further reviewed and
discussed by Jaffe (1968) and Robbins (1976). Shapiro and his
colleagues frequently found this mode of "defensive" perception
and behavior in the families they studied (Zinner 1972). The first
paragraph of Zinner's paper defines the mechanism and its
pivotal theoretical significance.

> Projective identification is an activity of the ego, which
> amoung its effects, modifies perception of the object and,
> in a reciprocal fashion, alters the image of the self.
> These conjoined changes in perception influence and may,
> in fact, govern behavior of the self toward the object.
> Thus, projective identification provides an important
> conceptual bridge between an individual and interpersonal
> psychology, since our awareness of the mechanism permits
> us to understand specific interaction *among* persons in
> terms of specific dynamic conflicts occuring within indi-
> viduals. [p. 573]

It is indeed a germinal concept, which describes a form of
narcissistic interaction that Freud described so eloquently but did
not conceptualize in his paper on narcissism (see chapter 5). It has
certain relevance for all types of group behavior (see also Freud's
Group Psychology and the Analysis of the Ego 1921). What is
needed is a greater clarification of the distinctions between
normal and pathological forms of projective identification.
Shapiro et al. (1972) puts the question this way:

Depending upon the nature of the interaction of these factors, projective identification can endow a relationship with salutary empathic qualities or to the contrary, generate binding attributions to which the child remains a creature of parental defensive economy. [p. 526]

A-4. The Marital Relationship

When George Bernard Shaw, over fifty years ago, was invited to contribute an essay on marriage for *The Book of Marriage* (1926) edited by Keyserling, he replied, "No man dare write the truth about marriage while his wife lives. Unless, that is, he hates her, like Strindberg; and I don't. I shall read the volume with interest knowing that it will consist chiefly of evasions; but I will not contribute to it" (p. iii). While Shaw had much to say on the subject of marriage, he was reluctant to tackle the subject head on. Psychoanalysts, while dealing daily with issues of marital relations, seem to have shared with Shaw the reluctance of writing directly about the subject. We have touched upon the psychoanalyic literature on the mother-infant relationship, the parent-child relationship, and the family's relation to the adolescent and turn now to the quite sparse psychoanalytic literature on the marital relationship. The few (Horney 1928, Dicks 1953, Stein 1956) who have addressed the subject have all commented on the absence of any systematic study of the problems of marriage. A perusal of the *Index of the Psychoanalytic Study of the Child Vol. 1-25* (1975) reveals no substantive reference either to the marital relationship or to the interplay of the marriage relationship and child development. T. Lidz (1957, 1963) has been the only writer to consistently emphasize the importance of marital relations to child development. The contributions to this area by family therapists who have a psychoanalytic orientation will be discussed later.

Horney (1928) took as a point of departure a queston raised by Keyserling (1926) in the book, just mentioned, to which Shaw refused to contribute. To the queston of what impelled human beings into marriage in spite of the presence of matrimonial unhappiness throughout the ages, Horney, from the vantage point of psychoanalysis, replied that it was "clearly neither more nor less than the expectation that we shall find in it the fulfillment of all the old desires arising out of the oedipus situation in childhood" (p. 319). The inevitably frequent disillusionments, disappointments, and guilt arising out of the persistence of these unconscious oedipal wishes "gives rise to the problem of monogamy." In addition to the other channels of libidinal gratification such as sublimation, regressive cathexis of former objects, and the outlet through children, there is the impulse to seek after fresh objects" (p. 323). It is no doubt the strength of this impulse that led society through its religious institutions to try to enforce the monogamous ideal.

Horney goes on to point out the preoedipal instinctual contributions to the desire for monogamy, which in turn often creates further difficulties. The derivative of the oral phase takes "the form of the desire to incorporate the object in order to have sole possession of it" (p. 32). To this is added the anal-sadistic demand for possession. She concludes this most unusual paper with a characteristic psychoanalytic tone of scientific detachment and humility. She notes that the opposing monogamous and polygamous instincts arising as they do out of childhood conflicts are essentially *not* resolvable by any general principle. "We must leave it to the moralist," she writes, "to decide what is then the right course." Psychoanalytic insight, however, is seen as an aid in the face of such matrimonial conflicts.

> The discovery of the unconscious sources which feed them may so weaken not only the ideal of monogamy but also the polygamous tendencies, that it may be possible for the conflicts to be fought out. And the knowledge we have acquired helps us in yet another way: when we see the conflicts in the married life of two people we often involuntarily tend to think that the only solution is that they should separate. The deeper the understanding of the inevitability of these and other conflicts in every marriage, the more profound will be our conviction that our attitude

towards such unchecked personal impressions must be one
of complete reserve and the greater will be our ability to
control them in reality. [p. 331]

Stein's paper (1956) on "The Marital Bond," a more modest but
quite interesting contribution, noted a frequent unconscious
male fantasy of the marital bond that includes the wife as an
intrapsychic representation of the man's phallus. Stein does not
mention the description of Eve's creation in *Genesis,* but her birth
out of Adam's rib may be an early mythic example of this
unconscious fantasy. Her unconscious essentiality to the male's
sense of bodily integrity serves to further our sense of the earliest
beginnings of the conflicts between male and female. Also the
female arising out of Adam's rib is reflective of her dependence
upon man in a patriarchally organized society from biblical times
until the modern era. The perennial conflicts of the sexes are
further illustrated in this creation myth as Adam and Eve avoid
the responsibility for the newfound knowledge of sexuality by
blaming others when confronted with their eating the forbidden
fruit. Adam blames Eve who in turn blames the serpent. Horney
had already hinted that other unconscious meanings of the
marital bond may include oral incorporation and sadomasochistic
fantasies. Further study of such fantasies would contribute to a
better appreciation of the intrapsychic contributions to marital
disharmony.

Because of the complementary enactment of such unconscious
fantasies in marital relations, psychoanalytic treatments often
reached impasses. Oberndorf (1938) and Mittelman (1944, 1948)
experimented with the analytic treatment of both spouses to
manage such difficulties. This innovation did not become an
accepted analytic practice for obvious reasons. Rogers (1965)
many years later again attempted a concurrent psychotherapy of a
spouse, which he called a parameter of classical analytic
treatment. The unfolding of an analytic process would surely and
necessarily be complicated by the analyst also seeing the spouse.
To their credit, however, we can see that they were trying to
resolve impasses resulting from complementary neuroses. They

were thus the first clinicians to describe the interlocking neurotic relationships that over the years have come to be seen by family therapists as collusive family systems. The works of Oberndorf and Mittleman are cited again and again by analytically oriented family therapists as the forerunners of this new modality. The problem of the resistances to classical analytic therapy resulting from such "external object relations" has been best described theoretically by Giovacchini (1958, 1961). He feels that these resistances can be interpreted analytically while frequently also requiring referral of the spouse to another analyst.

Today more and more patients present specifically with marital problems manifesting the kind of pathological "mutual adaptations" described by Giovacchini. Often there is initially little motivation for individual psychoanalytic treatment, as the distress is experienced as the relationship and psychonalysis may be contraindicated or impractical for other reasons. Conjoint therapy helps to focus directly upon the neurotic interaction, thus helping to bring some resolution or at least clarification of the presenting problem. At times the differentiaton of each partner's neurotic contribution to the difficulty establishes motivation for more intensive psychoanalytic therapy (see chapter 9).

Influenced by the development of object-relations theory in England, H.V. Dicks (1953, 1963, 1967) began his studies of marriage from an analytic framework. He began to describe the multifaceted ways in which marital relations were affected by experiences in each spouse's family of origin. He also noted the collusive process involving projective identification that we discussed in the previous part on adolescence. (See also Rosenbaum and Alger 1967, Sager 1966, 1976, Skynner 1976, Zinner 1974, Martin 1976, Flugel 1920, and Willi 1976.)

A-5. The Later Years (the Third Separation-Individuation Process?)

As noted in chapter 3, the elderly in our society are in a most precarious position. The demands of the modern family life cycle tend to separate the nuclear family from the elderly. The first separation-individuation process, which gives "psychological birth" to the infant, is followed by the second separation-individuation process of adolescence, which gives birth in a sociological sense. The adolescent leaves his family of origin to ultimately form a new family of procreation. Following marriage and child rearing, the individual is again faced with separations, but the prospect this third time is often isolating decline rather than "a new start in life."

Partly for the above reasons but mainly because psychoanalytic treatment usually comes to be a lengthy process of intrapsychic restructuring of the personality, the problems of the aged were not commonly addressed in the psychoanalytic literature. Freud set the tone by a pessimistic view, feeling that the aged have less psychological elasticity. Abraham (1919) tried to counter this pessimism with the report of some successful analytic interventions with older patients. Kaufman (1940) made some relevant observations about the tendency of persons in the "climacterium" to enact important earlier conflicts with their own parents in relationships with their children. How insistently many grandparents are in terror of depending upon their children in their later years. They are often reworking the dependency conflicts of their own childhood. He saw a revival of conflicts similar to those of puberty with the tendency to reverse the generations. In the same article he also called attention to the role of society's positive and negative "transferential" attitudes toward the aged and foresaw a time when psychoanalytic research would have a place in the investigation of the problems of aging. This prophecy found fulfillment in two volumes arising out of symposia sponsored by the Boston Society for Gerontologic Psychiatry. (See Zinberg and Kaufman 1963, Berezin and Cath 1965.)

These two volumes present an unprecedented application of psychoanalytic thinking to the aging process together with an openness to nonanalytic methodology that is rare in this literature survey. It could be that when faced with clinical problems where psychoanalytic treatment is rarely a realistic consideration, psychoanalysts could approach the crisis-ridden process of aging (with its losses and depletions) and recognize that a host of alternate modalities are required to support the failing defenses of the elderly. (See also Butler and Lewis 1973, Meerloo 1955, and Bibring 1966.)

B. Issues of Therapeutic Intervention

In the last chapter we reviewed Freud's early experimentation with hypnosis (1893) in the treatment of a woman with a postpartum illness (also see chapter 8). She was still living with her parents and unable to feed her new born infant; Freud gave her a hypnotic suggestion to cry out at her mother for not having fed her properly. This intuitive, interpersonal intervention given under hypnosis led Freud to go deeper and ask what lay beneath such symptoms and interpersonal disturbances. The psychoanalytic revolution was here in embryonic form. In a few short years the discoveries of the unconscious and infantile sexuality were to form the foundation of a new psychological theory that has left its stamp upon Western thought as well as upon the field of psychiatry. What is remarkable and paradoxical is that psychoanalysis, which so illuminated and widened our view of the nature of man and influenced so many other disciplines of thought and activity, has as a treatment modality been of such limited general value.

This is in part because (1) in Freud's own words, psychoanalysis promises no more than "the substitution of ordinary unhappiness for neurotic misery," (2) the training of competent psychoanalysts involves an unusual amount of time and money, thus precluding the training of large numbers of analysts (the length of training being similar to that of a neurosurgeon), (3) the number of patients treatable by classical psychoanalysis is limited by a host of considerations related to the capacity to verbalize, the presence of significant motivation, adequate financial resources, as well as the presence of largely internalized neurotic conflict, and (4) psychoanalysis has in recent years lost its dominant influence in American psychiatry. This is partly because of its inability to fulfill the hope placed in it as well as the recent return to prominence of biological psychiatry fueled by the awareness that any national health insurance may pay only for the more medically based emotional disturbances.

As has already been noted in the previous parts, many children, adolescents, and adults are often enmeshed in complementary pathological relations that prove to be obstacles for individually oriented therapists whose hard work with patients was being undone by such external resistances to change in the patient's behavior. Some observers were noting the impact of changes in a patient upon the family's equilibrium. V. Rosen (Eisenstein 1956), for example, speculated upon the impact upon family members of a relative being in psychoanalytic treatment.

While the neurotic interaction of family members led Oberndorf and Mittelman, as we have mentioned, to treat each spouse, child psychiatrists and analysts struggled with what to do about the frequently encountered disturbed parent-child relationship. The round-the-clock daily involvement of parents and their children created a host of technical problems for therapists who hoped to treat internalized conflicts in the traditional one-to-one therapeutic relationship. Empirically a child was usually treated by a primary therapist, while the mother, and rarely the father, were treated separately either by advisory child guidance or a simultaneous psychotherapy or analysis. The collaboration of their therapists then led to a series of clinical papers describing the extraordinary interplay of unconscious elements in parent and child and how regularly the child could only progress in his treatment if the unconscious forces in the parent were addressed (Levy 1960, Hellman et al. 1960, Kolansky et al. 1966, Johnson et al. 1942, Elles 1962, Fries 1946, Sperling 1950). The question of whether it was better for one or two therapists to see the mother and child was discussed by Burlingham (1951). She leaned toward the same therapist seeing both mother and child. Complementary neurotic conflicts were thus repeatedly described, but psychoanalytic theory had not yet changed to incorporate these observations in developing further parameters of treatment. A related development that reflected the recognition of the parent's significant role in child development were attempts to treat the child via the parent, a model actually suggested by Freud's treatment (1909) of little Hans via his father (Ruben 1946, Fries 1946, Bonnard 1950, Furman 1957).

An approach that seemed a combination of these was the inclusion of the mother in the child's treatment (Schwartz 1950). One observation, which has been rarely explored in the psychoanalytic literature, had to do with the conflicts of loyalty felt by a child going to an individual therapist (see Boszormenyi-Nagy 1973 for a fuller discussion of this problem).

A. Freud (1968) finally reviewed, after twenty years or so of clinical experience, the question of the indications and contra-indications for child analysis. She concluded that only children with well-internalized conflicts would benefit optimally. But the many children whose difficulties are not neurotically self-inflicted but "caused and maintained by active, ongoing influences lodged in the environment . . . are in need of therapeutic help, but the type of help is not clearly indicated, nor the therapist's role in the process clearly circumscribed" (*Abstracts and Index*, p. 113).

This summary statement reflects the glaring absence of a theory of psychoanalytic psychotherapy for children despite the presence of a most comprehensive theory of child development. C. Kramer (1968) is a child psychiatrist and analyst who began to extend psychoanalytic theory and technique by working with families when classical psychoanalysis was not appropriate. A. Ornstein (1976) has also recently addressed this issue in a most thoughtful and informed way. Sensitive to the great theoretical differences between child- and family-focused treatment, she utilizes the insights of each of these modes of treatment and moves toward an integration in the treatment of children of intrapsychic and interpersonal factors. She argues for "the conceptualization of the totality of the treatment as a single process, regardless of who is in treatment" (p. 28). She then proposes a somewhat simplified beginning model that takes into account the family as a whole, its members' intrapsychic as well as interpersonal aspects.

The model is a simple one but the first such attempt by a child analyst to include the family-as-a-system concept into any theory of the psychoanalytic therapy with children. While there is no adequate theory of the psychoanalytic therapy of the child, there

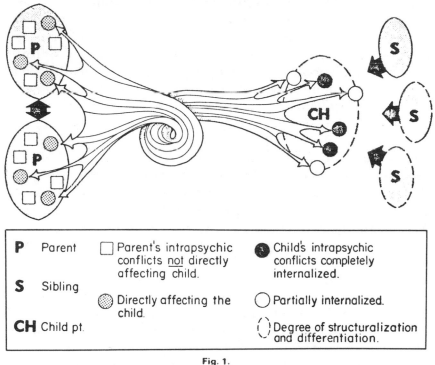

Fig. 1.

From: Ornstein, A., *Comprehensive Psychiatry*, 1976

is also no theory of the psychoanalytic therapy of the family. Some isolated papers have addressed the question of transference and countertransference in family therapy (Sager 1967) and the problem of interpretation (Titchener 1966), but a comprehensive theory of psychoanalytically oriented family therapy remains a challenge for the future. (See also Bird and Martin 1956, Mosse 1954, Pine 1976.)

C. Metapsychology

The revolution in psychology brought about by Freud's discovery of the unconscious required a *metapsychology* (meaning literally "beyond psychology"). The assumption of an unconscious necessitated a level of explanation other than existed in the prevailing psychology of the day. Metapsychology came to represent a higher level of abstraction in the continuum from clinical observation to theory. It has served as an orienting and systematizing framework around which clinical data and lower level psychoanalytic propositions could be organized.

Inasmuch as psychoanalysis has utilized data for the most part generated by the classical psychoanalytic method, metapsychology has naturally emphasized intrapsychic processes. Psychoanalysts have perenially been struggling with how much data derived from other methods falls within the boundaries of psychoanalysis. This is again raised in the most recent critical assessment of the future of psychoanalysis (Miller 1975), where the question of what is central to psychoanalysis and what peripheral was asked. This is a legitimate question, one reflecting the dilemma that psychoanalysis continues to face, namely, how it relates to the other behavioral sciences. The importance of interdisciplinary approaches are encouraged with the usual caveat that the "central," "core," pure gold of analysis not be alloyed or diluted.

The relatively recent, increasing psychoanalytic attention paid to the individual *and his relation to the outside world* was set in motion by Freud's introduction of the structural model in 1923. The newer tripartite division of the personality into ego, id, and superego facilitated the study of the ego's adaptation to the external world (see Hartmann 1958) as well as the role of external influences in the development of both the ego and the superego.

A nodal point in the development of psychoanalytic metapsychology was Waelder's "The Principle of Multiple Function" (1930). In that seminal paper Waelder noted that the problems faced by the ego reflect conflicts between itself and the following other agencies: the superego, the id, the compulsion to repeat, *and* the outside world. Inasmuch as the compulsion to repeat participates with the ego and the id, I have excluded it from the following diagram, which illustrates Waelder's model. It was his point that any attempted solution of a conflict (e.g., between the ego and the superego) must inevitably and simultaneously attempt solutions of other sets of problems as well.

First, this schematic drawing illustrates psychoanalysis's emphasis on the individual in placing the ego, influenced by and acting upon the other agencies, *at the center of the model.* It is, in a sense, an early but skewed version of what has come in recent years to be called general systems theory (though here with an egocentric focus).

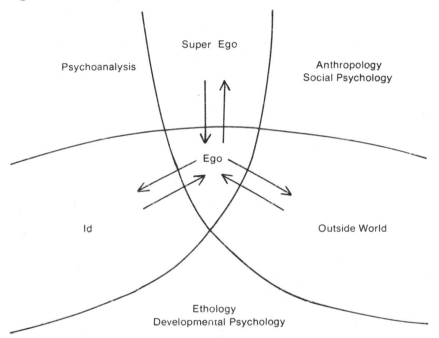

The drawing also illustrates the necessary narrowing of focus of the varying behavioral sciences in their specialized approaches to the study of man. Each of the behavioral sciences must exclude certain variables in order to more fully develop their disciplines. Psychoanalysis thus deemphasizes external reality while most social scientists pay less attention to the biological bases of behavior, and developmental psychologists, ethologists, and biologically oriented psychiatrists tend to ignore the superego in their observations.

This model did permit psychoanalysis to widen its scope of observation, giving rise to an ego psychology, which such theorists as Hartmann (1958), hoped would achieve a level of generality so as to subsume the other behavioral sciences. This expansion did facilitate the further evolution of psychoanalytic metapsychology through research in child development, which in turn facilitated its integration with object relations theory. Jacobson's *The Self and the Object World* (1964), for example, illustrates the greater incorporation of the external world in psychoanalytic theory, while retaining the basic emphasis on intrapsychic structure. A further integration of direct observations of family interaction beside that of mother-infant interaction remains problematical and quite rudimentary. Some papers that point in this direction are mentioned below.

When Freud first introduced the concept of *primary gain*, he was contrasting this new idea with the already existing, somewhat moralistic concept of *secondary gain*. Whereas secondary gain consisted in those benefits accruing to a person from the outside world as a result of falling ill, primary gain was a manifestation of the direct discharge of internal (i.e., primary) drives in symptom formation. Freud's early discussion of these concepts (Freud 1905, p. 43) recognized their greater complexity, but it was not until Katz's metapsychological review and discussion (1963) that these terms, which attempt to separate internal from external factors, could be clarified. Based upon later psychoanalytic theory Katz concluded that these concepts were ultimately inseparable. The reinforcement of symptomatology in a patient by significant others can now be better conceptualized as a result of more recent studies in narcissistic object ties and in terms of such inter-personal defenses as "the evocation of a proxy" (Wangh 1962). Wangh enlarged upon a defensive process first described by A. Freud as "altruistic surrender" (mentioned earlier in this chapter in the discussion of adolescence). In this process "another person may be used by the ego for defensive purposes" (Wangh 1962, p. 453). An obvious corollary question, though rarely asked, is what is the psychology of this "other person" who allows himself to be so used. This process was elegantly demonstrated by

Johnson and Szurek (1952), who showed how a child can be encouraged to act out unconscious impulses of a parent while simultaneously expressing his own impulses. Bird (1957) elaborated on the interpersonal aspects of such acting out as well as the problems of its management in the psychoanalytic situation. Altman (1957) noted the role of the oral drive in the varied participants of such *mutual* acting out. Pollock (1964) pulled together many of these strands in a paper that described various symbioticlike behaviors in nonpsychotic individuals. This led him to postulate a hierarchy of symbiotic relationships occurring "at all developmental levels" (p. 25). The above writers for the most part utilized data obtained from the context of individual therapy. Zinner and Shapiro (1972), on the other hand, as well as Brodey (1965) and Stierlin (1973, 1976), further elaborated on these processes based upon *actual observations* of family interaction. Bruch (1970) applied such conceptual refinements to her studies of eating disorders by noting the importance of the interplay of interpersonal experience and "instinct." All of the above studies rely heavily upon the often misunderstood concepts of projection and externalization. Novick and Kelly (1970) have attempted to clarify the differences between these related concepts and have indicated the prevalence and role of these mechanisms in the interpersonal field of many disturbed families.

As already stated, these papers are but a rudimentary start in integrating interpersonal observations with psychoanalytic metapsychology. The application of psychoanalytic theory to the treatment of couples and families has thus been quite limited. We turn now to the few family therapists who have attempted this integration. (See also Benedek 1970, Muir 1975, Lomas 1961, Friedman 1975, Pine 1979, and Ross and Dunn, in press.)

FAMILY THERAPY AND PSYCHOANALYTIC THEORY

The previous part of the chapter reviewed the observations about marriage and the family made by psychoanalysts whose primary professional commitment is to classical psychoanalysis. We will now deal with those clinicians who began doing family therapy with a psychoanalytic orientation. As mentioned earlier this division is somewhat arbitrary but does reflect the political reality involving these manifestly disparate modalities. Most clinicians by virtue of training and temperament, as well as their organizational loyalties, favor either one modality or the other, thereby sustaining and contributing to an unfortunate polarity. The unreceptivity of psychoanalysis and, for quite some time, of general psychiatry, to the innovation of family therapy has contributed to this polarization as it led a number of family therapists (Bowen, Minuchin, Jackson, Watzlawick, Haley, Whitaker) to develop approaches that were antithetical to the psychoanalytic point of view as well as being critical of the medical model generally. Their work is taken up in chapter eight. Their approaches have also been included in the course described in the next chapter. The reader interested in the family systems/psychoanalysis controversy and in comparing these different approaches will find the reviews of Beels and Ferber (1969) and First (1975) of interest.

There are noteworthy exceptions to this tendency toward polarization. Spiegel's writings (1971), for example, reflect an eclecticism that combines his psychoanalytic training with his years of research and teaching in Harvard's Department of Social Relations. He can be so intellectually evenhanded, in part, because he presently practices neither psychoanalysis nor family therapy, but has come to be more interested in the role of wider social and cultural forces in human behavior.

Martin's *A Marital Therapy Manual* (1976) also reflects an amalgamation of family therapy principles and psychoanalysis. He is a clinician with whom I share a conviction that individual therapy and family therapy are modalities that are applicable to different clinical situations and thus are not incompatible.

Nathan Ackerman is most often credited with having originated the field of family therapy. His early papers on families and family diagnosis appeared about the same time as T.S. Eliot anticipated family therapy in *The Cocktail Party* (see chapter 2).

His verbatim case reports (1967) together with films of his work demonstrate his uncanny intuition into family dynamics. His appreciation of the role of oedipal and preoedipal forces indicate his debt to psychoanalysis, though his interviewing style was anything but analytic. He was especially gifted at noting the significant nonverbal behavior in a family, thus gaining faster access to a family's core relationship disturbances. The warmth he conveyed to the family served as a kind of anesthesia for the rapid, almost surgical uncovering of painful family conflicts. His aggressive and charismatic personality, so often seen in pioneers, offended many of his colleagues while endearing him to his followers. However one views his therapeutic style there is no denying that more than anyone he helped turn the attention of the mental health professions to the family unit. His writings, unfortunately, did not advance our theoretical understanding.

In the mid-1950s V. Eisenstein edited a somewhat uneven yet fascinating collection of essays under the title *Neurotic Interaction in Marriage* (1956), containing contributions by both psychoanalysts and family therapists. Many of the germinal ideas expressed in these pages were rarely followed up. There is for instance an article with speculations by V. Rosen on the possible impact on a family of the psychoanalysis of one of its members. Family systems therapists have subsequently emphasized the impact upon the equilibrium of a family of any effective psychotherapeutic intervention. This has still not been systematically studied. When a young adult patient of mine in psychoanalytic treatment began making significant changes in his life situation, his father reported a dream to him in which my patient came into the marital bed and displaced his father. Needless to say the patient's working through of his oedipal conflict in his analysis stirred the residual corresponding conflict in his father.

The Eisenstein volume, together with the results of the scientific meeting of the Academy of Psychoanalysis in 1958, published in Volume II of the *Science and Psychoanalysis* annual (edited by Masserman 1959), reflects the early restless experiments with altering the classical method to handle those cases that were doing poorly primarily because of the interferences of family pathology. Articles included in this volume are by Grotjahn, Ackerman, Jackson, Lidz, and Spiegel. There is an awareness of family homeostatic resistances to change in any of its members. So, as mentioned earlier, some analysts tried to analyze both marital partners (Oberndorf 1938, Mittelman 1948, and Thomas 1956). Martin and Bird (1953) developed a "stereoscopic" technique in which separate therapists treating family members would consult with one another periodically. Grotjahn reviewed these developments and described his own efforts to overcome insurmountable resistances by bringing spouses for consultations in a group therapy setting. He was thereby attempting to interrupt what he called the marriage neuroses to make the identified partner more amenable to traditional treatment. These clinicians noted the tendency of so many of these patients (who today would probably be diagnosed as borderline or narcissistic) to use the defenses of projection and acting out. It is to the credit of these clinicians that they recognized the need to alter their treatment method when their treatments failed to effect meaningful change. In reading these volumes, one senses the strain that such modifications created in these clinicians' professional lives as they struggled with what they viewed as the orthodoxy of classical psychoanalysis.

We noted in chapter 5 that Freud was also quite aware of the surrounding family pathology of so many patients. He did have the opportunity, however, of treating patients on the healthier end of the spectrum who were more differentiated from their families. It has been my experience that where acting out, projection, externalizaton, and poor self-object differentiation exists, conjoint family therapy is often the logical place to begin. If this is successful, patients can then, when indicated and where there is sufficient motivation, be referred for further individual therapy (See chapter 9). One senses in reading these early papers of the 1950s that the practitioners were encountering new data but were not sure how to conceptualize their findings. Largely they defined themselves in contrast to the prevailing individual approaches, especially the psychoanalytic approach.

Ehrenwald (1963) wrote in the same vein as Grotjahn (1960),

referring repeatedly to family neuroses. These clinicians could not easily apply the standard concepts of psychoanalytic theory to the observations they were making. Ehrenwald introduced the concept of psychosocial defense to complement the standard psychoanalytic defenses. It was an awkward and somewhat clumsy attempt to develop new concepts. With an interest in epidemiology Ehrenwald would use a word such as *contagion* as an organizing concept to explain the clustering of certain types of pathology in families. His book, in fact, includes his extensive contacts over many years with four generations of the same family.

In 1965 Boszormenyi-Nagy and Framo edited their now classic *Intensive Family Therapy,* which pulled together the work of the most substantial contributors to this new field. As stated in their preface, the volume "represented nearly every major family worker who operates in a psychoanalytically-oriented manner based on psychodynamic principles with the goal of deep reconstructive change both in the family group and its individual members."

In particular, Nagy attempted the most ambitious integration of ego psychology, object relations theory and family therapy that was attempted up to that time and for that matter to the present. I shall quote here but one paragraph from his chapter, titled "A Theory of Relationships: Experience and Transaction," that illustrates his way of seeing the complex interaction of intra-psychic and transactional forces:

> The family therapist will tend to be equally interested in the relational or transactional aspects of any impulse discharge and in its possible intrapsychic ramifications. A daughter's vicarious acting out of her mother's repressed impulses is a good example here. Viewed in isolation, the prudish mother could be regarded as a person using the "intrapsychic" defense of "reactive character formation" against her overtly unacceptable impulses, and the overt transactional system of acting out seems to consist in this instance of the acting-out daughter and a man. Yet,

identification between mother and daughter may make them joint subjects of an impulse, which is transacted toward the man as its object. Self-Other delineation takes on an implicitly plural Self character here, based on the covert motivational fusion of mother and daughter. A dialectical or transactional orientation to psychopathology would tend to focus on the dynamic factors that prevented a Self-Other distinction between this mother and daughter, rather than on the intrapsychic motivational roots of the particular impulse responsible for the daughter's acting out. [p. 40]

Since the publication of this book there have been negligible advances toward a psychoanalytically oriented family therapy. One notable exception is H.V. Dicks, one of those practitioners who is also less easily classified in the present dichotimous way. He is therefore also mentioned earlier in the discussion of the marriage relationship. His attempt to integrate the object relations school of Fairbairn and Guntrip with conjoint family therapy (1967) was a significant advance. Sager (1976) and Skynner (1976) have each recently written books on marital and family therapy that retain an appreciation of the role unconscious and intrapsychic forces play in family disturbances. But there have been no studies comparable to Mahler's work on the mother-infant relationship, R. Shapiro's and his group's on the family of the adolescent, or Benedek's writings on parenthood. In-depth psychoanalytic studies of the marital relationship are virtually nonexistent. At a time when the divorce rate is approaching 40-50 percent, such a study has as important a place as the study of hysteria seventy-five years ago.

In this and the previous chapter the contributions by psychoanalysts and analytically oriented family therapists to an understanding of marriage and the family were noted. The contributions of the systems-oriented practitioners represent a larger segment of the family therapy literature. The next chapter describes a didactic and eclectic course, designed by C.C. Beels and myself, that introduces the family therapy trainee to the vast and often confusing general literature of this burgeoning field.

REFERENCES

Abelin, E.L. (1971). The role of the father in the separation-individuation process. In *Separation-Individuation: Essays in Honor of Margaret S. Mahler*, ed. J.B. McDevitt and C.F. Settlage. New York: International Universities Press.

———(1975). Some further observations and comments on the earliest role of the father. *International Journal of Psycho-Analysis* 56:293-302.

Abraham, H., and Freud, E., eds. (1965). *A Psychoanalytic Dialogue: The Letters of Sigmund Freud and Karl Abraham, 1907-1926.* New York: Basic Books.

Abraham, K. (1919). The applicability of psychoanalytic treatment to patients at an advanced age. In *Selected Papers*. London: Hogarth, 1950.

Abstracts and Index to The Psychoanalytic Study of the Child (1975). New Haven: Yale University Press.

Ackerman, N. (1967). *Treating the Troubled Family*. New York: Basic Books.

Altman, L. (1957). On the oral nature of acting out. *Journal of the American Psychoanalytic Association* 5:648-662.

Anthony, E.J., and Benedek, T., eds. (1970). *Parenthood: Its Psychology and Psychopathology*. Boston: Little Brown.

Barnett, J. (1971). Narcissism and dependency in the obsessional-hysteric marriage. *Family Process* 10:750-783.

Beels, C.C., and Ferber, A. (1969). Family therapy: a view. *Family Process* 8:280-318.

Benedek, T. (1959). Parenthood as a development phase. *Journal of the American Psychoanalytic Association* 7:389-417.

———(1970). The family as a psychologic field. In *Parenthood: Its Psychology and Psychopathology*, ed. E.J. Anthony and T. Benedek. Boston: Little, Brown.

Berezin, M., and Catherine, S., eds. (1965). *Geriatric Psychiatry*. New York: International Universities Press.

Berkowitz, D.A., Shapiro, R.L., Zinner, J., and Shapiro, E.R. (1947). Family Contributions to Narcissistic Disturbances in Adolescents. *International Review of Psycho-Analysis* 1:353-362.

Bibring, A.L., Dwyer, Thomas F., Huntington, Dorothy S., and Valenstein, Arthur, F. (1961). A study of the psychological processes in pregnancy and of the earliest mother-child relationship. *Psychoanalytic Study of the Child* 16:9-72.

Bibring, G. (1966). Old age: its liabilities and its assets. In *Psychoanalysis: A General Psychology*, ed. R. Loewenstein et al. New York: International Universities Press.

Bird, B. (1957). A specific peculiarity of acting out. *Journal of the American Psychoanalytic Association* 5:630-647.

Bird, H.W., and Martin, P.A. (1956). Countertransference in the psychotherapy of marriage partners. *Psychiatry* 19:353-360.

Blos, P. (1967). The second individuation process of adolescence. *Psychoanalytic Study of the Child* 22:162-186.

Bonnard, A. (1950). The mother as therapist in a case of obsessional neurosis. *Psychoanalytic Study of the Child* 5:391-405.

Boszormenyi-Nagy, I., and Framo, J. (1965). *Intensive Family Therapy*. New York: Hoeber.

Boszormenyi-Nagy, I., and Spark, G.M. (1973). *Invisible Loyalties*. Hagerstown, Maryland: Harper and Row.

Bowen, M. (1966). The use of family theory in clinical practice. *Comprehensive Psychiatry* 7:345-374. Reprinted in M. Bowen, *Family Therapy in Clinical Practice*. New York: Jason Aronson, 1978.

Boyer, L. B. (1956). On maternal overstimulation and ego defects. *Psychoanalytic Study of the Child* 11: 236-256.

Brodey, W. M. (1965). On the dynamics of narcissism: I. externalization and early ego development. *Psychoanalytic Study of the Child* 20:165-193.

Bruch, H. (1970). Instinct and interpersonal experience. *Comprehensive Psychiatry* 11:495-506.

Burlingham, D. (1951). Present trends in handling the mother-child relationship during the therapeutic process. *Psychoanalytic Study of the Child* 6:31-37.

———(1973). The pre-oedipal infant-father relationship. *Psychoanalytic Study of the Child* 28:33-47

Butler, R., and Lewis, M. (1973). *Aging and Mental Health*. St. Louis: C.V. Mosby.

Buxbaum, E. (1964). The parents' role in the etiology of learning disabilities. *Psychoanalytic Study of the Child* 19:421-447.

Cavenar, J.O., and Buits, N. (1978). Unconscious communication between father and son. *American Journal of Psychiatry* 136:344-345.

Chicago Psychoanalytic Literature Index: 1920-1970 (1971). Chicago: Chicago Processing Laboratories.

Coleman, R. W., Kris, E., and Provence, S. (1953). The study of variations of early parental attitudes: a preliminary report. *Psychoanalytic Study of the Child* 8:20-47.

Dicks, H.V. (1953). Clinical studies in marriage and the family. *British Journal of Medical Psychology* 26:181-196.

———(1963). Object relations theory and marital studies. *British Journal of Medical Psychology* 36:125-129.

———(1967). *Marital Tensions*. New York: Basic Books.

Ehrenwald, J. (1963). *Neurosis in the Family and Patterns of Psychosocial Defense*. New York: Hoeber.

Eisenstein, V., ed. (1956). *Neurotic Interaction in Marriage*. New York: Basic Books.

Eissler, K.R. (1971). *Discourse on Hamlet and* Hamlet. New York: International Universities Press.

Elles, G. (1962). The mute sad-eyed child: collateral analysis in a disturbed family. *International Journal of Psycho-Analysis* 43:40-49.

Erikson, E. (1950). *Childhood and Society*. New York: Norton.

First, E. (1957). Family therapy. *New York Review of Books* Vol. 22, February 20, 1975.

Flugel. J.C. (1920). On the character and married life of Henry VIII. *International Journal of Psycho-Analysis* 1:24-55.

———(1921). *The Psychoanalytic Study of the Family*. London: Hogarth Press.

Fraiberg, S. (1977). *Every Child's Birthright*. New York: Basic Books.

Freud, A. (1936). *The Ego and the Mechanisms of Defense*. New York: International Universities Press.

———(1968). Indications and contraindications for child analysis. *Psychoanalytic Study of the Child* 23:37-46.

Freud, A., and Burlingham, D. (1944). *Infants Without Families*.

Reprinted in *The Writings of Anna Freud,* Vol. III. New York: International Universities Press, 1973.

Freud, S. (1905). Fragment of an analysis of a case of hysteria. *Standard Edition* 7:7-124.

———(1909). Analysis of a phobia in a five-year-old boy. *Standard Edition* 10:3-152.

———(1911). Psychoanalytic notes on an autobiographical account of a case of paranoia. *Standard Edition* 12:9-82.

———(1921). Group psychology and the analysis of the ego. *Standard Edition* 18:69-143.

———(1923). The ego and the id. *Standard Edition* 19:12-66.

Friedlander, K. (1949). Neurosis and home background: a preliminary report. *Psychoanalytic Study of the Child* 3/4:423-438.

Friedman, L. (1975). Current psychoanalytic object relations theory and its clinical implications. *International Journal of Psycho-Analysis* 56:137-146.

Friend, M. (1976). The role of family life in child development. *International Journal of Psycho-Analysis* 57:373-383.

Fries, M. (1946). The child's ego development and the training of adults in his environment. *Psychoanalytic Study of the Child* 2:85-112.

Fromm-Reichmann, F. (1948). Notes on the development of treatment of schizophrenics by psychoanalytic psychotherapy. *Psychiatry* 11:263-273.

Furman, E. (1957). Treatment of under fives by way of their parents. *Psychoanalytic Study of the Child* 12:250-262.

Galenson, E., and Roiphe, H. (1971). The impact of early sexual discovery on mood, defensive organization and symbolization. *Psychoanalytic Study of the Child* 26:195-216.

———(1976). Some suggested revisions concerning early female development. *Journal of the American Psychoanalytic Association* 24:29-57.

Giovacchini, P. (1958). Mutual adaption in various object relations. *International Journal of Psycho-Analysis* 39:547-554.

———(1961). Resistance and external object relations. *Inter-*

national *Journal of Psycho-Analysis* 42:246-254.

Goldstein, J., Freud, A., and Solnit, A. (1973). *Beyond the Best Interests of the Child.* New York: Free Press.

Greenacre, P. (1960). Considerations regarding the parent-infant relationship. *International Journal of Psycho-Analysis* 41:575-584.

Grotjahn, M. (1960). *Psychoanalysis and the Family Neurosis.* New York: Norton.

Haley, J., and Glick, I. (1971). *Family Therapy and Research.* New York: Grune and Stratton.

Hartmann, H. (1958). *Ego Psychology and the Problem of Adaption.* New York: International Universities Press.

Hellman, I., Friedman, O., and Shepheard E. (1960). Simultaneous analysis of mother and child. *Psychoanalytic Study of the Child* 15:358-377.

Horney, K. (1928). The problem of the monogamous ideal. *International Journal of Psychoanalysis* 9:318-331.

Jackson, E. B., and Klatskin, E.H. (1950). Rooming-in research project: development of methodology of parent-child relationship study in a clinical setting. *Psychoanalytic Study of the Child* 5:236-274.

Jackson, E.B., Klatskin, E.H., and Wilkin, L.C. (1952). Early child development in relation to degree of flexibility of maternal attitude. *Psychoanalytic Study of the Child* 7:393-428.

Jacobs, L. (1949). Methods used in the education of mothers. *Psychoanalytic Study of the Child* 3/4:409-422.

Jacobson, E. (1964). *The Self and the Object World.* New York: International Universities Press.

Jaffe D.S. (1968). The mechanism of projection: its dual role in object relations. *International Journal of Psycho-Analysis* 49:662-677.

Jessner, L., Lamont, J., Lang, R., Rollins, N., Whipple, B., and Prentice, N. (1955). Emotional impact of nearness and separation for the asthmatic child and his mother. *Psychoanalytic Study of the Child* 10:353-375.

Johnson, A., and Szurek, S.A. (1952). The genesis of antisocial acting out in children and adults. *Psychoanalytic Quarterly* 21.

Johnson, A., Szurek, S.A., and Falstein, E. (1942). Collaborative psychiatric therapy of parent-child problems, *American Journal Orthopsychiatry* 12:511-517.

Katz, J. (1963). On primary and secondary gain. *Psychoanalytic Study of the Child* 18:9-50.

Kaufman, M.R. (1940). The psychoanalytic point of view: old age and aging. *American Journal of Orthopsyciatry* 10:73-79.

Kernberg, O. (1975). *Borderline Conditions and Pathological Narcissism*. New York: Jason Aronson.

Keyserling, H., ed. (1926). *The Book of Marriage*. New York: Harcourt Brace.

Klein, M. (1946). Notes on some schizoid mechanisms. *International Journal of Psycho-Analysis* 27:99-110.

Kluckohn, F. (1953). Dominant and variant value orientations. In *Personality in Nature, Society and Culture*, ed. C. Kluckohn and H.A. Murray. New York: Knopf.

Kohut, H. (1971). *The Analysis of the Self*, New York: International Universities Press.

Kolansky, H., and Moore, W.T. (1966). Some comments on the simultaneous analysis of a father and his adolescent son. *Psychoanalytic Study of the Child* 21:237-268.

Kovel, J. (1970). *White Racism*. New York: Pantheon.

Kramer, C. (1968). The relationship between child and family psychopathology: a suggested extension of psychoanalytic theory and technique. Family Institute of Chicago.

Kris, E. (1962). Decline and recovery in the life of a three year old; or: data in psychoanalytic perspective on the mother-child relationship. *Psychoanalytic Study of the Child* 17:175-215.

Kuhn, T.S. (1962). *The Structure of Scientific Revolutions*, Chicago: University of Chicago Press.

Levy, K. (1960). Simultaneous analysis of a mother and her adolescent daughter: the mother's contribution to the loosening of the infantile object tie. *Psychoanalytic Study of the Child* 15:378-391.

Lidz, T. (1963). *The Family and Human Adaptation*. New York: International Universities Press.

———(1975). *Hamlet's Enemy*. New York: Basic Books.

Lidz, T., Cornelison, A., et al. (1957). The intrafamilial environment of schizophrenic patients: III. marital schism and marital skew. *American Journal of Psychiatry* 114:241-248.

Loewald, H.W. (1951). Ego and reality. *International Journal of Psycho-Analysis* 32:10-18.

Lomas, P. (1961). Family role and identity formation. *International Journal of Psycho-Analysis* 42:371-380.

Mahler, M.S. (1963). Thoughts about development and individuation. *Psychoanalytic Study of the Child* 18:307-324.

Mahler, M.S., and Gosliner, B.J. (1955). On symbiotic child psychosis: genetic, dynamic, and restitutive aspects. *Psychoanalytic Study of the Child* 10:195-214.

Mahler, M., Pine, F., and Bergman, A., (1975). *The Psychological Birth of the Human Infant.* New York: Basic Books.

Martin, P. (1976). *A Marital Therapy Manual.* New York: Brunner-Mazel.

Martin, P., and Bird, H. (1953). An approach to the psychotherapy of marriage partners: the stereoscopic technique. *Psychiatry* 16:123-127.

Masserman, J., ed. (1959). *Science and Psychoanalysis: Vol. II. Individual and Family Dynamics.* New York: Grune and Stratton.

Mead, M. (1957). Changing patterns of parent-child relations in an urban culture. *International Journal of Psycho-Analysis* 38:369-378.

Meerloo, J. (1955). Transference and resistance in geriatric psychotherapy. *Psychoanalytic Review* 42:72-82.

Meissner, W.W. (1978). Conceptualization of marriage and family dynamics from a psychoanalytic perspective. In *Marriage and the Treatment of Marital Disorders: Psychoanalytic, Behavioral and Systems Theory Perspectives,* ed. J. Paulino and B. McCrady. New York: Brunner-Mazel.

Miller, I. reporter (1975). A critical assessment of the future of psychoanalysis. *Journal of American Psychoanalytic Association* 23:139-153.

Minuchin, S. (1974). *Families and Family Therapy* Cambridge: Harvard University Press.

Mitscherlich, A. (1970). *Society Without the Father*. New York: Schocken.

Mittelmann, B. (1944). Complimentary neurotic reactions in intimate relationships. *Psychoanalytic Quarterly* 13:479-491.

———(1948). The concurrent analysis of married couples. *Psychoanalytic Quarterly* 17:182-197.

Mosse, E.D. (1954). The handling of relatives in the psychoanalytic situation. *Psychoanalytic Review* 41:258-262.

Muir, R. (1975). The family and the problem of internalization. *British Journal of Medical Psychology* 48:267-272.

Neubauer, P.B. (1960). The one-parent child and his oedipal development. *Psychoanalytic Study of the Child* 15:286-309.

Niederland, W.G. (1959). The "miracled-up" world of schreber's childhood. *Psychoanalytic Study of the Child* 14:383-413.

Novick, J. and Kelly (Novick), K. (1970). Projection and externalization. *Psychoanalytic Study of the Child* 25:69-95.

Oberndorf, C. (1938). Psychoanalysis of married couples. *Psychoanalytic Review* 25:453-475.

Olden C. (1953). On adult empathy with children. *Psychoanalytic Study of the Child* 8:111-126.

Ornstein, A. (1976). Making contact with the inner world of the child: toward a theory of psychoanalytic psychotherapy with children. *Comprehensive Psychiatry* 17:3-36.

Parens, H., reporter (1975). Parenthood as a developmental phase. *Journal of the American Psychoanalytic Association* 23:154-165.

Pine, F. (1976). On the therapeutic change: a parent-child model. In *Psychoanalysis and Contemporary Science*, Vol. 5. New York: International Universities Press.

———(1979). On the pathology of the separation-individuation process as manifested in later clinical work: an attempt at delineation. *International Journal of Psychoanalysis* 60:225-242.

Pine, F., and Furer, M. (1963). Studies of the separation-individuation phase: a methodological overview. *Psychoanalytic Study of the Child* 18:325-342.

Pollock, G.H. (1964). On symbiosis and symbiotic neurosis. *Inter-*

national *Journal of Psycho-Analysis* 45:1-30.

Rangell, L. (1955). The return of the repressed "Oedipus." *Bulletin of the Menninger Clinic* 19:9-15.

Ritvo, S., and Solnit, A.J. (1958). Influences of early mother-child interaction on identification processes. *Psychoanalytic Study of the Child* 13:64-185.

Robbins, M. (1976). Borderline personality organization: the need for a new theory. *Journal of the American Psychoanalytic Association* 24:381.

Robertson, J. (1962). Mothering as an influence on early development: study of well-baby records. *Psychoanalytic Study of the Child* 17:245-264.

Rogers, T. (1965). A specific parameter: concurrent psychotherapy of the spouse of an analysand by the same analyst. *International Journal of Psycho-Analysis* 46:237-243.

Roiphe, H., and Galenson, E. (1972). Early genital activity and the castration complex. *Psychoanalytic Quarterly* 41:334-347.

Roman, M., and Haddad, W. (1978). *The Disposable Parent*. New York: Holt, Rhinehart and Winston.

Rosen, V. (1956). Changes in family equilibrium through psychoanalytic treatment. In *Neurotic Interaction in Marriage*, ed. V. Eisenstein. New York: Basic Books.

Rosenbaum, S., and Alger, I., eds. (1967). *The Marriage Relationship: Psychoanalytic Perspectives*. New York: Basic Books.

Ross, J.M., and Dunn, P.B. (in press). Notes on the genesis of pathological splitting. Accepted to appear in either the *International Journal of Psycho-Analysis* or the *International Review of Psycho-Analysis*.

Ruben, M. (1946). A contribution to the education of the parent. *Psychoanalytic Study of the Child* 1:247-261.

Rubinfine, D.L. (1962). Maternal stimulation, psychic structure, and early object relations with special reference to aggression and denial. *Psychoanalytic Study of the Child* 17:265-282.

Sager, C.J. (1966). The development of marriage therapy: an historical review. *American Journal of Orthopsychiatry* 36:458-466.

————(1967). Transference in conjoint treatment of married

couples. *Archives of General Psychiatry* 16:185-194.

———(1976). *Marriage Contracts and Couple Therapy.* New York: Brunner-Mazel.

Sandler, A.M., Daunton, E., and Schnurmann, A. (1957). Inconsistency in the mother as a factor in character development: a comparative study of three cases. *Psychoanalytic Study of the Child* 12:209-225.

Schatzman, M. (1973). *Soul Murder.* New York: Random House.

Schwarz, H. (1950). The mother in the consulting room: notes on the psychoanalytic treatment of two young children. *Psychoanalytic Study of the Child* 5:343-357.

Shapiro, E.R., Zinner, J., Shapiro, R.L., and Berkowitz, D.A. (1975). The influence of family experience on borderline personality development. *International Review of Psycho-Analysis* 2:399-411.

Skynner, A.C.R. (1976). *Systems of Family and Marital Psychotherapy.* New York: Brunner-Mazel.

Sperling, M. (1949). The role of the mother in psychosomatic disorders in children. *Psychosomatic Medicine* 11:377-385. Reprinted in M. Sperling, *Psychosomatic Disorders in Childhood.* New York: Jason Aronson, 1978.

———(1950). Children's interpretation and reaction to the unconscious of their mothers. *International Journal of Psycho-Analysis* 31:46-51. Reprinted in M. Sperling, *The Major Neuroses and Behavior Disorders in Children.* New York: Jason Aronson, 1974.

Spiegel, J., and Papajohn, J. (1971). *Transactions.* New York: Jason Aronson.

Spitz, R. (1945). Hospitalism: an inquiry into the genesis of psychiatric conditions in early childhood. *Psychoanalytic Study of the Child* 1:53-74.

———(1946). Hospitalism: a follow-up report. *Psychoanalytic Study of the Child* 2:113-117.

———(1950). Relevancy of direct infant observation. *Psychoanalytic Study of the Child* 5:66-73.

Stein, M. (1956). The marriage bond. *Psychoanalytic Quarterly* 25:238-259.

Stierlin, H. (1973). Interpersonal aspects of internalizations. *International Journal of Psychiatry* 54:203-213.

———(1974). *Separating Parents and Adolescents.* New York: Quadrangle.

———(1976). The dynamics of owning and disowning: psychoanalytic and family perspectives. *Family Process* 15:277-

———(1977). *Psychoanalysis and Family Therapy.* New York: Jason Aronson.

Thomas, A. (1956). Simultaneous psychotherapy with marital partners. *American Journal of Psychotherapy* 10:716-727.

Titchener, J.P. (1966). The problem of interpretation in marital therapy. *Comprehensive Psychiatry* 7:5 321-337.

Waelder, R. (1930). The principle of multiple function. *Psychoanalytic Quarterly* 5:45-62.

Wangh, M. (1962). The evocation of a proxy: a psychological maneuver, its use as a defense, its purposes and genesis. *Psychoanalytic Study of the Child* 17:451-469.

Weissman, P. (1963). The effects of the pre-oedipal paternal attitudes on development and character *International Journal of Psycho-Analysis* 44:121-131.

Willi, J. (1976). The hysterical marriage. In *Contemporary Marriage: Structure and Theory,* ed. H. Grunebaum and J. Christ. Boston: Little, Brown.

Winnicott, D.W. (1960). The theory of the parent-infant relationship *International Journal of Psycho-Analysis* 41:585-594.

Zinberg, N., and Kaufman, I., eds. (1963). *Normal Psychology of the Aging Process.* New York: International Universities Press.

Zinner, J. (1974). The implications of projective identification for marital interaction. In *Contemporary Marriage,* ed. H. Grunebaum and J. Christ. Boston: Little, Brown.

Zinner, J., and Shapiro, R.L. (1972). Projective identification as a mode of perception and behavior in families of adolescents. *International Journal of Psycho-Analysis* 53:523-529.

Zinner, J., and Shapiro, R.L. (1974). The family group as a single psychic entity: implications for acting out in adolescence. *International Review of Psycho-Analysis* Vol. 1:179-186.

Chapter Seven

THE FAMILY THERAPY
LITERATURE

The teaching of family therapy in most training programs is most often, and appropriately so, by the direct observation and live supervision of actual clinical interviews. The field is still so young that the systematic reading of relevant literature is usually not done. Further, since most training programs teach a particular school of family therapy, trainees will most probably be especially familiar, with the Bowen theory, Minuchin's structural theory, the communications approach, *or* the more psychoanalytically oriented point of view. To encourage the reading of the literature of family therapy and to counter the parochial tendencies of many training programs, my colleague C.C. Beels and I designed a course, originally taught at the Albert Einstein College of Medicine, that is described in the present chapter.

The course description was first published in *Family Process,* in 1970, and revised by me for *The Primer of Family Therapy* (Block 1973). To date, it is still the only published description of an eclectic course in family therapy, and it is reprinted here with minor changes. Since its publication, innumerable new books on family therapy have appeared. I shall mention a few of them here to bring the course syllabus more up to date. In 1974, Glick and Kessler published their textbook on marital and family therapy, which, at this time, is the only satisfactory overview of the field. Bowen's writings have, after many years, been brought together in one volume (1978) and Minuchin's recent book *Families and Family Therapy* (1974) represents the latest version of his structural theory. A most interesting and unique introduction to family therapy that is also an excellent teaching vehicle is Napier's and Whitaker's *The Family Crucible* (1978). Written in the form of a novel, it portrays the treatment of one family in such vivid detail that the somewhat controversial therapeutic interventions lend themselves to lively discussions of the varying family therapy theories and techniques. How these family therapy pioneers, as well as the "communications school" (Watzlawick et al. 1967, Haley 1973), conceptualize the individual within a family systems framework shall be taken up in Chapter 8.

CONTEXT OF FAMILY THERAPY

Where family and nation once stood, or Church and
Party, there will be hospital and theatre too.
— Philip Rieff

At historical moments of cultural change such as ours, it is with considerable anxiety that we witness our most stable institutions and deeply held convictions being called into question. Our parents are increasingly unable to transmit their culturally acquired wisdom to us; we as parents, in turn, sense our emerging obsolescence to our children. These doubts reflect more than the ubiquitous and perennial waves of generational conflict. There is, rather, a tide of cultural upheaval that defies our control and full understanding. We are too profoundly enmeshed in the swirl of events to view them clearly or dispassionately, and yet certain trends are becoming evident.

As Weston LaBarre (1970) has so convincingly documented in *The Ghost Dance*, it is at times of cultural crises that charismatic cult leaders emerge, satisfying regressive needs, and that pseudo-religious movements begin. Henry Ellenberger (1970) has shown how this pehonomenon is also true of the emergence of schools of pscyhotherapy, beginning, for example, with Mesmer in pre-revolutionary France. Where traditional religions have lost their sense of legitimacy, therapeutic institutions and varied "healers" have assumed a larger role in integrating man in his social order. Philip Rieff (1966) has called our age, and aptly has titled his recent book, *The Triumph of the Therapeutic.* As another "professional mourner at the wake of Christian culture," Rieff views with some apprehension the emergence of psychologic man, who has gained a "self" while lacking some compelling self-integrating communal purpose. He expects that "modern society will mount psychodramas far more frequently than its ancestors mounted miracle plays, with the patient-analysts acting out their inner lives" (p. 26).

No institution has been more altered by the rapidity of social change than that transmitter of culture and that crucible of personality formation, the family. This was discussed in chapter 2 as a primary factor in the emergence of the family therapy movement. This movement has both the characteristics of a revivalistic "Ghost Dance" and those of a new paradigm within the behavioral sciences. As the lens of the psychotherapeutic looking glass is changed, new structures are being seen and described. As mental illnesses are viewed increasingly as symptoms of family dysfuncton, new patterns of family interaction are being described. It is in this sense that Szasz's *The Myth of Mental Illness* (1961) can be seen better in historical perspective. He was one of the first to recognize the need for a paradigmatic change in the medical model of mental illness. By insisting that mental illnesses were more correctly viewed as "problems in living," he highlighted the limitations of that model. Inasmuch as these "problems in living" are partly interactional difficulties, the family and other immediate reference groups of an "identified patient" come into focus. By insisting, however, on the absolute separation of brain disease from "problems in living," Szasz's writings have, among other things, further polarized the nature-nurture controversy in psychology (Sander 1969).

This new attention to interpersonal patterns in natural groups is producing a vastly expanding literature. In this literature are reflected the multiple and varied approaches, philosophies, prejudices, and orientations of the many disciplines that have turned to the family as the unit of study. In 1971 Glick and Haley published a bibliography of writings in the field. Since the original publication of the didactic course described in this chapter, several anthologies related to family therapy have been published (Ackerman 1970, Erickson, G. and Hogan, T. 1976, Ferber et al. 1972, Guerin 1976, Haley 1971, Howells 1971, Paolino, T. Jr. and McGrady, B. 1978, Sager 1972, Skolnick and Skolnick 1972).

I shall outline the overview of our literature course for family therapy trainees, rather than attempt the presently impossible task of a comprehensive review of the literature. The last three sections of this chapter are drawn from the earlier description of our course.

The goals that we attempted to achieve with this course were: (1) some historical perspective on the family as an institution; (2) awareness of the multiple theoretical approaches to the understanding of family process; (3) an appreciation of the difficulties in the scientific study of family forces in the complex etiology of psychopathology; and (4) a comparison of writings of various family therapists with videotapes or films of their work.

HISTORICAL PERSPECTIVE AS SEEN IN FICTION

During the course of a yearlong, weekly, ninety-minute seminar, we spent three to four sessions on works of fiction that reflected changes in the structure and function of the family and its sociocultural contexts from biblical times to the present. The following capsule analyses illustrate our approach to the use of such materials. It was the use of such fictional material that were the seeds of this book.

The Book of Genesis (Abraham and Sarah)

> Be fruitful and multiply and replenish the earth, and subdue it. [Genesis 1:28]

To survive in the desert, nomads required a cohesive and authoritarian family. The survival of the family clan of 50-200 tent-dwelling shepherds demanded obedience to the father. Individual survival was linked directly to immediate and proximate membership in the family. To be out of this family group was tantamount to death. The constant dangers of hostile tribes, animals and disease made regular claims on their numbers and gave birth to a moral demand system whose first commandment was to be "fruitful and multiply."

This cultural demand-system led barren Sarah to entrust Hagar, her handmaiden, to Abraham for the purpose of bearing his child. The inevitable jealousies between Hagar and Sarah after the birth of Ishmael were followed by the arbitrary banishment of Hagar and Ishmael. This banishment and the later test of Abraham's faith in the sacrificing of Isaac illustrate the unquestioned acceptance of the requirements of obedience to the father (and God the Father) in this evolving patriarchal culture.

The role of arranged marriages is illustrated in the marriage of cousins Isaac and Rebecca. The incest taboo, endogamy requirements, and reduction of intertribal hostilities all were served by such arrangements.

Isaac, the younger of Abraham's sons, inherited the family line following the exile of Ishmael. This began a pattern, repeated in subsequent generations, of the preference of the younger son over the older. In reviewing this literature, our seminar speculated about the possible mechanisms for the generational transmission of such family patterns, while noting also how this theme of the "chosen son" resonated with the Jews' cultural self-representation as the "chosen people." Psychology, sociology, and culture were seen here as interwoven threads in the tapestry of Jewish history.

Jane Austen's *Pride and Prejudice* **(Elizabeth and Darcy)**

> It is a truth universally acknowledged, that a single man in possession of a good fortune must be in want of a wife. [*Pride and Prejudice*]

Marital arrangements among the eighteenth-century English aristocracy served to sustain and support a complex structure of property in the form of entitlements. The prophetic opening sentence above of Austen's novel reflects the demand system of that particular culture in the same sense that "to be fruitful and multiply" was part of the cultural demand system of the ancient Hebrews.

From the beginning Elizabeth and Darcy capture our interest because they represent some transcendence over the rigidified and mannered demands of their culture. The commands of the covenant in the Old Testament are replaced here by the pressures of social forms, but there is some room for autonomy. Jane Austen weaves their strivings for greater independence of their backgrounds with their ultimate reconciliation with it. Their marriage, based on love rather than on propertied arrangements, ultimately supports and sustains the social order at the same time that it satisfies their quest for individual autonomy. Family requirements and individual strivings here are balanced at this threshold of the industrial revolution. Elizabeth is also clearly a *forme fruste* of the "emancipated modern woman."

T.S. Eliot's *The Cocktail Party* **(Edward and Lavinia) and Edward Albee's** *Who's Afraid of Virginia Woolf?* **(George and Martha)**

Where the Old Testament's first commandment to be fruitful and multiply served to facilitate the survival of a people, we are for the first time in the history of our civilization aware that our future hinges on our ability to contradict that precept. Both of these contemporary plays are of interest in this regard because they portray childless marriages. *The Cocktail Party* dramatizes a modern couple devoid of extended kinship. Living in an urban apartment, they find that their relationship is stabilized by infidelities and ultimately by the ministrations of the first family therapist in literature. This play, written in 1949, interestingly preceded the emergence of the family therapy movement in the 1950s and illustrates the socioreligious role of the psychiatrist in secular society (see chapter 2).

In Albee's play, George and Martha battle endlessly as they desperately attempt to form a new family of friends and colleagues in a small college community. They do not sustain and support any viable culture, nor does any culture sustain and support them. They act out a "family romance" fantasy in which life is made bearable through the creation of an imaginary child (Blum 1969, also see chapter 3).

The historical perspective afforded by these readings in fiction highlights the emergence of the modern nuclear family as a unique structure, which still contains certain universal attributes dictated by the biologic trimorphism of mother, father, and developing child. These ideas can be studied further in the reading of various other disciplines in which theories regarding the institution of the family are offered.

THEORIES OF THE FAMILY

As psychiatry has little to offer in the way of a comprehensive theory of families, a brief survey of the theories and descriptions of other disciplines affords the student some beginning orientation to the family.

In our readings we considered the family as a social entity, its history and structure, rather than the individual family member, his biology and psychology. Beginning with Aries's *Centuries of Childhood* (1962) the student can view the historical development of the idea of "the family" and the rather recent appearance of such values as intimacy, privacy, and the specialness of children. One can contrast the cultural anthropology of Levi-Strauss (1956) and Margaret Mead (1950) with the primatological writings of

Jane van Lawick Goodall (1971) for two different views of the family's universality. One can then examine the extent to which some of its institutions, such as sex role differences, childbearing, and incest taboo, are biologically or socially obligatory. Readings in Parsons (1955) show how one sociologic theory attempted to integrate biology, psychoanalytic psychology, sociology, and anthropology. This ambitious and little-appreciated effort is clearly a neglected precursor of what is referred to today as general systems theory. Communication and system theorists such as Haley (1963, 1967, 1971), Jackson (1961, 1964, 1965, 1967), and Minuchin (1974) construct family theories that dispense with almost all the values, assumptions, and motivational forces the others have required. Such a quick tour of the field enables the reader to begin a second look at the theoretical assumptions on which clinical work is based. In our seminar we then reread such psychiatric theorists of family therapy as Boszormenyi-Nagy (1965), Laing (1967), and Dicks (1967) with the recognition that their task of building a bridge between the theories of individual and social function has only begun.

SCIENTIFIC BASIS

We thought we ought to ask a somewhat naive question: How much scientific evidence was there that family factors, in fact, could be viewed as etiologic agents in the production of mental illness? We chose what we felt were the better studies representing the clinical, epidemiologic, field, and laboratory approaches to this knotty problem.

One of the most interesting clinical descriptions of a family is to be found in Freud's case of Dora (1905). The correlation between family circumstances and Dora's symptoms is elegantly demonstrated. Historically the significance of this case is, of course, the discovery of the importance of infantile sexuality, the function of dreams, and intrapsychic factors in general. In fact, Freud's elucidation of Dora's complicity in the family system due to her oedipal and unconscious homosexual wishes reflects the present-day family systems view of the necessary collusion of all the members of any system to keep it going. The case lent itself beautifully to the age-old question perhaps best formulated by Shakespeare: whether it is in ourselves or in our stars that we are underlings. The relative significance of constitution, infantile experiences, and current social forces in the etiology of mental illness (hysteria in this case) were again considered.

Other psychoanalytic writers such as Main (1966) and Johnson and Szurek (1952) afforded a view of what additional theory is required by the shift to working concurrently (though not conjointly) with the relatives of the identified patient.

With the work of Thomas, Chess, and Birch (1963) we returned to the interplay, over time, of temperament and environment in a more systematic, although still primarily clinical, study. Problems of sampling, clinical biases, and interpretation of results were explored in greater detail. This book, by reemphasizing temperament, helps to shift the balance in the nature-nurture controversy away from the preponderant environmentalist bias of American culture and social science. It is a kind of scientific pacifier for a guilt-ridden parental generation tired of being blamed for all their children's ills.

We turned from these clinical impressions to read some material describing attempts at objective specification of the experience aspect of the temperament-experience interaction. We considered hard data such as family structure (Ferber et al. 1967), paternal absence (Anderson 1968), or maternal death (Barry and Lindemann 1968) and soft data such as Cheek's characterization of the mothers and fathers of schizophrenics (1964, 1965). Most of the studies could be seriously faulted for their methodology. Even the best, such as Wynne's and Singer's studies (1963, 1965) of the parental contribution to thought disorder in schizophrenia, were unsatisfying in the sense that they all seemed to represent such a small piece of the clinical picture. Wender's paper, "On Necessary and Sufficient Conditions in Psychiatric Explanation" (1967) summed up this problem quite well: The examination of single variables as partial causes of an event that occurs rarely and has many causes will yield a very low predictive grasp on the event even though it has a high level of statistical significance. Wender's own review of the genetic studies of schizophrenia, the most convincing paper we could find on the temperament aspect of the formula, suffers from the same difficulty (1969).

At this point we abandoned the medical model of first diagnosing a sick or deviant patient and then seeking the etiologic cause in his family. We assembled several papers that could be read as descriptions of the activity of the family as a disordered or malfunctioning group: Ravich (1969), Bauman and Roman (1966), and Reiss (1967). We then looked upon the Wynne and Singer, Reiss, and Cheek papers and viewed them in the same light. From this standpoint the family can be seen as setting out to accomplish a task (provided either by life or by the experimenter) and doing it well or badly. The trouble they are having with it appears to be strikingly the same in each study: They are spending time managing their relations with each other rather than thinking about the task. Once that point of view had been reached, we were ready to appreciate work such as Scheflen's on the ethology of the family as an interactive group (1968).

THERAPY

Having surveyed available theories of the family and the question of "scientific evidence," one can better read the writings of the major family therapists and compare them with films or videotapes of their work (Ackerman, Bowen, Haley, Jackson, Minuchin, Paul, Satir, Wynne, Whitaker, and Zuk).

We tried to appreciate what each of the therapists was trying to accomplish and to identify the special techniques used to get that result. In this way we concentrated on the unique characteristics of each one, their philosophy, personality, and tactics, rather than on what they all have in common. It is difficult to abstract a useful general theory or description of family therapy from the literature (see Beels and Ferber [1969], "Family Therapy: A View," for one such attempt). The most important benefit that can be gained from reading the literature of family therapy is to secure a collection of models and scenarios from which the student chooses the most appropriate for himself and the family he is treating.

CONCLUSION

This chapter describing an eclectic course on the literature of family therapy has made little mention of techniques. This is due partly to the fact that the technical aspects of all therapies tend to be less written about than more theoretical considerations. The newness of the field also contributes to this problem, but of much greater significance is the substantial increase in the role of direct observation of therapy by the use of videotape, one-way screens, films, audiotapes, and live supervision. The impact of these nonliterary methods are substantial and will in many ways guide future theoretical advances. The role, for example, of varying types of feedback in social systems and the very profound, heretofore neglected, role of nonverbal communications arc already shaping theoretic advances. These technologic advances have already played and will continue to play a role in the teaching and practice of family therapy. The hard work of sorting out the wheat from the chaff in this technologic explosion remains ahead of us.

Meanwhile, the reading of both technical and literary works remains a time-tested medium for deepening our appreciation of the complexities before us. Hopefully, as "cool media," they will restrain our overzealous attempts to change and modify human behavior before we understand more fully either ourselves or the multiple forces impinging upon us.

In the concluding part we move from the burgeoning literature to the job ahead of integrating the individual and family approaches. In chapter 8 we shall review the predominant schools of family systems therapy to see how they do or do not deal with the individual in the family system. Chapter 9 examines some of the dramas encountered in the clinician's office before turning, in the final chapter, to Oscar Wilde's *Salome.* I attempt an integration of psychoanalytic and family systems concepts in a play that brings us full circle back to chapter 1, for Salome is a princess whose family structure is strikingly similar to Hamlet's. She must cope, as Hamlet did, with the murder of a father/king by a usurping uncle who marries the mother/queen.

REFERENCES

Ackerman, N.W. (1966). *Treating the Troubled Family*, chapters containing interview transcripts. New York: Basic Books.

———, ed. (1970). *Family Process*. New York: Basic Books.

———Movie of Hillcrest family (obtainable through Psychological Cinema Register, Pennsylvania State University, University Park).

Albee, E. (1962). *Who's Afraid of Virginia Woolf?* New York: Atheneum.

Anderson, R. (1968). Where's dad? *Archives of General Psychiatry* 18:641-649.

Aries, P. (1962). *Centuries of Childhood. A Social History of Family*. New York: Vintage Books.

Austen, J. (1950). *Pride and Prejudice*. New York: Modern Library.

Barry, Jr., H. and Lindemann, E. (1968). Critical ages for maternal bereavement in psychoneurosis. *Psychosomatic Medicine* 22:166-181.

Bauman, G., and Roman, M. (1966). Interaction testing in the study of marital dominance. *Family Process* 5:230-242.

Beels, C.C., and Ferber, A. (1969). Family therapy: a view. *Family Process* 8:280-318.

Block, D., ed. (1973). *The Primer of Family Therapy*. New York: Grune and Stratton.

Blum, H. (1969). A psychoanalytic view of *Who's Afraid of Virginia Woolf? Journal of the American Psychoanalytic Association* 17:888-903.

Boszormenyi-Nagy, I. (1965). A theory of relationships, experience, and transaction. In *Intensive Family Therapy*, ed. I. Boszormenyi-Nagy and J. Framo. New York: Harper and Row.

————(1965). Intensive family therapy as process. In *Intensive Family Therapy*, ed. I. Boszormenyi-Nagy and J. Framo. New York: Harper and Row.

Bowen, M. (1966). The use of family theory in clinical practice. *Comprehensive Psychiatry* 7:345-374.

————videotapes (obtainable through Dr. Murray Bowen, Department of Psychiatry, Medical College of Virginia, Richmond).

————(1978). *Family Therapy in Clinical Practice*. New York: Jason Aronson.

Cheek, F. (1964). Schizophrenic mothers in word and deed. *Family Process* 3:155-177.

————(1965). The father of the schizophrenic. *Archives of General Psychiatry* 13:336-345.

Dicks, H. (1967). *Marital Tensions*. New York: Basic Books.

Eliot, T.S. (1950). *The Cocktail Party*. New York: Harcourt, Brace.

Ellenberger, H. (1970). *The Discovery of the Unconscious*. New York: Basic Books.

Erickson, G., and Hogan, T. (1976). *Family Therapy*. New York: Jason Aronson.

Ferber, A., Kliger, D., Zwerling, I., et al. (1967). Current family structure: psychiatric emergencies and patient fate. *Archives of General Psychiatry* 16:659-667.

Ferber, A., Mendelsohn, M. Napier, A., eds. (1972). *The Book of Family Therapy*. New York: Science House.

Freud, S. (1905). Fragment of an analysis of a case of hysteria. *Standard Edition* 7:15-63.

Glick, I.D., and Haley, J. (1971). *Family Therapy and Research*. New York: Grune and Stratton.

Glick, I.D., and Kessler, D. (1974). *Marital and Family Therapy*. New York: Grune and Stratton.

Goodall, J. (1971). *In the Shadow of Man*. Boston: Houghton-Mifflin.

Guerin, P., ed. (1976). *Family Therapy: Theory and Practice*. New York: Gardner Press.

Haley, J. (1963). *Strategies of Psychotherapy*, chapters 6 and 7. New York: Grune and Stratton.

———(1967). Toward a theory of pathological families. In *Family Therapy and Disturbed Families*, eds. I. Boszormenyi-Nagy and G. Zuk. Palo Alto: Science and Behavior Books.

———, ed. (1971). *Changing Families: A Family Therapy Reader*. New York: Grune and Stratton.

Howells, J.G. (1971). *The Theory and Practice of Family Psychiatry*. New York: Brunner-Mazel.

Jackson, D. (1965). The study of the family. *Family Process* 4:1-20.

Jackson, D., and Weakland, J. (1961). Conjoint family therapy: some considerations on theory, technique, and results. *Psychiatry* 24:30-45.

———Movie of the Hillcrest family (obtainable through Psychological Cinema Register, Pennsylvania State University, University Park).

Jackson, D., Weakland, J., and Yalom, I. (1964). An example of family homeostasis and patient change. In *Current Psychiatric Therapies*, vol. 4, ed. J. Masserman. New York: Grune and Stratton.

Johnson, A., and Szurek, S.A. (1952). The genesis of antisocial acting out in children and adults. *Psychoanalytic Quarterly* 21:323-343.

LaBarre, W. (1970). *The Ghost Dance*. New York: Doubleday.

Laing, R.D. (1967). Individual and family structure. In *The Predicament of the Family*, ed. P. Thomas. London: Hogarth.

Levi-Strauss, C. (1956). The family. In *Man, Culture, and Society*, ed. H.L. Shapiro. London: Oxford University Press.

Main, T.F. (1966). Mutual projection in a marriage. *Comprehensive Psychiatry* 7:432-439.

Mead, M. (1950). *Sex and Temperament in Three Primitive Societies*, chapters 17 and 18. New York: New American Library.

Minuchin, S. (1974). *Families and Family Therapy*. Cambridge: Harvard University Press.

Minuchin, S., Montalvo, B., Guerney, B., et al. (1967). *Families of the Slums*. New York: Basic Books.

Napier, A., and Whitaker, C. (1978). *The Family Crucible*. New York: Harper and Row.

Paolino, T., and McGrady, B., eds. (1978). *Marriage and Marital*

Therapy. Psychoanalytic, Behavioral, and Systems Theory Perspectives. New York: Brunner-Mazel.

Parsons, T. (1955). The American family: its relation to personality and to the social structure. In *Family Socialization and Interaction Process,* ed. T. Parsons and R.F. Bales. Glencoe, Ill.: Free Press.

————(1955). Family structure and the socialization of the child. In *Family Socialization and Interacton Process,* ed. T. Parsons and R.F. Bales. Glencoe, Ill.: Free Press.

Paul, N. (1967). The role of mourning and empathy in conjoint marital therapy. In *Family Therapy and Disturbed Families,* ed. I. Boszormenyi-Nagy and G. Zuk. Palo Alto: Science and Behavior Books.

Paul, N., and Grosser, G. (1965). Operational mourning and its role in conjoint family therapy. *Community Mental Health Journal* 1:339-345.

Ravich, R.A. (1969). The use of an interpersonal game-test in conjoint marital psychotherapy. *American Journal of Psychotherapy* 23:217-229.

Reiss, D. (1967). Individual thinking and family interaction. *Archives of General Psychiatry* 5:80-93.

Rieff, P. (1966). *The Triumph of the Therapeutic.* New York: Harper and Row.

Sager, C.T., and Kaplan, H.S., eds. (1972). *Progress in Group and Family Therapy.* New York: Brunner-Mazel.

Sander, F. (1969). Some thoughts on Thomas Szasz. *American Journal of Psychiatry* 125:135-137.

Sander, F., and Beels, C.C. (1970). A didactic course for family therapy trainees. *Family Process* 9:411-423.

Satir, V. (1964). *Conjoint Family Therapy.* Palo Alto: Science and Behavior Books.

Schaffer, L., Wynne, L., Day, J., et al. (1962). On the nature and sources of the psychiatrist's experience with the family of the schizophrenic. *Psychiatry* 25:23-45.

Scheflen, A. (1968). Human communication: behavioral programs and their integration in interaction. *Behavioral Science* 13:44-55.

Skolnick, A.S., and Skolnick, J.H. (1971). *Family in Transition*. Boston: Little, Brown.

Szasz, T. (1961). *The Myth of Mental Illness*. New York: Harper and Row.

Thomas, A., Chess, S., and Birch, H. (1963). *Temperament and Behavior Disorder in Children*. New York: New York University Press.

Watzlawick, P., Beavin, J., and Jackson, D.D. (1967). *The Pragmatics of Human Communications*. New York: Norton.

Wender, P. (1967). On necessary and sufficient conditions in psychiatric explanation. *Archives of General Psychiatry* 16:41-47.

_____(1969). The role of genetics in the etiology of the schizophrenias. *American Journal of Orthopsychiatry* 39:447-458.

Whitaker, C. (1958). Psychotherapy with couples. *American Journal of Psychotherapy* 12:18-23.

_____(1965). Acting out in family psychotherapy. In *Acting Out: Theoretical and Clinical Aspects*, ed. L.E. Abt and S.L. Weismann. New York: Grune and Stratton.

_____Movie of the Hillcrest family (obtainable through Psychological Cinema Register, Pennsylvania State University, University Park).

Wynne, L. (1961). The study of intrafamilial alignments and splits in exploratory family therapy. In *Exploring the Base for Family Therapy*, ed. N.W. Ackerman, F. Beatman, and S. Sherman. New York: Family Service Association.

_____(1965). Some indications and contraindications for exploring family therapy. In *Intensive Family Therapy*, ed. I. Boszormenyi-Nagy and J. Framo. New York: Harper and Row.

Wynne, L., and Singer, M.T. (1963). Thought disorder and family relations of schizophrenics. Parts I,II. *Archives of General Psychiatry* 9:191-206.

_____(1965). Thought disorder and family relations of schizophrenics. Parts III,IV. *Archives of General Psychiatry* 12:186-212.

Zuk, G. (1971). *Family Therapy: A Triadic Approach*. New York: Behavioral Publications.

Part III

INTRAPSYCHIC AND INTERPERSONAL FACTORS IN FAMILIES

Chapter Eight

CLINICAL PRACTICES OF
FAMILY THERAPISTS

In the thirty years since T.S. Eliot first dramatized the innovation of family therapy (see chapter 2), the numbers of family systems theories, family training programs, and family therapists have been increasing at an unimaginable rate. This uncontrolled development is characteristic of what Kuhn (1962) described in *The Structure of Scientific Revolutions* (see chapter 1) as a revolution's

> pre-paradigm period when there is a multiplicity of competing schools.... This is the period during which individuals practice science, but in which the results of their enterprise do not add up to a science as we know it.... With respect to normal science, then, part of the answer to the problem of progress lies simply in the eye of the beholder. Scientific progress is not different in kind from progress in other fields, but the absence, at most times, of competing schools that question each other's aims and standards makes the progress of a normal scientific community far easier to see.... Once the reception of a common paradigm has freed the scientific community from the need constantly to re-

examine its first principles, the members of that community can concentrate exclusively upon the subtlest and most esoteric of the phenomena that concern it. [pp. 162-163]

Most pioneers of the family therapy revolution have until now favored the openness and unstructured development of this multiplicity of schools. But the proliferation has now come to haunt the profession. Sooner or later a discipline must develop professional standards, credentialing procedures, training accreditation and legitimized theories. To begin to address these questions an American Family Therapy Association has now been formed with Murray Bowen as its first president. At the same time, AAMFT, the American Association of Marriage and Family Therapists (formerly the American Association of Marriage Counselors), a large, older organization with an altogether different history and tradition, has recently been recognized by the Department of Health, Education, and Welfare as the national accrediting body for training institutions for marriage and family therapy. In an attempt to avert a collision between these organizations, Donald S. Williamson, president of AAMFT, suggested in a recent memorandum (1979) that "the two organizations are twin wings of a single movement which has now naturally and irretrievably fused as far as theory, therapeutic biases, and professional personnel are concerned. From the beginning the commitment to perceive and understand human behavior in inter-relational terms and to generate treatment interventions from this framework has been the incipient bond between these two traditions and communities."

This bit of rhetoric attempts to gloss over differences for the sake of political harmony. In my view the field is far from having achieved sufficient consensus to warrant a credentialing and accrediting status. For the time being it seems best for the traditional disciplines of psychiatry, social work, psychology, and psychoanalysis to continue their already difficult tasks of giving credentials and accrediting while family systems concepts, theories, and techniques are introduced as they are developed and researched. We must try to clarify what the various "schools" of family therapy do have in common and in what important ways they differ. I shall in this chapter survey the clinical approaches of some major contributors to the family systems approach from the perspective of the underlying premise of this book, i.e., that the polarization of individual/intrapsychic and family/interpersonal approaches is an artificial one. We need to understand in what ways the individual approach affects individuals and family systems as we need to know how the family systems approaches affect change in families and individuals.

FREUD'S AND HALEY'S UNCOMMON THERAPIES: COMPARING THE BEGINNINGS OF PSYCHOANALYSIS AND FAMILY THERAPY

The Beels and Ferber (1969) review of the field of family therapy was the first and is still the most comprehensive attempt at comparing the various family therapists' approaches. Before describing major differences in techniques, the authors correctly note what unifies all the schools of family therapy, "the goal of changing the family system of interaction" with "... individual change occurring as a by-product of system change" (p. 283).

It is natural and understandable for therapists to want to change the individuals and families who come to them for help. In the prepsychoanalytic period, reviewed in chapter 5, we noted how Freud, while experimenting with hypnosis, was also eager to actively change and "cure" the individual disturbances referred to him.

In his 1893 paper "A Case of Successful Treatment by Hypnotism," Freud dramatically intervened in a strategic way that had obvious and immediate ramifications along both intrapsychic and transactional pathways, and it has much in common with some of the recent developments in family systems therapy.

Almost ninety years ago Freud was consulted by the family of a young woman in her mid-twenties who was unable to feed her newborn infant. The woman vomited all her food, became agitated when it was brought to her bedside and was completely unable to sleep. After a thorough abdominal examination, Freud hypnotized her, using ocular fixation, and suggested away her symptoms. Cured for a day she then relapsed as anticipated by her husband, who in fact feared her nerves would altogether be ruined by hypnosis. A second hypnosis was attempted the following day.

> I told the patient that five minutes after my departure she would break out against her family with some acrimony: what happened to her dinner? did they mean for her to starve? how could she feed the baby if she had nothing to eat herself? and so on.
>   When I returned on the third evening, the patient refused to have any further treatment. There was nothing more wrong with her, she said: she had an excellent appetite and plenty of milk for the baby, there was not the slightest difficulty when it was put to her breast, and so on. Her husband thought it rather queer that after my departure the evening before she had clamored violently for food and had remonstrated with her mother in a way quite unlike herself. But since then, he added, everything had gone all right. [p. 120]

We can only speculate as to the basis of this remarkable "hit-and-run," symptomatic cure. It is commonplace in many family therapies to encourage more open expression of feelings among family members and to "prescribe" behaviors. Such interventions are rarely welcome and require the tactful handling of family resistances. Was the intervention successful due to the "abreaction" of her "strangulated affects," a formulation developed with Breuer (1893) and/or due to the anxiety in herself and the family members created by the uncharacteristic, rule-breaking expression of her suppressed hostility.

In his discussion of the mechanism of his patient's disorder, Freud demonstrated his earliest plummeting into dynamic psychic determinism. It was the beginning of an unparalleled voyage into the depths of psychic functioning. He postulated the presence in his patient of "distressing antithetical ideas," that is, ideas running counter to intentions. The patient had every intention of feeding her child. However, "counter intentions in neurotics are removed from association with the intentions and continue to exist as a disconnected idea, often unconsciously to the patient" (p. 122). These novel formulations of unconscious motivations and of ambivalence were the beginnings of the elaborate and comprehensive theory of mental functioning that was to become psychoanalysis.

The case however, even as unelaborated in details as this one, suggests the presence of ongoing interpersonal conflicts, as well as intrapsychic forces. In her regressed state, unable to feed her baby, she simultaneously identified with the ungiving mother and the unfed child, thus acting out with her child her ambivalence conflict with her own mother. That she was not allowed expression of her conflict in the family setting is implied in her becoming "unlike her (usual) self" in the rebellious attitude set off by Freud's suggestion. That her husband may have expected her dysfunctioning is suggested by his prediction that her nerves would be altogether ruined by hypnosis.

In getting his patient to remonstrate with her mother in a way quite unlike herself and thereby losing her symptoms, Freud had achieved an optimum family therapy goal: changing the family system of interaction. In this instance Freud was intervening in what Haley, in his recent book *Uncommon Therapy: The Psychiatric Techniques of Milton Erickson, M.D.* (1973), would call an overinvolved dyad (pp. 36-37). By inducing her anger Freud could help the patient begin to disengage from her intense overinvolvement with her mother and gain control over her symptom of vomiting. The intervention also participated in the paradoxical component Haley has noted in all hypnotic therapy. "The hypnotist directs another person to spontaneously change his behavior. Since a person cannot respond spontaneously if he's following a directive, the hypnotic approach poses a paradox. The way the subject adapts to such a conflicting set of directives is to undergo a change and behave in a way described as trance behavior" (p. 21). Freud's intervention was doubly paradoxical in that he told the patient who was vomiting all her food to angrily ask for more food if she was to feed the baby she had said she was unable to feed. This element demonstrates the point made by Don Jackson about the ambiguity regarding the patient's ability or inability to control his symptoms. Before Freud such symptoms were seen as manipulative and as manifestations of malingering. Freud introduced the idea of unconscious ideas motivating symptoms (Freud and Breuer 1895) and later explored the role of secondary gain in symptom formation (1905, pp. 42-44). This question of secondary gain is, I believe, one of the major points of linkage between psychoanalytic theory and family systems theory, which more recently has come to see symptoms as induced or expected of the identified patient by the immediate context.

The case is almost identical in family structure to the one Haley uses to illustrate illness in the childbirth phase of the family life cycle (pp. 185-188). In fact, it coincides in its family aspects with almost every case of postpartem illness I have seen. In addition to the regression in the identified patient, there is an uncanny collusive participation of the husband and either or both sets of grandparents. In their eagerness to take over the nurturing function of the new mother, they compound and reinforce the patient's maladaptation.

Haley's emphasis upon employing, as foci of psychiatric intervention, the difficulties attendant upon the transitions in the family life cycle is the very considerable contribution of his book. He illustrates again and again the participation of other family members in the identified patient's illness. The families are, in fact, having difficulty carrying out the functions of their stage of development. By highlighting the stages of family development, he lays the groundwork for the next theoretical step of linking these stages developmentally with one another as Erik Erikson (1950, pp. 219-234) did so elegantly within the framework of individual psychology (see chapter 3). Perhaps as we develop our family theories further, we can go beyond the miraculous-sounding strategies outlined in *Uncommon Therapy*. Haley's need, however, to debunk insight, intrapsychic forces, the unconscious, and long-term intensive therapy, none of which is centrally relevant to the management of family crises or psychiatric emergencies, mars his otherwise excellent book. Psychoanalysis is not the indicated therapy in crises. Because its theories were probably overutilized when no other theories or models were available is no reason to discard its hard-won insights.

As imaginative as the miraculous-sounding strategies described by Haley are, they nonetheless sound like attempts to outsmart the patient and terminate the contact as quickly as possible. This approach leaves unanswered the question of how long-lasting the changes brought about will be and what the bases of these changes are. In this regard, Freud observed that his patient relapsed with the birth of her next child. He went beyond his uncommon hypnosis of the 1890s to develop the even more uncommon therapy of psychoanalysis. Not to ask these questions concerning follow-up and the dynamics of change is to relegate such therapeutic innovations to the long list of successful, uncommon faith healers that have marked the history of psychotherapy. The history of psychotherapy is replete with illustrations of symptom alleviation from the days of Aesclepius to the fads of the 1960s and 1970s (see Buckley and Sander 1974). The advancement of psychotherapy as a science rests upon the greater insight gained into the processes — biological, psychological, and social — of symptom formation and "abnormal behavior." The family systems paradigm assumes that significant portions of human behavior and experiences are (to degrees never fully realized) overdetermined by the social field and has demonstrated that as a modality it too can achieve symptomatic improvement. But to embrace behavioral change as a raison d'etre of family therapy will doom its further development.

The importance of and for many the centrality of the social field has been rediscovered by the family therapy movement. The most radical exponents of this view have been the communications school of family therapists, which include Don Jackson, Paul Watzlawick, John Weakland, Jay Haley, and more recently Mara Palazzoli and Salvador Minuchin. They are all indebted to

Gregory Bateson; the title of his recent collection of writings (*Steps to an Ecology of the Mind* 1975) marks the pole toward which the systems theory purists are traveling. It was this group that first described the concept of the double bind (Bateson, Jackson, Haley, and Weakland 1956) and saw schizophrenia as a manifestation of profoundly disturbed, rule-governed communication processes between people. It is this group that has written most lucidly about communication in family systems (see especially Watzlawick et al. 1967) and that has developed a model that is primarily change oriented. This emphasis is in striking contrast to a principle of psychoanalytic treatment, most recently restated by Gedo (1979), that "the analyst should not approach his or her clinical work with the personal need to be a healer; to require patients to improve is an illegitimate infringement on their autonomy" (p. 649).

It is one of the ironies in the history of the family therapy revolution that in the eagerness to do away with "the medical model" the most radical family therapists have incorporated the underlying attitude of that very same model, that is, the active intervention and change of a dysfunctioning entity, be it an individual or a family. We see this trend most elaborated in the work of Minuchin, to whom we now turn.

MINUCHIN'S STRUCTURAL FAMILY THERAPY

Significantly influenced by the communications theorists just mentioned, Salvador Minuchin has risen to national prominence as the proponent of the structural family therapy approach. This theory, developed at the Philadelphia Child Guidance Clinic, forms the framework for a therapy that is, as stated on the second page of his *Families and Family Therapy* (1974), "directed toward changing the organization of the family." He reiterates that "structural family therapy is a therapy of action. The tool of the therapy is to modify the present, not to explore and interpret the past" (p. 14). Clearly his framework is established in diametrical opposition to what he imagines is the individual psychoanalytic approach. It is a common misunderstanding to think that psychoanalytic treatment begins and ends with the past. The present transference relationship, which repeats the past, is the actual focus of the unfolding work.

To better understand his revolutionary stance, we would do well to look at the patient population out of which his theories evolved. His earliest contribution was a result of his work in a project at the Wiltwyck School for Boys, which culminated in *The Families of the Slums* (1967). The delinquents treated in that project came from very "disorganized" families that required "restructuring." The treatment formats developed emphasized the necessity of creating appropriate role boundaries for the family's subsystems, be they for spouse, parent, or sibling. Common in the early treatment strategies was the tendency to use the one-way screen to demarcate family subsystems. A grand-mother, for example, who tended intrusively to control a family's interaction, might be asked to stay behind the one-way screen while the mother and father discussed their child-rearing difficulties. In this early work we see the beginnings of what was to become the structural family therapy notation system. Healthy families include a gratifying spouse/parent affiliation

$$F = M$$

in contrast to a conflictual relationship

$$F \dashv \vdash M$$

that in turn related to "overinvolvement" of a parent and child.

$$
\begin{array}{c}
P \\
\text{||||} \\
C
\end{array}
$$

Boundaries tended to be rigid (_____), with detachment,
    diffuse (..........), with enmeshment, or
    clear   (_ _ _ _ _).

While we may look at this work today and see it as the application
of common sense, in the fifties and early sixties, the mental health
professions, for reasons explored in the next chapter, were
reluctant to adopt a family systems approach while attempting
the near impossible individual treatment of the casualties of these
disorganized families (see Meers 1975 for a psychoanalytic
discussion of this clinical population).

Families of the slums are not the only families in need of
structural support or change, and this accounts for much of the
success and wider popularity of Minuchin's approach. At this
stage in our social history, as we noted in the second chapter, the
structure and functioning of American families are changing
rapidly. The high divorce and remarriage rate has created many
families where parenting roles become highly fragmented.
Minuchin's diagrammatic and programmatic approach is easily
taught to trainees who attempt to help families establish
appropriate role boundaries, alliances, and coalitions. A trainee
in one of my seminars, after reading Minuchin's book, had the
parents of a family, after two sessions, move into the parental
bedroom, which had been given over to the children.

Beyond the ubiquitous sociological upheavals the structural
family therapy approach also appears relevant to patients with
severe psychosomatic illnesses (see Minuchin 1978) and often
with families of behaviorally symptomatic children. Minuchin
and his coworkers have repeatedly exposed the ineffectiveness and
inappropriateness of the individual treatment approach when
families are functioning in a manifestly malignant manner.

The case reports and edited teaching tapes that have been
produced over the years by the Philadelphia Child Guidance
Clinic as well as such publicity as a recent lead article in the *New
Yorker* (Malcolm 1977) have established the Minuchin approach
as a leading school in the family therapy movement.

We should nonetheless ask whether this approach is any further
in its development than psychoanalysis in its early days. In a
teaching tape titled "A Modern Little Hans" (also briefly
discussed in *Families and Family Therapy*, 1974, p. 153), the
approach is used to cure a young boy's dog phobia by
"restructuring" the family. The initial ("before") structural

diagram of the family is like that of many in which the child is the identified patient.

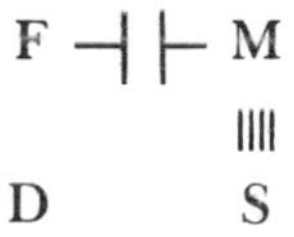

Fig. 1

There is a marked marital conflict and an overly close relationship between the mother and the identified patient. The obvious solution for the structural therapist is to arrange a closer relation between the boy and his father and foster improvement in the marital relationship.

> In "A Modern Little Hans," a child comes into therapy with a dog phobia that is so severe he is almost confined to the house. The therapist's diagnosis is that the symptom is supported by an implicit, unresolved conflict between the spouses, manifested in an affiliation between the mother and son that excludes the father. His strategy is to increase the affiliation between the father and son before tackling the spouse subsystem problems. Therefore, he encourages the father, who is a mailman "and therefore an expert in dealing with dogs," to teach his son how to deal with strange dogs. The child, who is adopted, in turn adopts a dog, and the father and son join in transactions around the dog. This activity strengthens their relationship and promotes a separation between mother and son. As the symptom disappears, the therapist praises both parents for their successful handling of the child. He then moves to work with the husband-wife conflicts. [p. 153]

The cure is accomplished in a short period of time, leading to an "after" treatment diagram:

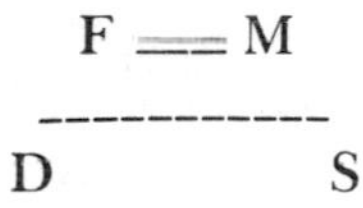

F ═══ M

D   S

Fig. 2

There is no mention in the tape or case report that father, mother, and daughter are all visibly overweight. It is sufficient that the dog phobia has been cured.

The structural family therapists tell us that a family structure such as that in Fig. 1 is pathogenic, as it interferes with the child's development of autonomy. Such a generalized theory tells us little of the more discrete aspects of development. Why after all should the modern Little Hans have been fearful of dogs? It is, of course, fascinating that the case lends itself, as intended, to comparison with the original Little Hans case, for there too, by having the father, though not by therapeutic design, treat his own son, Freud was increasing the "affiliation" between those oedipal rivals.

The family structures of each little Hans complicate development by threatening the fulfillment of oedipal wishes and undermining autonomous strivings. Figure 1 symbolizes the realization of the intrapsychic oedipal wishes. Dogs, the animals presumably threatening his father on his postal route, may well have been a repository simultaneously of the child's aggressive impulses (by projection) as well as the feared retaliation from his father (through displacement). The symptom, of course, like Little Hans's horse phobia, kept him home with mother, thereby further reinforcing the phobia. We see that family systems data can potentially enrich our understanding of how intrapsychic reality relates to the realities of family interaction.

For better or for worse one of the consequences of the family systems revolution involves turning the privacy and confidentiality of individual therapy into a far more public and often dramatic affair. Reflecting this change, the courts have just recently questioned the therapist's privilege of confidentiality in the family therapy context on the ground that by its very structure it is not confidential (*Psychiatric News*, 5/4/79). The one-way screen, with its multiple observers, as well as videotape replay are testimonies of the technological changes that have turned the world of therapy literally inside out. "The One-Way Screen," the title of Janet Malcolm's *New Yorker* account (1977) of Minuchin and the family systems revolution, describes her direct observations of family therapy interviews conducted at the Philadelphia Child Guidance Clinic.

The family, a couple in their forties with a young fifteen-year-old daughter who has been deteriorating and is about to be hospitalized are referred for family therapy. The family is treated by a trainee, while Minuchin directs and orchestrates the therapy by phoning in suggestions and at other times entering the interview room with observations, pronouncements, and "attacks":

> Mr. Braun began to complain about his wife. He said that she "screamed and hollered." Mrs. Braun began to cry. He went on to report that she had said she couldn't take it anymore and was going to leave. Mrs. Braun, through her tears, accused her husband of leaving everything to her; it was all too much for her, she said.
> In the observation room, Minuchin listened to the argument and then said, *"I'm going to attack the mother again."* He reentered the treatment room and said sternly to Mrs. Braun, "I am concerned about what you are saying. I am concerned that when you leave here today your daughter will go crazy again. And I think the reason she will do it is to save your marriage. Children sometimes act in very weird ways to save their parents' marriage." He turned to the girl and said, "Yvonne, I suggest that you go quite crazy today, so that your parents can become concerned about you. Then things will be O.K. between them. You seem to be a good daughter, so you will go crazy, and your father will support your mother in taking care of you, and things will be O.K." To the parents, he went on, "I think that your daughter is trying to save your marriage. It is a bizarre thing to say, I know. But sometimes children are so protective of their parents that they sacrifice themselves. I think that Yvonne has kind of perceived that you are at the deep end, and she is saving you by being crazy, so you will organize yourselves." He started to leave, and then, pausing in the doorway, he said to the girl, "You're a good daughter, and if you see a danger, go crazy."
> The parents started talking about their marriage, and Lee [the therapist] told the girl that she could leave if she wanted

to, since what her parents were saying didn't concern her. "Do you think you'll go crazy when you get home?" Lee asked her. [p. 40]

How are we to understand such interventions as helpful? Those investigators who have studied, whether individually (e.g., Lidz 1965) or conjointly (e.g., Wynne et al. 1958), the family members of seriously disturbed adolescents have described the severest disturbances in object relations and communication patterns involving the entire family. The very fact of bringing such families for treatment rather than specifying an identified patient allows the examination and often the amelioration of an organismic family process in which one member sacrifices himself for the sake of the psychological stability of one parent (see chapter 3) or, as Minuchin suggests in this case, for the stabilization of the parents' marriage. This intense pathological triangling and family undifferentiatedness has been noted by many students of the family, and the process can be temporarily interrupted by family treatment. In the present case Malcolm visits the family a month or so after they ended their brief treatment and notes that while the acute problem has been relieved, the chronic relational disturbances remain.

THE BOWEN THEORY: THE DIFFERENTIATION OF SELF

The popularity of Bowen's theory is comparable with that of Minuchin's, and Bowen, like Minuchin, has trained large numbers of practitioners whose thinking and approach mark them as Bowenians. Bowen too has developed a deceptively simple schema, the key concept of which is the differentiation of self from the undifferentiated family ego mass (1978). Bowen's theory must also be understood, in part, as stemming from a specific clinical experience. In the 1950s Bowen began to study families of schizophrenic patients at the National Institute of Mental Health. In these early studies the whole family was often hospitalized. Any clinician who has worked with families in which the schizophrenic process is operative will recognize the aptness of the concept of the undifferentiated family ego mass, as these family members often speak and act as if they had but one skin. Ego boundaries are hard to recognize. Bowen's descriptions can immediately be correlated with the individual paradigm's emphasis on intrapsychic self-object undifferentiatedness and symbiotic trends. Bowen demonstrated that this is as much a relational as an intrapsychic process.

The problem with the concept is that it is overgeneralized. While differentiation of the self should go on throughout the life cycles of individuals and families, this developmental concept becomes a kind of catchall explanation, perhaps comparable to psychoanalysis's early emphasis upon the oedipal conflict as the common denominator of all neuroses.

Nonetheless, for a number of reasons, Bowen's approach, though he would probably deny it, has more in common with the psychoanalytic paradigm than the other schools of family therapy. His emphasis upon the importance of self-differentiation parallels the ultimate goal of a psychoanalysis.

The psychoanalyst attempts through the analysis of the transference to undo the neurotic distortions that have been internalized over the years. Bowen eschews or deflects such transference developments in therapy and does much of his therapy by having his "clients," with his coaching, work directly with members of their family of origin. This approach often diffuses marital conflicts that became the arena for displaced struggles with parents and siblings. This approach may also reduce the guilt associated with attempts to resolve conflicts by "leaving home." In other words, you must go home again. There is much that Bowen has in common with Boszormenyi-Nagy in this regard, whose book *Invisible Loyalties* (1973) traces somewhat moralistically the subterranean, cross-generational loyalty ties, which are so often disrupted. The presence and degree of unconscious guilt would probably limit this approach in certain cases.

Bowen, with his emphasis upon generational transmission of

emotional disorders, introduces an historical perspective that is absent in the communications and structural schools. He appreciates that the process of change is not a simple one achieved by a quick strategy. His disavowal of the medical model by refusing to call his clients "patients" is an awkward semantic evasion. Whether those seen in psychotherapy are called patients, clients, or students is less material than the actual nature of the therapeutic interaction, which is not determined primarily by labels. In psychoanalysis, for example, a patient's view of himself as "patient" and his view of "cure" are analyzed for their associated unconscious meanings. What Bowen does emphasize, in this position, is his primary orientation to research, which has much in common with psychoanalysis. He feels as do most psychoanalysts that such an orientation goes further in "helping" patients than the active-change methods of almost all other individual and family approaches. Like the analyst he refuses to collude and collaborate in the clients' attempts to satisfy transference demands, and he is similarly criticized for this stance of technical abstinence.

CARL WHITAKER: EXISTENTIAL ENIGMA

In Napier and Whitaker's *The Family Crucible* (1978) we have a most readable and controversial introduction to the field of family therapy. The experience of working with families is conveyed through the depiction of a composite of families the authors have seen. What emerges is a very recognizable, American, middle-class version of "Everyfamily."

The dramatic portrayal of this family's struggles, as well as the therapists' "war" against its resistances to change, alternate with remarkably lucid and jargon-free "theoretical" chapters. Family homeostasis, the inevitable tendency toward triangulation, the role of the families of origin, marriage as an attempt to heal past wounds, are ideas developed out of the "clinical" material. As in most good novels, the universality of family conflicts is convincingly presented, and again we can trace the roots and manifestations of pathology.

The portrayal of this family is as naturalistic as its treatment is controversial. Most schools of family therapy, while in accord with the overall viewpoint, will also find issues with which to quarrel. Followers of Bowen will question the degree of involvement of the therapists. The structuralists will question the retention of an intrapsychic perspective. The interventions, however, are so graphically presented that one can readily compare and contrast one's own theory and approach. Discussion is thus easily stimulated, making this book an excellent teaching vehicle.

Unfortunately the authors misunderstand the place of Freud, and their discussion of him is full of distortions. Freud was not "the source of the entire psychotherapeutic movement" (p. 30). Actually, psychoanalysis as repeatedly noted in this book represents the latest and most fully developed theory and practice of individual treatment, a modality that goes back to man's beginnings when his diseases were responded to by "healing" the individual sufferer. Nor did Freud "avoid seeing that his disturbed patients were members of disturbed families" (p. 41). He just candidly expressed his inability to deal with families (see chapter 5). In relation to Freud's "scornful attitude toward humanity" (p. 43) — more correctly a pessimistic outlook — one sees little to warrant Napier's optimism or his quest for a "science of the higher person" (p. 43). Napier disdains the instinctual bases of psychoanalytic theory, incorrectly implying that they preclude examination of man's creativity and achievements. He thus joins the current wave of "repression" and repudiation of the findings of the Freudian revolution (cf. Jacoby 1976).

Despite the book's manifestly antipsychoanalytic bias, unconscious processes are introduced repeatedly. The emphasis upon the repetition of familial disturbances across generations (p. 119) and the appreciation of transference (p. 107) are testimony to psychoanalytic concepts, i.e., the repetition compulsion (p. 159). Although the authors note the importance of identifications in this process, the dynamic of guilt in the perpetuation of self-destructive neurotic interaction is omitted. Here Napier and Whitaker share with many family therapists an aversion to "why" questions. Why are family systems so difficult to change? Why do so many individuals and families persist in self-defeating patterns? Psychoanalysis, while shying away from family treatment, has some compelling answers to such questions. Separation anxiety, for example, certainly contributes to what the authors call "family-wide symbiosis" (p. 88) and what Bowen calls the "undifferentiated family ego mass" and Minuchin sees as family "enmeshment." Further, the authors' essential interventions involve the Oedipus situation. First they disengage the family's adolescent daughter and later the son from oedipal triangles that are aggravated by the parents' conflictual marriage.

> For Don [the son] was indeed the victim of a family process which created in him the fantasy that he was older, smarter, and stronger than he actually was. Without meaning to, his parents had trained him in a kind of subtle delusional thinking about himself, one that implied that he could beat his father in a contest of strength and that he could be his mother's substitute mate. [p. 179]

Don is disabused of this fantasy of physical strength in the "therapeutic moment" of a spontaneous but "unconsciously" enacted wrestling match with Whitaker.

Napier and Whitaker repeatedly and actively enter the therapeutic exchange with an explicit acceptance of the role of surrogate, "symbolic" parents. They see themselves as a "professional marriage" (p. 91), offering warmth (p. 10), parenting (pp. 11, 185) with toughness (p. 20), caring (p. 210), and presenting "maybe a superior model" of parenting (p. 80). With interpretations, confrontations, advice, and "just being with the family," they try to interrupt the cycles of disappointment and of blaming "the other" for inadequacies in "the self" (p. 197); by sparking a renewal of the marriage, they attempt to free the children to develop more naturally.

Napier and Whitaker thus become "real objects" to their patients in ways that psychoanalytic therapists usually reserve for sicker patients. While they, after many years of experience and their own eight personal therapies, may know the right dosage of such personal involvement, many students will take their model too literally, thereby infantilizing their patients.

On the other hand, although their "parenting" therapy is quite pervasive, the authors repeatedly insist, especially in their excellent chapter on divorce, that the family members must take ultimate responsibility for their own lives. This seeming contradiction is potentially confusing to both patients and students. When Whitaker asks the family to turn to the therapists for help rather than to each other, the father poignantly asks, "Where does that leave us when you guys aren't around?" (p. 121). That is something, of course, we will never know with this fictionalized family, as we rarely know with most real families.

One does feel by the end, however, that this "family" has learned better ways of approaching their problems. The authors, unlike so many therapists these days, do not make grand claims of success. They acknowledge that the work of growth and change is difficult and interminable and that the family or individual members may again come for help in the future with similar or new problems. The appropriateness of family treatment for this kind of crisis is most convincing.

The book written by Napier describes the work of a pioneer family therapist who, unlike Bowen and Minuchin, has not founded a school because, wary of the pitfalls of theory, he refuses to write about theory, and his approach is so idiosyncratic and "existential" that it is virtually unteachable.

REFERENCES

Bateson, G. (1975). *Steps to an Ecology of the Mind.* New York: Ballantine.

Bateson, G., Jackson, D.D., Haley, J., and Weakland, J.H. (1956). Towards a theory of schizophrenia. *Behavioral Science* 1:251-264.

Beels, C.C., and Ferber, A. (1969). Family therapy: a view. *Family Process* 8:280-318.

Boszormenyi-Nagy, I., and Spark, G. (1973). *Invisible Loyalties.* New York: Harper and Row.

Bowen, M. (1978). *Family Therapy in Clinical Practice*. New York: Jason Aronson.

Buckley, P., and Sander, F.M. (1974). The history of psychiatry from the patient's viewpoint. *American Journal of Psychiatry* 131:1146-1150.

Erikson, E. (1950). *Childhood and Society*. New York: Norton.

Freud, S. (1893). A case of successful treatment by hypnotism. *Standard Edition* 1.

———(1905). Fragment of an analysis of a case of hysteria. *Standard Edition* 7.

———(1909). Analysis of a phobia in a five-year-old boy. *Standard Edition* 10.

Freud, S., and Breuer, J. (1893). On the psychical mechanism of hysterical phenomena: preliminary communication. *Standard Edition* 2: pp. 3-17.

———(1895). Studies in hysteria. *Standard Edition* 2.

Gedo, J. (1979). A psychoanalyst reports at mid-career. *American Journal of Psychiatry* 136:646-649.

Haley, J. (1973). *Uncommon Therapy: The Psychiatric Techniques of Milton Erikson, M.D.* New York: Norton.

Jacoby, R. (1976). *Social Amnesia: A Critique of Conformist Psychology from Adler to Laing*. Boston: Beacon Press.

Kuhn, T.S. (1962). *The Structure of Scientific Revolutions*. Chicago: University of Chicago Press.

Lidz, T., et al. (1965). *Schizophrenia and the Family*. New York: International Universities Press.

Malcolm, J. (1977). The one-way screen. *New Yorker*, May 15, 1977.

Meers, D. (1970). Contributions of a ghetto culture to symptom formation: psychoanalytic studies of ego anomalies in childhood. *Psychoanalytic Study of the Child* 25:209-230.

Minuchin, S. (1974). *Families and Family Therapy*. Cambridge: Harvard University Press.

Minuchin, S., et al. (1967). *Families of the Slums*. New York: Basic Books.

———(1978). *Psychosomatic Families: Anorexia Nervosa in Context*. Cambridge: Harvard University Press.

Napier, A. and Whitaker, C. (1978). *The Family Crucible.* New York: Harper and Row.

Psychiatric News (1979). Privilege denied in joint therapy. May 4.

Watzlowick, P., et al. (1967). *Pragmatics of Human Communication.* New York: Norton.

Williamson, D. (1979). *AAMFT Newsletter.* March 1979.

Wynne, L., et al. (1958). Pseudo-mutuality in the family relations of schizophrenics. *Psychiatry* 21:205-222.

Chapter Nine

FAMILY DRAMAS IN CLINICAL PRACTICE

INDIVIDUAL AND/OR FAMILY THERAPY

Dramatis Personae

Mrs. B.: About forty, housewife and graduate student, was referred by her individual therapist whom she had been seeing for about one year. She was unhappy with her marriage, and there had been no change. Her therapist agreed and referred her and her husband for marital therapy. She has had the bulk of the responsibility for their three children ranging in age from eight to twelve and for the home generally, doing minor home repairs, caring for the yard, etc. She feels the marriage lacks intimacy and a sense of partnership. During most of the conjoint therapy, which has lasted about four months, she has continually been the expressor of any feelings.

Mr. B.: Also about forty, a biological researcher working long hours, including weekends when he is writing grant applications. He comes to marital therapy reluctantly, as he is happy in his marriage, unhappy only in that she is not satisfied.

Dr. S.: About forty, calm, curious, generally letting his patients develop their agenda. In this scene he more actively tries to shift the focus from her unhappiness to eliciting more of his feelings.

Setting

The 1970s, a psychotherapist's office, books lining two walls; the titles on one wall are about the family and family therapy; on the other they are about psychoanalysis. There is a couch and four chairs, three of which are arranged to form a triangle. Mrs. B. enters followed by Dr. S.

Mrs. B.: I don't know why Allen is late. Things are quiet at home, but it is as if there is a cold war going on. Underneath there seems to be a lot of anger.

Mr. B.: (Arrives looking at his watch) You must have started early. (Takes his seat and looks abstracted, as if he were still in the lab. Catches himself, looks directly at his wife.) So, what's on your mind?

Dr. S.: You still want Ann to start off. What is on *your* mind?

Mr. B.: For some reason Ann has not wanted to make love the last two weeks. (Matter of factly)

Dr. S.: How do you feel about that?

Mr. B.: I feel she is disabled. There is something wrong with her. She is clearly unhappy and that makes me unhappy. That's why we are here. (Mrs. B. is visibly more unhappy as he says this but remains silent. Mr. B. looks directly at Dr. S.) If your wife were disabled with some illness, you wouldn't get angry with her, would you? (said somewhat challengingly)

Dr. S.: You seem more annoyed about being here today. How do you feel about being here?

Mr. B.: I don't like it much; I was in the middle of an experiment.

Dr. S.: What keeps you from saying that?

Mr. B.: I don't want to hurt your feelings. You are a decent enough person. You haven't done anything to me.

Mrs. B.: I know so little of what goes on inside of you; all you talk about is your work. (encouraged by the therapist's lead)

Mr. B.: I just can't do it. I admire how the kids can come right out and say what they feel, like Lizzie did yesterday. I still remember when I ran in to tell my parents something exciting.

My father threw me out. (Mrs. B. moves up in her seat, seems interested)

Dr. S.: How would you feel if the marriage broke up?

Mr. B.: (Almost as if it were a fact) I would survive. When the wife of one of my professors died, he went back to work the next day. I would be sad because of the children, but I would survive. (Pause) You keep implying there is something wrong with the relationship. Aren't you interested in seeing it that way because you see couples. If she were psychoanalyzed and got over her feelings toward her father, or whatever, she'd be happier and we wouldn't be here now.

Dr. S.: Did you notice that when you insist that Ann is the problem she becomes cooler and when you talk more of how you feel she is more interested; yet you still feel you will be thrown out, as you were by your father, if you express how you feel.

Mr. B.: I do remember a lot of bad feelings in the past. I don't want to be reminded of them, or feel them again.

This scene, a common one in the family therapist's office, illustrates the pervasiveness of the traditional common-sense viewpoint that emotional disturbances reside usually [within another person] rather than within *and* between people. We saw in *Hamlet* (chapter 1) that all the major characters saw Hamlet as the identified patient, in part, to ward off some painful aspects of themselves. Mr. B. would similarly prefer to see any unhappiness residing in his wife. That this externalizing defense comes to plague him is in fact an example of the Freudian concept of the return of the repressed. In the usual, fully internalized conflict the repressed most often returns in the form of dreams and symptoms. When families are seen where externalizing defenses predominate, the repressed aspects of one person are often evoked and provoked in another. When this happens, the separation of intrapsychic processes and interpersonal processes is quite artificial as these processes are always mutually influencing one another. It is however quite difficult to study these levels simultaneously, and understandably therapists tend to simplify the task by doing either family therapy or individual therapy. These modalities, however, like the varying lenses of the microscope distort one level while another is being illuminated.

Mr. B. is partly correct when he states that his wife's unhappiness is the problem. He is also partly correct in his assumption that something in her past history is "responsible" for her unhappiness. Were it not for her discontent he could get on with his research without this unpleasant intrusion of therapy. Nonetheless his labeling and treating her as disabled serves his defensive needs and intensifies her emotional withdrawal and their current impasse. It also simultaneously sustains the level of detachment that Mr. B. has been comfortable with for reasons of his own history and psychic economy. Lest it look like all that is required is his becoming less defended, I should add that subsequently in a dramatic reversal he felt in his guts that should the marriage break up it would be largely because of him. This relevation led his wife to respond limply as she began asking herself whether she indeed did want more intimacy. She was more comfortable, in fact, in maintaining herself (out of a sense of guilt) as being unloved. Her response confirmed his feelings that he is best off remaining detached. This new awareness made it even clearer that this couple unconsciously chose one another to keep a distance that suited each of them. Their mutual awareness in the conjoint sessions of this shared dynamic in fact paved the way for further resolution.

Because of the tendency to focus only upon the individual, the practitioner of individual treatment tended not to concern himself with changes in the patient's family. Yet any effective individual treatment, including chemotherapy, has unpredictable and mostly unstudied effects upon other members of the family. A number of years ago I saw a family where the mother, after many years of manic-depressive illness, was cured of this manifest illness by the discovery of Lithium. One might have thought this to be a most welcome event in the life of her family. The father, who for years had been overfunctioning in relation to his wife's disorder, became unaccountably depressed (see Jacobson 1956 for an early analytic view of such interaction). It was as if they shared an unconscious need for a "caretaking" relationship within the marriage. The introduction of Lithium in this case for a clear-cut mental illness nonetheless disturbed their object-relational balance, requiring further intervention. Clinical psychiatry abounds with such family systems effects of traditional treatment. The successful treatment of a child, for example, is not always a welcome event if the child's illness also serves regressive needs of one or both of the parents.

The very nature of the individual paradigm precludes studying the systems effects of individual treatment. This is graphically illustrated in a letter Freud wrote to his colleague Abraham over sixty years ago. Quite matter of factly he noted the frequency with which psychoanalytic treatment resulted in the patient's divorce. This observation, off the scientific record, was not then considered of any particular relevance. Only in the past decade or so, with the advent of the family systems paradigm, have researchers thought to look at what impact individual and family treatments have upon the family. (See Gurman and Kniskern 1978 for an excellent recent review.) Because we now study and treat the family, Freud's aside in a letter now serves as a stimulus for questioning when, why, and how individual therapy leads to divorce or to an improvement in family relations. A corollary question is how can family therapy effect meaningful changes in individuals. These questions are not merely of theoretical interest. A significant number of my consultations involve couples whose marital relationship has become threatened after one member has been in treatment for a number of years. Their conscious and unconscious needs no longer complement one another, and their marriage "contract" (see Sager 1976) has changed. Because of changes in the marital equilibrium catalyzed by individual treatment, the spouse in treatment or often the untreated spouse decides he or she wants a separation. While this may often be an appropriate and welcome outcome for all concerned, it is not necessarily a fortuitous one and may be a disequilibrium that can be corrected by involvement of the spouse in treatment. A husband in such a situation commented that in retrospect his wife seemed to stop talking to him around the time she started her individual therapy. It may have suited him not to talk with her at the time, but again, we see that individual treatment sets in motion complex changes in family interaction that are often out of awareness and of course never studied. Financial resources are often strained at these times, and the individual therapy itself is often jeopardized by the budgetary changes that come with a separation.

Whitaker and Miller (1969) have already stressed the possible untoward impact of individual therapy "when divorce impends." Where they urge a family evaluation at such times, I would go further to state that a family evaluation is also indicated when a patient comes for marital problems *before* divorce impends. This may sound like the family paradigm is overly preoccupied with preserving the family's structural integrity rather than elucidating the relevant dynamics. This is often a problem with practitioners of either modality who because of their own values and countertransference try to influence (often unconsciously) the outcome of their patients' life circumstances. To minimize such tendencies, practitioners of either modality in my view optimally ought to have had a personal analytic treatment (see Wynne 1965).

When a practitioner works "analytically" in either modality, the goal is the greater autonomy and individuation of each person ideally through the greater awareness and working through of the roots and less conscious dynamics of their relationships. The result, as distinguished from that goal, may be an improvement in the relationship and at other times in its dissolution. In beginning a family therapy, I exlicitly state that the goal is not the preservation of the marriage but the greater individuation of each member through an appreciation of factors often out of their awareness that have contributed to their difficulties. This approach differs from many therapists who see themselves primarily as behavioral ("system") change agents and "insight" as a relic of the old individual paradigm. Except in cases of the more acute psychosomatic and psychiatric disorders, acute family crises, or in the more chronic, undifferentiated family systems, I find such emphasis on change seriously flawed by the therapist's imposition of his own values and need to manage others.

NONCLINICAL FACTORS INFLUENCING PARADIGM CHOICE

We have established that in reality, intrapsychic and interpersonal determinants are always at work. The question remains, When is it most appropriate to do individual and/or family therapy? Before turning to that question, I shall raise a preliminary question of the nonclinical factors that determine paradigm choice. This will be discussed under three headings: (1) therapist factors, (2) client factors, and (3) sociocultural and institutional factors.

Therapist Factors

There is, of course, the obvious factor of the relative newness of the field. For this reason many older clinicians never trained in this specialty practice only individual therapy. Beyond that historical factor it is clear that younger trainees when exposed to both of these approaches seem to gravitate to one or the other of them for reasons of personal temperament. Training programs ought to be aware of such early preferences as they may reflect correctible limitations of particular trainees.

The single most important factor and the one that probably explains the long history and persistence of the individual modality is the almost universal preference for the privacy and intimacy of the dyadic relationship. The most natural, almost instinctive reaction of an individual in pain is to seek aid from a helping individual. It is a natural, almost instinctive reaction for the helping person, by varying degrees of identification and empathy with the sufferer's pain, to respond to the plea for help. This felicitous fit is first established in all of us by having participated in the caretaking mother-infant dyad. Within the psychoanalytic situation this is an inherent part of the relationship that must also be analyzed (see Stone 1961).

There are many trainees and family therapy "purists" who will not see individuals because they are uncomfortable with these more regressive transference and countertransference pulls. They are often more comfortable with greater therapeutic activity and management. One sees this trend toward therapeutic activism most fully explicated in Minuchin's structural approach (1974) (see chapter 8). He advocates the active restructuring of family systems from the very start. The popularity of this approach fits well with the activist temperament of many, especially trainees overly eager to help. It also fits in with the American value of active mastery of problems, be they technological or psychological. With many families this approach is necessary, but, with many families such activism undermines their autonomy and coping capacities. On the other hand, and far more frequently, some trainees and "purist" individual therapists temperamentally avoid family and group therapy. They may defensively prefer the individual therapy setting because of discomfort with the greater "activism" family treatment usually requires. Also family therapy is inherently more complex. There is a multiplication of data in seeing more than one patient at a time. Also there is multiplication of the resistances, which must be dealt with in all modalities. Families are no more eager to change than individuals are.

The temperamental preferences for individual and family therapy are inevitable, and most competent individual or family therapists need not learn the other modality. It is important, however, that those involved in diagnostic screening evaluations and deciding which modality is most appropriate be familiar with both. We now turn to the patient and family forces that determine choice of modality.

Client Factors

Just as therapists gravitate toward certain modalities for personal reasons, patients also defensively seek out modalities that may be more comfortable than therapeutic. When, for example, a child's symptomatology is largely reactive to a marital problem and the parents do not want to deal with their marriage, they will be more comfortable if the child is seen as the indentified patient and treated in individual therapy. Many having marital problems may also choose individual therapy, hoping for an ally or using the therapist as a "transitional object" to help achieve a marital separation. On the other hand, many families will insist on family therapy in the hope of stemming the independent strivings of an adolescent or one of the spouses. Separation anxiety may thus play a defensive role in the preference for either modality. The therapist, aware of such determinants, will less likely collude with them while working toward the autonomy and individuation of all involved. Bowen (1978) has emphasized that in most families there are relatively equal levels of undifferentiatedness among most of the members. The treatment of one member of a family will sooner or later have an impact on others in the family. All of them are thus potential patients, often leading to numerous individual therapies which, except for the very wealthy, is usually prohibitive. This needs to be considered in starting an individual therapy, as financial economics as well as psychic economics come into play when other members of the family begin to need and seek treatment in response to a relative's therapy.

Sociocultural and Institutional Factors

The newness of family therapy and more importantly the radical shift from the individual as the identified patient to the family as the patient creates a host of difficulties that have as yet not been resolved. A most formidable problem is that of reimbursement. Health insurance has now become a major form of reimbursement for most medical and psychiatric treatments. Third-party payers, however, have as yet rarely recognized this new modality. Insurance forms usually require the naming of one identified patient with an "insurable" illness. When the diagnosis "marital adjustment," which exists in the American Psychiatric Association's diagnostic nomenclature, is noted, the form is usually returned for a more individual-sounding diagnosis.

There is still no diagnostic nomenclature for families that can serve as a basis for third-party reimbursement. There is also no agreed-upon theory of family functioning or method of intervention.

Some third-party payers such as Medicaid in New York have recently begun to reimburse clinics doing family therapy by multiplying the individual fee by the number of family members (i.e. patients) present. This multiplication of the hourly rate of reimbursement suddenly made family therapy a much more popular modality. Such is the irrationality of our bureaucracies in dealing with innovation and change. There is a much larger problem involving reimbursement in the field of medicine, for insurance companies increasingly reimburse doctors for procedures rather than for time spent with patients. This "objectification" has disrupted the doctor-patient relationship and created an out-of-control inflationary spiral in the cost of medical care. Hosts of laboratory fees and technological procedures now supplement the fee for the history and physical examination. This is especially problematical for the practitioners of either of the modalities under discussion, as they do not "do procedures." Little wonder that psychiatry has doubled its efforts to return to its medical roots.

Then there is the problem of record keeping. Should there be records for families or for each family member? This has further discouraged the introduction of this modality into clinic settings. The keeping of individual records makes sense for a number of reasons. First, it encourages a more thorough evaluation of each family member. Second, as family membership is often changing, it makes sense to have a record for each individual patient, placing copies of family treatment summaries in each patient's chart. Individual records are thus a reminder that a family system, whatever the degree of its undifferentiatedness, is still composed of individuals in interaction.

There is yet another quite practical consideration that adds to the difficulty of doing family therapy. As family members often work and go to school the actual times that families can assemble are often in the evenings or at least in the afternoons. Scheduling individuals is thus vastly easier.

INDIVIDUAL AND FAMILY THERAPY — WHEN?

Aware that significant intrapsychic and interpersonal forces are usually present in most patients and with some awareness of those just reviewed, nonclinical considerations that determine choice of modality, we ask the critical question, "When do we utilize these modalities?"

As most patients seeking psychotherapeutic help are enmeshed in complex relationships with significant others, the initial conjoint evaluation of such relationships affords a more balanced unraveling of their mutual interpersonal and intrapsychic difficulties. These are cases in which there is often a transitional crisis in the family life cycle (e.g. a pregnancy wanted by one member and not the other, the problems of the "empty nest," and on up to the interpersonal difficulties precipitated by one spouse's retirement). A period of conjoint therapy will often resolve a presenting problem to their mutual satisfaction. At other times the reduction of externalizing defenses such as the conscious or unconscious blaming of others leads many individuals to want to further resolve their difficulties, in individual treatment or psychoanalysis. Exceptions, of course, to such family evaluations are patients who are single and living apart from their families. They are, in fact, often between families, between their family of origin and their family of procreation, or between marriages. Also, married patients who come primarily with clear intra-psychic conflicts such as a success neurosis, depression following a loss, and symptoms of anxiety, with little involvement of others with their symptoms (i.e., with minimal secondary gain) are generally more suitable for individual treatment. Unless a patient is such an obvious candidate for individual treatment, I almost always first see the family or marital couple in the evaluation stage. This follows Freud's 1905 warning to look carefully at the "family circumstances" of a patient and Dr. Harcourt-Reilly's rationale for family consultations in Eliot's *The Cocktail Party* that "it is often the case that my patients / Are only pieces of a total

situation / Which I have to explore. The single patient / Who is
ill by himself, is rather the exception" (Eliot 1952, p. 350; see
chapter 2, this volume).

I shall briefly present two cases that illustrate the use of family
therapy in dealing with a family crisis and, in the second case,
preparing individuals for more intensive individual therapy.
Both cases began as family life cycle crises. The first was around
what has come to be called the "empty nest" syndrome (the Ns).
The second couple (the Ps) came with conflicts around having a
first child.

The Empty Nest

Mrs. N., a woman in her mid-forties, was referred for individual
therapy because of depression and marital difficulties that
included her "provoking" her husband to beat her. When she
called for an appointment, I suggested that initially she and her
husband might come together. She claimed that that was
unnecessary as "she was the problem" and that if she were less
depressed the marriage would be fine, as there was nothing wrong
with her husband. I indicated that she might be right and that she
might benefit from individual treatment, but that nonetheless I
would prefer to see them together initially. She agreed to ask her
husband, who came quite readily.

They were an attractive couple; she dressed more elegantly than
her husband. She took the lead in the sessions and the
responsibility for their difficulties. Their four children ranging in
age from seventeen to twenty-four were now all out of the home.
Their oldest son had just recently been married. Their twenty-
four-year-old marriage had had many ups and downs, precipitated
by job changes and many moves over the years. She had
"sacrificed" herself to his erratic work schedule, which included
frequent periods of travel.

The past six months of depression and marital fights made
separation seem inevitable. If not, someone "might get killed," as
their fights ended with each one black and blue. The fights tended
to occur in the bedroom after some drinking. A sexual advance on

her part was seen as a demand for genital performance. This led to his withdrawal and her becoming violent and accusing him of longstanding intermittent impotence and not loving her.

Her past history was remarkable in this regard because her biological father, a "wife beater," left his wife, the patient, and her sister when she was an infant. Her mother remarried a man who was initially quite good to her, "warmer than my mother, who was cold and always working, though he also beat me for wrong doings." By the time she reached adolescence, her stepfather began forcing himself upon her sexually. This lasted several years and was accompanied with threats that if she were to tell anyone he would have her put away. Her initial willingness to come for individual therapy saying there was nothing wrong with her husband paralleled the experience of her adolescence. She would not expose her stepfather's sexual advances or her husband's sexual dysfunction. She wreaked symbolic revenge on her stepfather and self-destruction upon herself in these dramatic nighttime brawls. She thus acted out her guilt over her sexual and aggressive impulses.

We know that such interaction requires the neurotic complicity of both partners. Mr. N. had, as is so often the case, certain parallel childhood experiences that facilitated the collusion of such mutually reinforcing self-destructive trends. He was an only child whose father died when he was an infant, and he had a stepfather briefly when he was about 4. After that he lived with his mother and maternal grandparents. He saw nothing unusual about his childhood, felt it was a happy one, and did not feel it had any relevance to his present life. In the once-weekly conjoint sessions he was extremely deferential and saw their problems as primarily caused by his wife's "multiple personalities." They would have a good week followed by another disastrous blowout as she turned from a loving person to her other personality, "the witch."

Her "sexual needs" were examined more closely and acknowledged as primarily wishes to be close and nurtured. When he withdrew sexually, she felt he was a "stone," like her mother, thereby provoking her violent rages. As she began to make these needs for nurturance rather than genital satisfaction more explicit, Mr. N. was less threatened and far more responsive. If he were not under pressure to "perform," he could enjoy their sexual relations. By the fourth month of treatment this change in their sexual interaction had generalized to an unprecedented and prolonged, for them, period of good feeling, as well as a sense of renewal of their marriage. They were redecorating their home and felt like newlyweds. Her menstrual period was two weeks overdue, and she thought she might be pregnant, almost repeating the beginning of their marriage when she became pregnant in the second week.

They felt so good about their relationship that they wished to continue without further treatment, to "cut the cord" of dependence upon me. This precipitous termination seemed in keeping with the other many dislocations in their marriage. Should they return, if the improvement does not sustain itself, they will have had the recent period of unprecedented good feeling as an experience of possibilities they had not thought possible. To have seen her as an individual patient, as she was referred and as she requested, would have colluded with her definition of herself as the bad one or the victim. In their last session when I asked her about that, she said that even though she had asked for individual treatment, she felt sure the therapist would have sooner or later involved her husband. Their six months of severe difficulties began the same month as the marriage of their oldest child and when their youngest was about to leave for college. They were for the first time in twenty-four years and the only time in their marriage left alone together, just the two of them. At such transitions it is often better to see all the persons involved. With Mr. and Mrs. N., after the crisis abated there was little interest in delving any further. They were delighted with the positive changes and eager to terminate therapy. I left the door open should they feel the need for further work.

We turn now to another developmental, individual, and family crisis, this time around the readiness to start a family.

On Not Starting a Family

Mr. and Mrs. P. both in their late twenties came after seven years of marriage. Mrs. P. was pregnant and wanted to have their child. Her husband, a lawyer working for the government, did not want the child. In the first session, with their immediate conflict pressing, Mr. P. took time to note that he had an "additional neurosis." His parents had divorced when he was seven, and he grew up with his mother, a "powerful matriarchal" grandmother, and a very resented younger brother. He had always thought that his father had abandoned the family but found out later that he was kicked out for philandering, by the grandmother.

Mrs. P. in the same session expressed her fear of yet "another abortion." She had had one when she was about to start college and met Mr. P. shortly thereafter. He was very supportive and comforting at the time. He had just been through a similar situation as a girlfriend of his had just had an abortion. They seemed united by this shared experience. As therapy developed, this shared experience had its deeper counterpart in that she also had a younger brother toward whom there was marked, though more unconscious, resentment.

They came to a decision about the pregnancy rather quickly. He felt unable to become a father at the time, and she felt she was "the stronger" of the two and could survive another abortion better than he could manage fatherhood. They agreed that they needed to better understand what had led them to this juncture, and they started marital therapy.

He was having casual affairs at the time, which he stopped when the therapy began. During the course of a year's treatment Mr. P. came to see that he was retreating from fatherhood out of guilt over his oedipal success and recalled breaking down in tears at age twenty when his mother remarried. His first dream in the therapy was that he was sitting in my chair while a high school rival sat in his chair making love to his wife. Becoming a father was simultaneously equated with being ousted by a rival. Just as

George in *Who's Afraid of Virginia Woolf?* (see chapter 3) could not become a real father less he fall victim to projected patricidal impulses, Mr. P. was tempted to remain childless. The unconscious passive yearnings toward the father in this conflict could not be resolved in the marital therapy. This became more apparent when later in the year he somewhat compulsively resumed his extramarital affairs despite a general improvement in the marital relationship. This finally brought the marriage to an end, with a sense of sadness and relief for both of them as well as an awareness that they each had individual problems to work out. Throughout the early phase of treatment they felt they were married to the wrong partners. She felt he was too passive and unreliable, and he felt she no longer "turned him on." By the end of a year of treatment he had a wish to overcome his own conflict and saw the necessity for a personal analysis, which he subsequently began upon referral to a colleague.

Mrs. P. was less convinced that she had a comparable neurosis but agreed to continue in once-weekly psychotherapy, where she began to see her own retreat from oedipal strivings.

Her first dream also dealt manifestly with oedipal wishes. She was giving a party in her mother's house, and she was in charge. Her mother was not in sight. Guilt over these wishes in a subsequent intimate relationship led her to tolerate the occasional "straying" of her friend. Again she saw herself as the "stronger one," and her friend who "needed" these outside relationships as reflecting the general weakness of men. This rationalization masked her masochism in "losing" to the other women.

Mr. and Mrs. P. came to treatment as so many families do when facing a life cycle transition. Within a relatively short period their respective, well-internalized neuroses became manifest, and they saw the need for individual treatment. With the full span of adult life ahead of them they were more motivated to resolve underlying conflicts than the Ns, who, having launched their four children, longed for a harmonious "empty nest" phase of their lives. They never fully acknowledged that they had any individual problems, and should they return for further help, the family modality would again be most appropriate.

REFERENCES

Bowen, M. (1978). *Family Therapy in Clinical Practice*. New York: Jason Aronson.

Eliot, T.S. (1952). *The Complete Poems and Plays (1909-1950)*. New York: Harcourt, Brace and World.

Gurman, A.S. and Kniskern, D.P. (1978). Deterioration in marital and family therapy: empirical, clinical, and conceptual issues. *Family Process* 17:3-20.

Jacobson, E. (1956). Manic-depressive partners. In *Neurotic Interaction in Marriage*, ed. V. Eisenstein. New York: Basic Books.

Minuchin, S. (1974). *Families and Family Therapy*. Cambridge: Harvard University Press.

Sager, C. (1976). *Marriage Contracts and Couple Therapy*. New York: Brunner-Mazel.

Stone, L. (1961). *The Psychoanalytic Situation*. New York: International Universities Press.

Whitaker, C. and Miller, M. (1969). A re-evaluation of "psychiatric help" when divorce impends. *American Journal of Psychiatry* 126:611-616.

Wynne, L. (1965). Some indications and contraindications for exploratory family therapy. In *Intensive Family Therapy*, eds. I. Boszormenyi-Nagy and J. Framo. New York: Harper and Row.

Chapter Ten

INTEGRATION OF INDIVIDUAL AND INTERPERSONAL FACTORS

In the first chapter we revisited *Hamlet* and introduced the central paradigmatic question raised by the emergence of the family therapy movement. Can a disturbed individual be viewed as a symptom of a family disorder? What is the interrelation of the identified patient and his or her surrounding dysfunctional family? We noted that from a general systems point of view abnormal behavior, depending on the level of analysis, may be explained in terms of disturbances in genetic and biochemical factors, psychological forces, dysfunctional familial patterning, and at times cultural disparities. In the end the mental health sciences subsume nothing less than the interdependence of these points of view or "approaches to the mind."

We turn in this chapter to Oscar Wilde's one-act play *Salome*, which shocked the literary world at the same time as Freud was beginning to shock the scientific world with his discoveries. The play, written in 1891, representative of the fin de siècle literature of the 1890s, was to have starred Sarah Bernhardt. It could not be produced in England because of a law against the dramatic portrayal of Biblical characters, and after Richard Strauss wrote his highly controversial, sensual adaptation of this decadent play, censors in Vienna also forbade its production and the Kaiser cancelled a Berlin production. The first operatic performance of this study in perversity finally took place in Dresden the same year that Freud (1905) published his account of the polymorphous perverse sexuality of children in his *Three Essays on Sexuality*.

The American premiere of the opera in 1907, while receiving a highly favorable review by the *New York Times*, nonetheless was so offensive in content that it was not seen again at the Metropolitan for twenty-seven years! As the *Times* reported the event:

> When Mme. Fremstad (playing the lead) began to sing to the head before her, the horror of the thing started a party of men and women from the front row and from Boxes 27 and 29 in the Golden Horseshoe. Two parties tumbled precipitously into the corridors and called for their carriages. But in the galleries men and women left their seats to stand so they might look down upon the prima donna as she kissed the dead lips of the head of John the Baptist. Then they sank back in their chairs and shuddered! [1/23/07]

I have chosen *Salome* for this concluding chapter because of the striking similarity to the familial structure of *Hamlet*. To my knowledge this similarity has not, at least in the psychological literature, previously been noted. It allows us to view, from both psychoanalytic and family systems frameworks, a play in which we see a female version of *Hamlet*. Faced, as Hamlet was, with the *actualization* of childhood oedipal wishes, Salome moves toward a homosexual resolution by turning against the father representative and back toward her mother.

BRIEF PLOT SUMMARY

Both Oscar Wilde's play and Strauss's opera, which is an almost verbatim rendering of the play, rewrites the biblical story of

Salome. Wilde once said in keeping with his view of the primacy of the artistic endeavor that the artist's only duty to history was to rewrite it. In this short, dramatic rewriting of history, Salome enters the stage, having just left a royal banquet from which she escapes the lecherous stares of her stepfather, King Herod. She asks the palace guards to let her speak with John the Baptist, the religious prophet and follower of Christ. He is a prisoner of Herod held in an underground cistern. We then learn that it is the same cistern that once held Salome's father, the previous king and older brother of Herod. After his brother was in the prison for twelve years, Herod finally had him killed.[1]

John, ghostlike, comes out of the cistern, condemns and rebuffs Salome's seductive advances toward him, while also condemning the incestuous marriage of Herod and Salome's mother, Herodias. Cursing Salome as a daughter of adultery and of Sodom, John returns to his prison. Herod, whose wife repeatedly rebukes him for his attention to Salome, leaves the banquet in search of his beautiful stepdaughter. The tension mounts as Herod repeatedly pleads with Salome to dance for him, even offering her her mother's throne, even half his kingdom. She finally agrees to dance after extracting Herod's fateful oath to fulfill any wish of hers. After the dance she demands the head of John. She is thus reconciled to her mother who had wanted to have John silenced. At the same time she kills and possesses the man who had rejected her. The drama ends as she kisses the dead head, and Herod, in horror, gives his order, "Kill that woman!"

SIMILARITIES TO HAMLET: REVIEW OF THE LITERATURE

The few psychoanalytic studies of Salome that have appeared illustrate Bergmann's recent caveat (1973) regarding psychoanalytic studies of biography and literature. Such studies usually illuminate more about the state of contemporary psychoanalytic theory than about the work or person being studied. Coriat's very

---

1. This rather important detail of the murder is curiously omitted from the opera libretto.

brief paper (1914) on Salome emphasizes the role of sadism in her personality and reflects the interest of psychoanalysis of that period in the psychosexual stages of development that Freud had just previously elaborated. Plokker (1940) discussed Salome as representing a woman with a masculinity complex pervaded by an oral fixation. Salome wishes to bite off the penis as a type of revenge against the man. He feels the play's power rests in the expression of this common unconscious fantasy. Bergler (1954), writing in commemoration of the centenary of Wilde's birth, discusses the writing of *Salome* as a turning point in Wilde's life. The paper, which is rather unconvincing, reflects the interest of the psychoanalytic theory of the day in the role of the mother-child relationship. He argues that Wilde had sought refuge from the cruel giantess image of his mother in his 1886 marriage to a nonentity of a wife. In *Salome* (1891) Wilde's view of the cruelty of women found its fullest expression and paralleled, according to Bergler, his flight into a reckless homosexual life. The subsequent ruinous libel trial with the paranoid Marquess of Queensbury brought about Wilde's imprisonment and ultimate downfall. In fact, Wilde was serving his prison sentence in 1896 when *Salome* was first produced in Paris.

None of these writers noted the interesting parallel structure to Hamlet's family, reproduced in the following diagram:

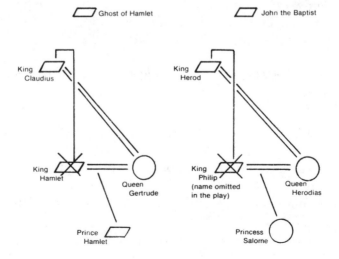

The parallels between the plays are further reinforced in the opening scenes as we note the similarities between the Ghost and John the Baptist.

Both plays open outside the respective castle (Hamlet) and palace (Salome) with the conversations of the guards as they come in contact with the speechless Ghost of Hamlet and the disembodied, ghostlike voice of John. In each play the guards try to protect Hamlet and Salome from their fateful meetings with these representations of their dead fathers.

> *Marcellus*: You shall not go, my Lord. [I. iv. 88]
> *The Young Syrian*: Do not

> stay here Princess, I beseech you. [p. 401]

Both John and the Ghost rise as if (or from) the dead. John's identity with Salome's father is obvious, as they occupied the same tomblike prison. Displacement to John of her feelings toward her father is thus facilitated. Salome's desire to speak with this representation of her dead father finds parallel in Hamlet's eagerness to speak with his dead father. Both the Ghost and John condemn the similar incestuous and adulterous marriages while recommending quite different solutions to Hamlet's and Salome's questions.

Hamlet: What should we do? [I. iv. 61]
Ghost: Revenge (my) foul and unnatural murder. [I. v. 30]
Ay that incestuous, that adulterous beast, [I. v. 49]

Salome: Speak again! Speak again and tell me what I must do. [p. 402]
John: Daughter of Sodom, come not near me! But cover thy face with a veil ... and get thee to the desert and seek out the Son of Man. [p. 402] Daughter of adultery, there is but one who can save thee ... Go seek Him ... ask of Him the remission of thy sins. [p. 405]

Where the Ghost calls Hamlet to revenge, John, speaking from the cradle of Christianity, tells Salome to seek out redemption and Christ. There are further details that reflect similar themes, for just as we learn that Fortinbras's father, also a king, had been killed by King Hamlet, the Young Syrian's father, also a king, had been killed by Herod. The similarities border on the uncanny.

There is no evidence that Wilde was consciously changing the Salome story to resemble the beginning of Hamlet, but the resemblance deserves some note. The resemblance is in sharper focus as we note the degree to which Wilde rewrote the original story. The historical version differs from Wilde's adaptation in the following significant ways.

1. Salome's father, whose name was Philip, was *not* a ruler, but a wealthy half brother of Herod, and he was not imprisoned or killed, but lived in Rome.
2. It was because he was not a ruler that Herodias left him to become Herod's wife and queen, thus committing the adultery that John the Baptist condemned.
3. It was for this reason that Herodias wanted John killed and asked for his head through her daughter, who in the biblical version innocently asked her mother what she should ask of her stepfather after the dance.
4. Salome was not killed, but in fact, ended up marrying another man named Philip.

In rewriting this story, Oscar Wilde has changed the plot to resemble a female Hamlet figure who moves toward a homosexual resolution.

THE HOMOSEXUAL RESOLUTION OF THE OEDIPAL CONFLICT

In the earlier review of Freud's writings on marriage and the family (see chapter 5), I noted his early observations on the neurosogenic impact of severe marital discord on a child's oedipal development. The disharmony between parents creates an opportunity for a child to side with the parent of the opposite sex, thereby attempting fulfillment of his oedipal wishes, or siding with the parent of the same sex, thereby denying or repressing the oedipal rivalry with that parent. Extended into adult life, the choice of someone of the same sex as a love object constitutes the regressive homosexual resolution of the oedipal conflict.

For the female the regression reestablishes her primary attachment to the mother, while for the male the regression is often an identification with this first love object. Both are set in motion by the castration or Oedipus complex while more determined by earlier preoedipal fixations. These alternatives have come to be called the positive and negative sides of the oedipal conflict. The following diagram showing these alternatives for the boy and girl cites the mythological figures often associated with them. I have placed the name of Salome in the fourth box as there has not been a legendary figure that has become associated with the girl's negative oedipal conflict.

	Positive Oedipus	Negative Oedipus (Homosexual)
Boy	Oedipus	Orestes
Girl	Electra	Salome

In the open conflict between Herod and Herodias, Salome flees the incestuous tie to the stepfather while attempting briefly to enact it with a direct substitute for her father, John the Baptist. The blatant transparency of the oedipal relation, as we read the play today, makes one wonder if Wilde, as so many modern writers, was not writing under the influence of Freudian ideas. Such "contamination" is however not possible as Freud's first published discussion of the Oedipus complex in *The Interpreta-*

tion of Dreams (1900) came nine years after Wilde wrote his *Salome.*

When Herod repeatedly asks Salome to dance for him, as her mother protests vehemently, Salome seems to give in while asking the fateful oath of Herod. After the dance she claims as her prize the head of John the Baptist, to her mother's triumphant delight and Herod's mortification. She thus, for the moment, is reconciled with her mother and is perversely and unconsciously united with her dead father.

Bergmann (1976) has recently called attention to the phenomena of "love that follows upon murder in works of art" that has particular relevance to the subsequent discussion of preoedipal ambivalence. As he notes, once the murderous impulse has been enacted, the love toward the object finds expression. The request for his head also however, threatens Herod's authority as his subjects have begun to worship this disciple of Christ. Thus her reconciliation with her mother and father is indeed brief as Herod then has her killed.

THE PREOEDIPAL FACTORS: AMBIVALENCE AND THE ROLE OF SPLITTING

In the previous section we discussed the oedipal conflict of Salome as it was intensified by the murder of her father and the later seductive approaches of her stepfather. The homosexual resolution of the Oedipus complex inevitably has its roots in the preoedipal relation to the mother. In males the preoedipal relationship is usually dealt with by identification with the maternal object. In the female the conflictual preoedipal relationship is handled by a wish to return to a blissful preambivalent tie to her. If the mother-infant relationship has been pathological the child often turns to the father in search of such nurturance.

This tendency is enacted in Salome's approaches to John the Baptist whom we have already shown to be a direct substitute for her father. She, however, does not seek genital sexual gratification but rather a more primitive contact with the maternal body (i.e., the "good" idealized breast). And when John rejects these advances, the "body" she had idealized immediately turns into the "bad" persecutory object.

Salome: I am amorous of thy body, Jokanaan! Thy body is white like the lilies of a field that the mower hath never mowed. Thy body is white like the snows that lie on the mountains of Judea, and come down into the valleys. The roses in the garden of the Queen of Arabia are not so white as thy body. Neither the roses of the garden of the Queen of Arabia, the garden of spices of the Queen of Arabia, nor the feet of the dawn when they light on the leaves, nor the breast of the moon when she lies on the breast of the sea . . . There is nothing in the world so white as thy body. Suffer me to touch thy body.

Jokanaan: Back! daughter of Babylon! By woman came evil into the world. Speak not to me. I will not listen to thee. I listen but to the voice of the Lord God.

Salome: Thy body is hideous. It is like the body of a leper. It is like a plastered wall where vipers have crawled; like a plastered wall where the scorpions have made their nest. It is like a whitened sepulchre full of loathsome things. It is horrible, thy body is horrible. It is thy hair that I am enamoured of, Jokanaan. Thy hair is like clusters of grapes, like the clusters of black grapes that hang from the vine-trees of Edom in the land of the Edomites. Thy hair is like the cedars of Lebanon, like the great cedars of Lebanon that give their shade to the lions and to the robbers who would hide them by day. The long black nights, when the moon hides her face, when the stars are afraid, are not so black as thy hair. The silence that dwells in the forest is not so black. There is nothing in the world that is so black as thy hair . . . Suffer me to touch thy hair.

Jokanaan: Back, daughter of Sodom! Touch me not. Profane not the temple of the Lord God.

Salome: Thy hair is horrible. It is covered with mire and

dust. It is like a knot of serpents coiled around thy neck. I love not thy hair ... It is thy mouth that I desire, Jokanaan. Thy mouth is like a band of scarlet on a tower of ivory. It is like a pomegranate cut in twain with a knife of ivory. The pomegranate flowers that blossom in the gardens of Tyre, and are redder than roses, are not so red. The red blasts of trumpets that herald the approach of kings, and make afraid the enemy, are not so red. Thy mouth is redder than the feet of the doves who inhabit the temples and are fed by the priests. It is redder than the feet of him who cometh from a forest where he hath slain a lion, and seen gilded tigers. Thy mouth is like a branch of coral that fishers have found in the twilight of the sea, the coral that they keep for the kings! ... It is like the vermilion that the Moabites find in the mines of Moab, the vermilion that the kings take from them. It is like the bow of the King of the Persians, that is painted with vermilion, and is tipped with coral. There is nothing in the world so red as thy mouth ... Suffer me to kiss thy mouth.

Jokanaan: Never! daughter of Babylon! Daughter of Sodom! Never.

Salome: I will kiss thy mouth, Jokanaan. I will kiss thy mouth. [pp. 403-404]

There have been some recent "hair-splitting" debates as to the precise definition of splitting, most recently by Robbins (1976). In the just-quoted passages we see a richly elaborated example of a precursor of splitting in an infant's first object relationship. In the infant's ambivalent attitude to the breast, the libido is directed toward an idealized breast and aggression toward the persecutory one.

The portrayal of Herodias is of a rather jealous, angry, cold, unmaternal woman, in keeping with the image Wilde seems to have had of women as unfaithful, ravenous, and power hungry. Behind the image of Salome's sexuality and acclaimed beauty, we see her yearning for reunion with a life-giving good mother. Her beauty, which is acclaimed in the opening line of the play, is immediately contrasted with her identification with death.

> *The Young Syrian*: How beautiful is the Princess Salome tonight!
>
> *Page of Herodias*: Look at the moon. How strange the moon seems! She is like a woman rising from a tomb. She is like a dead woman. One might fancy she was looking for dead things. [pp. 392-393]

Indeed, she is looking for her dead father whom she may have wished to have nurtured her and protected her from the cruel mother. Her desperate, unsatisfied thirst causes her to kill the object of her desire, which then brings about her own destruction. One of the earliest hallmarks of the mother-infant relationship is the smile response and the role of mirroring behavior in the earliest differentiation of the child from its mother. Repeatedly in the play the dangers of looking too much at a love object are emphasized. Usually it is couched in sexual terms; the Syrian looks too much at Salome, Salome looks too much at John, and Herod looks too much at Salome. This looking is latently expressive of preoedipal longing, and at the end of the play its full import is expressed in Herod's despair when Salome asks for the head of John:

> *Herod*: No, no, thou wouldst not have that. Thou sayest that but to trouble me, because I have looked at thee and ceased not this night. Thy beauty has troubled me. Thy beauty has grievously troubled me and I have looked at thee over much. Nay, but I will look at thee no more. *One should not look at anything. Neither at things nor at people should one look. Only in mirrors is it well to look for mirrors do but show us masks.* [p. 423, italics mine]

Herod, in his despair, turns away from the faces of others, preferring the masks of his narcissistic reflection. Also when Salome gets the head she has longed for, through massive denial of his death, she begins to kiss and bite it as she notes his unresponsive eyes.

Salome: But wherefore dost thou not look at me, Jokannen? Thine eyes that were so terrible, so full of rage and scorn are shut now. Wherefore are they shut? Open thine eyes. Lift up thine eyelids, Jokannen. Wherefore dost thou not look at me?....

Ah! wherefore didst thou not look at me Jokannen? With the cloak of thine hands and with the cloak of thy blasphemies thou didst hide thy face. Thou didst put upon thine eyes the covering of him who would see his God. Well, thou hast seen thy God, Jokannen, but me, me thou didst never see. If thou hadst seen me thou hadst loved me. I saw thee and I loved thee. [pp. 427-428]

Thus to be seen, to be recognized, is to be loved. Despairing of such object love, Herod seeks resolution in turning in upon himself and Salome in destruction of the love object. Actually in the killing of the love object, Salome enacts a wish to finally possess that which she could not have, the love of her father and mother. She longs, as she was described in the first scene, for death where she can be reunited with the lost objects of her past.

THE OEDIPUS COMPLEX SEEN TRANSACTIONALLY

The Oedipus complex, which remains a cornerstone of the psychoanalytic theory of neurosis, has generally been descriptive of each person's developmental struggle with his or her parents viewed generally from within or intrapsychically and taking place in childhood. While psychoanalysis has a keen appreciation of the role of life experiences upon the developing ego, the descriptions and theories nonetheless tend to emphasize the internalized facets of the personality, especially in its early formation and functioning. This is so because the primary data of psychoanalysis remains the productions of the individual patient on the couch. The more unconscious and instinctual elements of the personality, laid down, repressed, to be sure in the earliest years, continue to exert themselves in character structure, symptoms, reenactments, and transformations in later life. When reenacted in the transference neurosis of a psychoanalytic treatment, these internal forces can be moderated.

Quite often the interpersonal dramas of families remain the unfolding and interweaving of parts of each member's internalized past life. In *Salome* we know little of Herod's or Herodias' lives except that, just as Claudius and Gertrude, they have committed adultery, incest, and murder. They have *enacted* the oedipal crime with its attendant tragic consequences. When internal conflict is thus averted or superseded by perverse or psychopathic *acts*, the interpersonal ramifications are multiple and amplified.

In *Salome* the most recent elaboration of the multiple unfoldings is in the present dramatic interaction of Herod, Herodias, and Salome. The usurpation of the throne did not put to rest the conflicts and desires of Herod and Herodias. The ambivalence between husband and wife quickly involve them with Salome in another oedipal triangle leading them to ruin. Herod antagonizes his wife by his attraction to his stepdaughter. Herodias drives Herod further toward his stepdaughter by her self-fulfilling accusations and criticisms of Herod. Herodias thus plays a part in losing the man she had gained at such cost. In lusting after his stepdaughter, Herod offends both his wife and stepdaughter, who later vent their rage at his authority in asking for the head of John the Baptist. Salome unsuccessfully tries to escape the triangle and finally allows herself to be the instrument of the constellation when she agrees to dance for her stepfather, bringing the tension to its climax.

What is critical here is the way in which each person is inextricably bound to the triangle. It is a major contribution of the family therapy movement to have noted how the participants of a disturbed family are collusively bound in such pathological triangles, from which there seems to be no exit and in which repetitive interactional patterns predominate. The following portion of the play will illustrate this here-and-now aspect of the oedipal constellation. The text of the play is here presented with my comments in parentheses.

Midway through the one-act play Herod slips on the blood of

the Young Syrian who, enamored of Salome, had committed suicide as he watched Salome try to seduce John. Unsettled, recalling that he had driven the Young Syrian's father, also a king, from his kingdom and made the Syrian captain of his guard, Herod hallucinates the Angel of Death. Herodias tries to reassure him.

Herodias: I tell you there is nothing. You are ill. Let us go within. (She tries to get Herod back into the palace and away from Salome.)

Herod: I am not ill. It's your daughter who is sick to death. Never have I seen her so pale. (Herod rebuffs his wife and attends to his stepdaughter.)

Herodias: I have told you not to look at her. (She again charges her husband with incestuous glances; in most of these communications the content message is thus expressed as a command, conveying an attitude of authority toward Herod.)

Herod: Pour me forth wine. Salome come drink a little wine with me. I have here wine that is exquisite. Caesar himself sent it to me. Dip into it thy little red lips, that I may drain the cup. (Herod defies his wife's command and openly tries to woo Salome.)

Salome: I am not thirsty, Tetrarch. (She declines his offer.)

Herod: You hear how she answers me, this daughter of yours. (He, rather than reply directly to Salome's refusal, blames his wife.)

Herodias: She does right. Why are you always gazing at her? (She is pleased with her daughter and reproaches her husband again.)

Herod: Bring me ripe fruits. Salome, come and eat fruits with me. I love to see in a fruit the mark of thy little teeth. Bite but a little of this fruit that I may eat what is left. (In response Herod continues the pattern of provocation.)

Salome: I am not hungry, Tetrarch. (She declines again.)

Herod: You see how you have brought up this daughter of yours. (He again blames his wife for her daughter's response, continuing the triangling process.)

Herodias: My daughter and I come of a royal race. As for thee, thy father was a camel driver! He was a thief and robber to boot! (Herodias reverts to insults, identifying herself with her daughter.)

Herod: Thou liest!

Herodias: Thou knowest well that it is true.

Herod: Salome, come and sit next to me. I will give thee the throne of thy mother. (Again Herod uses Salome to get back at his wife, in fact, offers her throne to rest upon.)

Salome: I am not tired, Tetrarch. [p. 409]

This repetitive sequence is here interrupted by John's voice from below forecasting doom. Moments later the cycle resumes, this time with Herod asking that Salome dance for him. She repeatedly refuses until she extracts from him the fateful oath to give her "whatever she shall ask."

The rising interpersonal (and presumably intrapsychic) tension thus moves toward a runaway resolution. Salome may have whatever her heart desires. No simple matter of asking the child in the consultation room his three wishes to catch a glimpse of the id. Salome shall have John's head. In this brief replay of the oedipal entanglement of Salome, Herod, and Herodias, we are reminded again of the emphasis or point of view of family therapy. The family is "a system" in which each person's activity or inactivity, thoughts and feelings, and part or role, affects to varying degrees the activity, thoughts, and feelings of the others.

While the novel is often also quite dramatic, it differs from drama in giving us more of a picture of the motivations and private thoughts of the characters. For this reason the novel lends itself more readily to psychoanalytic study, where the drama is more frequently suitable to illustrate the interpersonal concepts of family therapy.

Salome illustrates again the family therapy emphasis upon the importance of examining the here-and-now interaction as a clue to a clinical situation or problem. The interaction was all too clear. The earlier psychoanalytic examination of her use of displacement and splitting in the interaction with John the Baptist, whom she had never before met, led us to *infer* a desire to be reunited with her dead father and with the further aim of establishing with him a preoedipal tie to an ambivalently experienced maternal object.

The intensity of that wish for reunion with the mother is thus added to the constellation of interpersonal forces that bring the oedipal crisis to a tragic conclusion.

It is the appreciation and understanding of the confluence of such past developmental and present interpersonal forces that hold promise for a psychoanalytically oriented family therapy that integrates the insights of both psychoanalysis and family therapy[2] while helping those patients with whom classical psychoanalysis is not possible.

REFERENCES

Bergler, E. (1956). "Salome": The turning point in the life of Oscar Wilde. *Psychoanalytic Review* 43:97-103.

Bergmann, Martin S. (1973). Limitations of method in psychoanalytic biography: an historical inquiry. *Journal of the American Psychoanalytic Association* 21:833-850.

2. A sociopolitical interpretation that underscores the intrapsychic and interpersonal family dynamics has been put forth by Marcus (1974). She sees in Salome an early representation of modern woman's quest for equality and her rebellion against patriarchal authority.

In the lecherous advances toward his stepdaughter Herod reflects the patriarchal abuse of women in its most decadent form. Salome and her mother turn against this callous treatment. Seen as a threat to the established authorities, Salome is crushed to death by a symbol of the State's authority, the shield of Herod's soldiers. Marcus goes on to see her death as paralleling Christ's martyrdom.

This is an intriguing interpretation, which touches upon the present upheaval in the changing roles of women. All our traditional institutions, such as religions, political structures, and the family are being shaken by these changes, which while clearly liberating are also contributing to the present instability of the modern family. It is this factor in addition to other structural changes in the family over the past 100 years that has contributed to society's attempt to manage this instability through the mental health professions, more specifically through the emergence of family therapy (see chapter 2).

————(1976). Love that follows upon murder in works of art. *American Imago* 33:98-101.

Coriot, I. (1914). Sadism in Oscar Wilde's "Salome." *Psychoanalytic Review* 1:257-259.

Hyde, H.M. (1975). *Oscar Wilde: A Biography*. New York: Farrar, Straus, and Giroux.

Freud, S. (1900). The interpretation of dreams. *Standard Edition* 4, p. 257 ff.

————(1905). Three essays on the theory of sexuality. *Standard Edition* 7.

Marcus, J. (1974). Salome: the Jewish princess was a new woman. *Bulletin of the New York Public Library*, Autumn, 1974.

New York Times, Review of Opera "Salome." 1/23/07.

Plokker, J.H. (1940). Psychoanalytic study of Salome. *Ned. Tijdschr. Psychol.* 7:449-462.

Robbins, M. (1976). Borderline personality organization: the need for a new theory. *Journal of the American Pychoanalytic Association* 24:831-853.

Shakespeare, W. *Hamlet*. New York: Washington Square Press.

Wilde, O. (1891). *Salome*. In *The Portable Oscar Wilde*. New York: Penguin Books, 1977.

INDEX